INTRODUCTION TO REFLECTION AND ACTION FOR TEACHER RESEARCHERS

Introduction to Critical Reflection and Action for Teacher Researchers provides crucial direction for educators looking to improve their teaching and maximise learning. While many students can grasp the basic elements of researching their practice and can write about practitioner research, some need guidance and assistance to reflect meaningfully on their teaching practice so as to articulate their educational values. This book provides this guidance.

By exploring how to engage in an authentic, practical and personalised framework, the book encourages critical reflection and action on educational practice. Moving through the process of reflecting on practice, engaging in critical thinking and planning and taking action, it helps the reader to subsequently generate educational theory from their own personal learning. Examples from the authors' experiences illustrate the issues raised in each section, with 'Pause and Reflect' activities, guidelines for conducting a research project and annotated further reading available for every chapter.

Introduction to Critical Reflection and Action for Teacher Researchers is based on the idea that reflection is in itself a deliberate action and something we must live – it is key to understanding our practice and is a core component of action research. This book is a valuable guide for teachers, trainee teachers and researchers interested in reflecting on and enhancing their teaching practice.

Bernie Sullivan is a former principal of a primary school in Dublin, Ireland. She currently works as a tutor for second-level student teachers on school placement at St. Patrick's College, Thurles, and also supervises action research projects for mathematics teachers undertaking postgraduate studies at the University of Limerick, Ireland.

Máirín Glenn works in Co. Mayo, Ireland, as a primary school teacher and school principal. She also works as a part-time tutor in the area of self-study action research with students on Masters programmes at St. Angela's College, Sligo; St. Patrick's College, Dublin and Hibernia College, Ireland.

Mary Roche is Senior Lecturer in Education at St Patrick's College, Thurles, Ireland. Following a career in primary teaching, Mary lectured in Primary English at Mary Immaculate College, Limerick (BEd) and on Action Research (MEd) at University College Cork, Ireland. She is the author of *Developing Children's Critical Thinking through Picturebooks*, which was highly commended for the UKLA Academic Book Award 2015.

Caitriona McDonagh spent many years as a primary teacher. Recently, she has supported teacher continuous professional learning and initial teacher education across a number of settings and teacher education colleges in Ireland.

INTRODUCTION TO CRITICAL REFLECTION AND ACTION FOR TEACHER RESEARCHERS

Bernie Sullivan, Máirín Glenn, Mary Roche and Caitriona McDonagh

Routledge
Taylor & Francis Group

LONDON AND NEW YORK

First published 2016
by Routledge
2 Park Square, Milton Park, Abingdon, Oxon OX14 4RN

and by Routledge
711 Third Avenue, New York, NY 10017

Routledge is an imprint of the Taylor & Francis Group, an informa business

British Library Cataloguing in Publication Data
A catalogue record for this book is available from the British Library

Library of Congress Cataloging in Publication Data
Names: Sullivan, Bernie, author. | Roche, Mary (Lecturer in education), author. | McDonagh, Caitriona, author. | Glenn, Máirín, author.
Title: Introduction to critical reflection and action for teacher researchers / Bernie Sullivan, Mary Roche, Caitriona McDonagh, and Máirín Glenn.
Description: New York, NY : Routledge, 2016.
Identifiers: LCCN 2015046947| ISBN 9781138911048 (hardback) | ISBN 9781138911055 (pbk.) | ISBN 9781315693033 (ebook)
Subjects: LCSH: Action research in education. | Reflective teaching.
Classification: LCC LB1028.24 .S89 2016 | DDC 370.72–dc23LC record available at http://lccn.loc.gov/2015046947

ISBN: 978-1-138-91104-8 (hbk)
ISBN: 978-1-138-91105-5 (pbk)
ISBN: 978-1-315-69303-3 (ebk)

Typeset in Interstate
by Cenveo Publisher Services

DEDICATION

We dedicate this book to teacher researchers everywhere.

CONTENTS

Conclusion 145

ACKNOWLEDGEMENTS

We authors are scattered around the island of Ireland and, every now and again, we need to find time and space to get together for an intensive burst of writing. We would like to thank everyone who helped and inspired us to write this book. A special thanks to our husbands and families who supported us throughout our writing endeavours. We are grateful to the teachers, educational researchers and students who engaged with us as we journeyed towards an understanding of our practice as teacher researchers, while at the same time supporting fellow teacher researchers as they undertook similar journeys of reflection and action.

INTRODUCTION

Dear reader,

In this book we invite you to explore how you might engage in an authentic, practical and personalised framework for conducting critical reflection and action on your educational practice. We, the authors, draw on current theory in action research and also draw on our own practical experiences. We guide you through the process of reflecting on your practice, engaging in critical thinking, planning and taking action, and generating new theory from your learning throughout. We feel passionate about the importance of critical reflection on the practice of teaching and learning because we are convinced that, in its absence, teaching could become murky, mundane and repetitive – something to be avoided. Our suggestions throughout the book are invitational and we hope that they will be useful as you engage in your research journey. We agree with Larrivee (2000) who suggests that each teacher researcher needs to plan their own research route, rather than adhering to a prescribed format: 'The path to developing as a critically reflective teacher cannot be prescribed with an intervention formula. The route cannot be preplanned – it must be lived' (p. 30).

We authors are frequently invited to work on various postgraduate programmes in education, where students are required to reflect on their practice and engage in self-study action research so as to improve their practice, or their understanding of it, and to generate a theory of practice from their experiences. We have found that, while many students can grasp the basic elements of researching their practice and can write about practitioner research, some find it difficult to articulate their values, identify their learning and generate theory from it. This book will address these difficulties by offering a structured, practical framework for doing your project. We aim to guide you through the underpinning theory of action research as you work through the practicalities of doing an action research project, thus enabling you to subsequently generate your own educational theory from your learning.

We address the growing trend in educational contexts for teachers to engage in critical reflection (Brookfield 1995; Schön 1983) and to develop new forms of understanding of practice (Bradbury 2015). The book is highly supportive of all those engaged in undergraduate and postgraduate studies in reflective practice, in action research, in living theory and in leadership for professional development. Our book is a collaborative undertaking which brings to life our research on our individual practices. We feel that we are qualified to write this book because, collectively, we have nearly 140 years of teaching experience and 70 years of researching our practice as teachers, and these experiences underpin and enhance the content. We are convinced of the viability of practice-based research as a form of continuing professional development (CPD) and also of the potential of self-study for developing the habit of critical reflection for improving practice, as well as for increasing professional understanding. We know, too, that reflection is something we must choose to do wholeheartedly. Just like anything else that is good for you, it cannot be imposed from without: the motivation must come from within.

Reflection is something we must live and it is key to understanding our practice. It is also a core component of action research. Almost all teacher education courses have an element of reflective practice. In many teacher education contexts, both at undergraduate and postgraduate levels, teachers are encouraged to take responsibility for their professional actions and to become active agents in analysing their practice. We suggest that reflection is purposeful or intentional – we have a reason for doing it – and that it is sustained over some period of time. It is almost like having a dialogue, a 'conversation with ourselves that leads to even deeper understanding of our own values and beliefs' (Lindsey *et al.* 2015: 13). In this dialogue we need constantly to probe and query our own thinking. We have found that our reflection may highlight some uncomfortable professional truths for us, and we are aware that we each have within us the power to change or improve.

The learning outcomes of teacher education courses are peppered with references to critical thinking and metacognition – and rightly so. We teachers need to be able to think critically about our practice, and think critically about our own thinking. Critical thinking is a key element in critical reflection and, in this context, we draw on the work of McNiff and Whitehead (2011) and Brookfield (2012). Critical thinking could be said to be the opposite of passively accepting the thinking of others. Like any skill it needs practice and the more we do it the better we get at it. This implies that being a critical thinker can become a way of being as well as having a set of skills. Michael D. Higgins, President of Ireland, recognises the importance of critical thinking, both for schools and for society in general, when he asserts:

> Our schools' curricula and pedagogical methods reflect the kind of humanity our society seeks and nurtures. The society we so dearly wish for will not take shape unless we acknowledge the need for an education of character and desires, the need to encourage and support critical reflection and a more holistic approach to knowledge. (Cited in Humphreys 2015: 13)

Throughout this text we authors refer to action research, living theory and self-study action research almost interchangeably, as many of the ideas that underpin them are quite similar. All are concerned with reflecting on a situation, identifying an area that could be improved on, taking action to effect improvement, gathering data to indicate whether improvement has occurred and reviewing the changed situation. While there are many interpretations and understandings of the umbrella term 'action research', in this book we are addressing, specifically, the voice of the individual generating educational theory from their own learning. Reason and Bradbury (2013) perceive action research as a 'family of approaches' and use the term 'first person action research' to describe the stories and theories drawn from one's own practice, which is the focus of this book. (They use the term 'second person research' to describe when the researcher engages in face-to-face dialogue along with others to explore their learning and 'third person research' describes research from a wider community of enquiry (ibid.: 6).) Continuous reflection throughout the research process is a feature of all approaches, as is the necessity to keep a reflective journal for the purpose of documenting the story of one's learning during the course of the research.

Values are kernel to action research approaches, as they underpin the framing of one's research question and can also be used to formulate the criteria for assessing the research project. Values can evolve from different perspectives, the main categories being educational, ontological and epistemological. Educational values can be identified through naming the things you value around education, such as inclusion, social justice and democracy. Ontological values stem from one's way of being in the world, and can permeate our relationships with our fellow human beings, so respect would feature highly among these values. Epistemological values are determined by our view of knowledge: if we believe that knowledge is power (Foucault 1980), then our value around knowledge will not view it as a package to be delivered uncritically to students, but as something that can be co-created in a reciprocal relationship (Buber 1958) that values the knowledge contribution of our students. Sometimes, there can be overlap between the three types of values mentioned here. For example, respect can be an educational value if you show respect as a right to all the students with whom you work; it can be an ontological value if you believe that all people, irrespective of race, creed or colour are entitled to equality of respect; and it can be an epistemological value if you accept that students can contribute to the development of knowledge on an equal basis with teachers. Because of this interconnectivity, we sometimes use the three categories of values interchangeably in this book.

What you will encounter in this book

Each author has taken responsibility for one of the four sections of the book, and each section contains two chapters. Vignettes from the authors' lived experiences help to explain and illustrate many of the objectives of the sections and the issues raised in the chapters. 'Pause and reflect' activities form step-by-step guidelines for conducting a research project on one's own practice. At the end of each chapter, we provide a summary of issues discussed as an aide-memoire for the reader. A list of recommended reading and possible resources for viewing are attached to each chapter.

In Section I, Mary Roche accompanies you as you explore the notion of reflective practice and its implications for you as a teacher researcher. In Chapter 1 you will be invited to take a step back and look at what you value in education. You will be asked reflective questions that will help to guide you through beginning the process of thinking critically – first, on why you are an educator and, second, on the concept of education. You will be introduced to the work of key theorists in the area of reflection and reflective practice. In Chapter 2 Mary invites you to look at research, in particular educational research. You will be offered an overview of action research and of self-study action research, and you will explore how reflection plays a key role in this form of educational enquiry. You will then be asked to take a more critically reflective orientation to exploring the practice of teaching. You will begin to see why self-study action research can be considered an appropriate methodology for critically reflecting on practice. Finally, Mary suggests ways as to how you might experience critical pedagogy in your everyday work as she introduces you to the work of some of the major critical voices in education.

Section II encompasses Chapters 3 and 4 and examines the practicalities of critical thinking and reflection; Máirín Glenn discusses the pivotal role of values as you embark on an action research project. Chapter 3 asks you to examine the question 'Why do I do what I do?' as a practical starting point for linking critical thinking, reflection and taking actions to change things. You will explore critical thinking as a key element of reflective practice and you are introduced to cycles of reflection and action, the concept of praxis, how you might collaborate with colleagues and the idea of keeping a reflective diary. In Chapter 4, you will explore the concept of 'experiencing oneself as a living contradiction' (Whitehead 1989) in terms of launching a research project, exploring 'living theory', identifying your values and asking questions like 'How do I improve my practice?' You will also examine some of the key elements of preparing for an action research project and getting the groundwork done for the reconnaissance period.

Section III deals with action and the assessment of your research. Caitriona McDonagh calls on her experiences as a teacher researcher of pupils with special education needs and as an assessor of others' educational action research projects from pre-service to CPD, to show how you can conduct rigorous first-person action research to improve your practice. Chapter 5 takes a critical look at how can we provide evidence to convince others, who are grounded in positivist and external forms of knowledge, of the validity of our research. Caitriona invites you to find forms of data that are most relevant to your specific context. She shows how you can develop a chain of evidence from this data so that you can confidently claim new knowledge about improvement in your practice. This approach provides you with a path to convince others of the validity of your research which works within a more holistic approach to knowledge that is appropriate for learning. This theory of knowledge is grounded in personal and relational knowledge, which are important forms of knowledge relevant in teaching and learning. By articulating the knowledge base of your research you can demonstrate that it is quality research rather than merely professional development or system change. In Chapter 6 we find ways to challenge an unsupported belief that author bias can be removed from educational action research. We invite you to consider issues about all participants being part of the research. This requires teacher researchers to articulate the basis of the ethical standards in their research. Finally, we look at how your research may be evaluated so that you have the opportunity to demonstrate that you have conducted quality research.

Section IV contains Chapters 7 and 8. In Chapter 7, Bernie Sullivan engages with the concept of the teacher as an agent of change. She explores the idea of change in educational practice leading to improvement, and explains that the improvement can be in the practice or in the understanding of practice. She demonstrates how the learning emanating from reflection on your practice can be expressed as new knowledge about it, and how you can develop a new theory of practice in the process. She indicates how your action research can have significance for you, as researcher, for your students, for your colleagues and for the wider educational community. Chapter 8 gives you specific guidelines for writing up an action research project from various perspectives. Bernie outlines different methods of sharing your learning, depending on the purpose of the writing assignment. These include presenting work orally at conferences, writing articles for journals or online publications,

completing chapters for books and producing dissertations or theses for academic accreditation. Bernie suggests that learning communities represent another means of sharing the outcomes of your research, as well as constituting an opportunity for continuing your research
endeavours. This will ensure the sustainability of improvement in your educational practice
in the long term.

Mary, Máirín, Caitriona and Bernie are convinced that information about critical reflection alone will not enable you to become a teacher researcher who can reflect critically: to
achieve this you need to engage wholeheartedly with the living process of critical reflection and action in your classroom practice. So we have written this book for you in a way
that encompasses a holistic approach to knowledge creation that is hopefully conducive to
successful learning and teaching. We chose to write collaboratively rather than produce an
edited book, so that we could share and critique our personal learnings as teacher researchers with each other and with you, our reader. Critical reflection and dialogue are at the heart
of our approach. We begin the book by inviting you to develop a journal in which you could
dialogue with your ideas and your actions. We hope that you will go on to share the 'Pause
and reflect' suggestions with others, so that your collaborative dialogues will contribute to
your capability as a critically reflective teacher and researcher.

Finally, whether you dip into this book to support aspects of your research, or whether
you use its suggestions for pausing and reflecting to develop a critically reflective approach
in yourself, we hope that it will not only inspire you to engage in critical reflection, but that it
will also enable you to enjoy your experiences as a teacher researcher.

Yours
Bernie, Máirín, Mary and Caitriona

SECTION I

Where to begin?

Mary Roche

It is teachers who in the end will change the world of the school by understanding it.

Stenhouse 1981: 104

In this section we explore the notion of reflective practice and its implications for us as teacher researchers. We offer an overview of action research and of self-study action research, as we examine how reflection plays a key role in this form of educational enquiry. We explore how critical reflection might be developed as an important component of our everyday practice and we examine some relevant critical pedagogy theories.

Chapter 1 examines some of the key ideas and theories about reflection, reflection on practice and critical reflection. We invite you to take a step back and look at what you value in education. This will involve you being interrupted frequently in your reading as we ask reflective questions so as to guide you through beginning the process of thinking critically – first, on why you are an educator and, second, on the concept of education. We introduce you to the work of key theorists in the area of reflection and reflective practice. In later chapters we will examine in deeper detail some practical applications of these theories.

Chapter 2 looks at research, in particular educational research. We provide an overview of action research as a research paradigm. We explore self-study action research as an appropriate methodology for critically reflecting on practice. We examine how you might experience critical pedagogy in your everyday work as we look at the ideas of Paulo Freire, Maxine Greene and Joe Kincheloe, among others.

1 Pausing and reflecting

Introduction

As a teacher researcher you are located in a particular context. You know this context well. As a professional you can be seen as an expert. You are now beginning the process of closely studying your practice within this context with a view to understanding your practice better and, maybe, even improving it. This will require reflection and critical thinking about what you do and why.

We invite you to begin this process by examining some theories of reflection, and theories to do with educational research. This may seem at times to be heavy going. However, in order to get a sense of why reflection is a core element of self-study action research you will need to grapple with the theoretical frameworks – especially if you are studying for a postgraduate degree.

We begin by looking at Stenhouse, whose work has been very influential in developing an understanding of teacher research. As we said at the start of this section, Stenhouse argued that 'It is teachers who in the end will change the world of the school by understanding it' (1981: 104). McLaughlin (2004) links the idea of reflecting (so as to understand better the world of education) with the idea of being an 'extended professional' (Hoyle 1975). Citing Stenhouse (1975), she argues that being an extended professional involves teachers *themselves* studying their teaching rather than leaving it to other, outsider researchers to interpret the teachers' own practices (McLaughlin 2004: 128). This last point is hugely important. We authors guide you towards studying your own practice with a view to improving it; you are in the driving seat here rather than being a passenger waiting for outside others to tell you what you need to do. This resonates strongly with what Stenhouse proposed. Stenhouse (1980) argued that 'education is learning in the context of a search for truth... [and that] reaching towards the truth in education is a matter of situational professional judgement' (p. 3). This point is also very important because it tells us that teachers, situated in their own professional contexts, can make judgements about that context and their practice within it. We cannot do this however, without first reflecting on what we do and why we do it.

In this chapter:

- You will examine some of the key ideas about reflection, reflection on practice and critical reflection.
- You will take a step back and look at what you value in education.
- You will be guided through a process of reflecting on why you are an educator as you begin reflecting critically on the concept of education.
- You will be introduced to the work of key theorists in the area of reflection and reflective practice.

Key ideas about reflection, reflection on practice and critical reflection

Stenhouse, like Hoyle (1975), viewed the extended professional as someone who has a broad vision of education, who values the theory underpinning pedagogy and who can provide a critical rationale for their practice. Citing Stenhouse (1975: 143), McLaughlin (2004: 128) suggests that being an extended professional involves the commitment to systematic questioning of one's own teaching as a basis for development; the dedication and the skills to study one's own teaching; and the concern to question and to test theory in practice. Hammersley (1993: 428) adds a fourth point: 'readiness to allow others to observe your work and to discuss it with them on an honest, open basis'.

These elements resonate very much with what we authors believe. As we progress through each chapter in this book, we explore how you can become an extended professional by studying your own educational context, with a view to improving both your practice and your understanding of your practice. You might ask why all this reflection and thinking is even necessary. What is the point? As we work though this first section you may gain some clarity around this. For example, Noffke (1997) suggests that the reasons teachers give for engaging in research are to do with arriving at a better understanding and improvement of one's own teaching; hoping to produce knowledge that could be of benefit to other educators; wanting to contribute to greater equity and democracy in education in particular and society in general. This matches well with what we are hoping to achieve here. You might, at this stage be happy with the first of those reasons. As you gain a better understanding of critically reflective practice you might also appreciate that you can achieve the others as well.

If we unpack Stenhouse's assertion that 'it is teachers who in the end will change the world of the school by understanding it' we see that it involves *understanding so as to change*. As teacher researchers, trying to examine our practice so as to understand what we do, in order to improve or change what we do, we quickly come to realise that we, first of all, need to name or identify what it is we want to change. Our lecturers, supervisors and tutors, and the literatures, tell us that, in order to identify our research question (our area of focus), we need to reflect. That, however, is easier said than done. Where to begin? How do we 'do' reflection? Is it just like 'thinking about something'? What exactly is 'reflective thinking'?

The first point to recognise is that reflective thinking is usually very personal, even though you may be scaffolded or guided by questions from your tutors – or, as in the case of this book, by us. You will have to take aspects of your practice and think deliberately, purposefully and deeply about them, to see if you can gain insights and improvement. So, in this sense, reflection differs from ordinary thought.

Reflective thinking usually involves retrospection – looking back at some event and analysing it. It may not even be an event: reflective thinking could also be triggered by re-examining or looking anew at an idea or a concept or a teaching approach, or even an artefact such as an academic paper, a textbook or a teaching resource. It will, however, involve examining the event/idea/approach/artefact from as many different perspectives as possible, and then trying to explain the situation for yourself. You need to think deeply about the relevance of this event, idea, approach or artefact. However, reflection can also involve looking forward, as you try to imagine how a specific course of action might turn out, and what the relevance of that would be for you and for your pupils. Individual personal reflection is often the first step in the process, but you can also further develop your understanding by discussing your ideas with colleagues or friends. Your own reflections then, combined with dialogue with others, have the potential to be very powerful.

Pause and reflect

You need to begin keeping a reflective journal. We elaborate on this in later chapters. But you need to start one now. As you read this book, jot down things that strike you or questions that are raised for you. This will form a good basis for beginning what Lindsey *et al.* (2015: 13) called your 'dialogue with yourself'. Your reflective journal can become a 'window into your own pedagogical thoughts and actions' (Loughran 2006: 85).

We must also re-emphasise that this reflection will be all the more robust if you have a critical friend or friends with whom to continue that dialogue. Do you have a colleague who is supportive and open to the idea of reflective practice with whom you might discuss your practice or your ideas? In your journal perhaps you could note who this friend might be and how you might present your emerging ideas to them. (The idea of critical friends is further explored in later chapters.)

As we have said, reflective thinking about an event that has already happened is more than just recalling an event and describing it: it involves interpretation and explanation also. This is a skill just like any other and will improve with practice. We could say that reflective thinking involves all levels of Bloom's Taxonomy (1956). We deliberately recall an event and we try to understand it better by examining it practically and abstractly. We analyse it and, perhaps, look for recurrent patterns within it. We make connections or synthesise our own understanding with the views of others, including academic literatures, and we evaluate or judge it, and perhaps even create new knowledge for ourselves, and for others, in the process.

In Chapter 3 you will be given ample opportunities to hone this skill. For now, though, we begin by examining the act of reflection itself.

What do the experts say about reflection?

Reflection affords us a space in which to take stock of experience (Argyris & Schön 1978; Dewey 1933; Kolb 1984; Schön 1983). Bolton (2014: xix) suggests that reflection is 'a powerful process which takes [people] to the heart of what is significant for them, enables them to explore it, and then supports them to make changes which develop practice based on their learning.'

We authors see reflection as an essential component of learning and we argue that it is in itself an action: it requires *doing* something – in this case thinking with a specific purpose, what Di Stefano *et al.* (2015: 7) call 'purposeful and intentional action on the part of an individual' so as to 'synthesize, abstract, and articulate the key lessons learned from experience.' We agree with this definition and we concur, too, with Zwozdiak-Myers (2012) who also suggests that reflection represents a deliberate and conscious process. We acknowledge that reflection is related to the past because it is generally about action that has already taken place. However, as we said earlier, the purpose of reflection is related to the future.

Each teacher researcher must find their own way to becoming or being reflective. We acknowledge that some people are naturally more introspective and reflective than others. That said, however, we can improve and, with practice, becoming more reflective may even develop into a lifelong habit. We agree with Larrivee (2000) who argues that critical reflection is not only a way of approaching teaching but that it can develop into a way of life. The more teachers explore, she says, the more they discover. The more they question, the more they access new realms of possibility. She suggests that there are a variety of pathways to becoming a reflective practitioner and that each teacher must find his or her own path.

> Any path a teacher chooses must involve a willingness to be an active participant in a perpetual growth process requiring ongoing critical reflection on classroom practices. The journey involves infusing personal beliefs and values into a professional identity, resulting in developing a deliberate code of conduct.
>
> (Larrivee 2000: 306)

Hayes *et al.* (2014: 3) suggest that the 'original definition of reflection in education probably came from Dewey (1933) who discusses reflection in the light of professionalism', and this, they say, was developed further by Schön (1983) into a process he called 'reflective practice'. Hayes *et al.* (2014) provide several models of reflection (pp. 8-14). They examine how practitioners look for 'real solutions to real problems'. Altrichter *et al.* (2005: 206) suggest that action researchers must continuously examine the expected and unexpected consequences of their action. They continue:

> The results of reflection are continuously transformed into practice, and practice continuously throws up reasons for reflection and development of these practical theories. The term for this characteristic feature of action research is *reflexivity*.
>
> (Altrichter *et al.* 2005: 206)

Maybe you are beginning to see that reflection then, is about far more than just thinking back over or idly musing or pondering on an issue or an event. Reflection is complex and intentional and future oriented. It is an intellectual *activity* that aims at generating learning from experience (Stevens and Cooper 2009), and there are skills and dispositions required for engaging in reflection.

The dispositions needed for reflective practice

Dewey (1933: 33) identified the three traits or characteristics most required of reflective practitioners as wholeheartedness, openmindedness and intellectual responsibility.

Wholeheartedness implies that there is passion and enthusiasm and energy involved and seems to involve more than logic and rationality. Zeichner and Liston (1996: 9) suggest that reflection involves intuition, emotion and passion and, like Larrivee (2000) say it is not something that can be neatly packaged as a set of techniques for teachers.

Openmindedness implies generosity of spirit – an ability to take on board the views of others, even if they are contrary to one's own. It involves active listening, and processing, and critical engagement with ideas. It is the opposite of fundamentalist thinking or rigid adherence to uncritiqued points of view or beliefs. It implies that we accept that our thinking and our knowledge may be incomplete and partial and continuously under construction. We ask 'How can I understand better what I am doing?' or 'How might I teach better?' We share our current best thinking with critical friends and we invite feedback and constructive criticism. We examine education literature to see if we can find support or otherwise for our ideas.

Responsibility means we hold ourselves accountable for our thinking and actions. We disseminate or share our work-in-progress as well as our finished papers and books. We invite critique. We acknowledge that we are influenced by our assumptions and values and we ask ourselves why things are the way they are, as we seek viable and life-affirming alternatives. To Dewey's original three dispositions, we could add several other dispositions – such as diligence, curiosity, care, integrity, and professionalism.

As well as the skills and dispositions of reflection, there is the question of knowledge too: what we know and how we know is influenced by our background and contexts. We acknowledge that here too, our values play a significant role: our ability to reflect on the world and our place in it is influenced by our experiences, and our interpretations of them, underpinned by the values we hold.

By values, in this context, we mean the underpinning philosophy of teaching and learning that informs how we act as teachers. This is in turn influenced by the assumptions we hold about knowledge and about our relationships with others – particularly those with whom we work. Values about knowledge can be referred to as *epistemological* values, and those that involve how we see ourselves in relation with, and to, others can be referred to as *ontological* values or values about being (see also McDonagh *et al.* 2012: 27–45). In a little while we will guide you as you begin the process of reflecting on the values upon which your teaching life is built.

On the home page of our website (www.eari.ie) we have the following quote from Maxine Greene:

> To proceed unthinkingly is to be caught in the flux of things, to be 'caught up' in dailyness, in the sequences of tasks and routines. Of course we have to proceed that way a good deal of the time, but there should be moments when we deliberately try to draw meaning out of particular incidents and experiences. This requires a pause …
>
> (Greene 1984: 55)

We also concluded our previous book, McDonagh *et al.* (2012: 152), with the same quote because we feel that it encapsulates the first requirement of reflection – taking time. Stepping back and pausing takes time.

Pause and reflect

Now perhaps you might try to create your own definition of reflection. Record it in your journal and revisit it and, perhaps, add to it or amend it as you read on.

Write a paragraph about one incident or event in your teaching life that stands out for you as being something you enjoyed or of which you are proud. Analyse why that event is a significant one. Are there any literatures that might back up or support what you have written?

To revisit the issue of making time: write a paragraph in your reflective journal about where in your busy day you might make time for reflection. In my case I stopped watching television. This might be a step too far for you, but perhaps you could begin to be more discriminating in your viewing habits. When I embarked on my Master's and PhD studies, I was a fulltime teacher, wife and mother with all that *that* entails. TV watching was the only aspect of my life that I felt could be jettisoned. It has become a way of life for me: I now rarely watch television. One of my colleagues, embarking on his postgraduate studies, got up ninety minutes earlier every day and used that time to read and write. Another friend bought a new shed that she installed at the end of her garden and fitted out as a study. She spent her weekends in there. Her family were warned not to interrupt unless some crisis occurred.

Making time for reflection

We must give ourselves time because reflection requires a standing back from events or issues or contexts in order to try to make sense of them. However, bear in mind that memory can be unreliable and that this is where your reflective journal may become invaluable. For example Hayes *et al.* (2014: 3-4) caution against inaccurate memories: 'the further away in time you are from a situation the less you remember about it and, more disturbingly, you may even appear to remember things related to the event that never transpired.' They go on to describe how this is recognised in the legal profession and how witness accounts are considered less reliable after just twenty-four hours. It is important therefore to get into the habit of writing in your reflective journal every day. We advise that you record your thoughts and feelings as soon as possible after events: you can always go back and meta-reflect, that is, reflect on your reflections. You will be invited to do this as you read Chapter 4.

Greene (1984: 55) asks 'how often … do we reflect on what we are doing, given our incessant involvement in the activity of teaching, maintaining order, meeting needs, making plans?' There are myriads of other activities included in any teacher's role. Taking time out to reflect may seem like a luxury in the busy race for coverage of curriculum – what Dadds (2001: 49-53) called the 'hurry-along curriculum'. Restating our view that reflection is purposeful and deliberate action, we would argue that the busier the school day, the more need there is to stop and reflect on the micro of one's practice so as to begin the process of examining critically the macro of the world of education. Dadds (2001) links the hurry-along curriculum to teaching for coverage and posits, as an antidote, a 'wait-a-while' curriculum – based on understanding and reflection. It takes serious reflection though, to identify that a hurry-along curriculum is teacher-centred and grounded in transmission or delivery of facts and information and coverage of material on a syllabus, whereas a wait-a-while curriculum is learner-focused and grounded in meaning-making and understanding. All of these stances are underpinned by the values we hold about teaching and learning and our views about ourselves and others.

Pause and reflect

Do you agree or disagree with Dadds?

If you agree with Dadds, then try to identify when you are most likely to feel this sense of stress.

How might you begin to 'wait-a-while'? What could you do alone, or with colleagues, that could ease this hurry-along burden? Could you devolve more power to students?

Beginning the process of reflecting on why you are an educator and critically reflecting on the concept of education

What do we mean when we say 'reflect' on our practice?

The phrase 'our practice' refers to what we do every day as teachers. It includes the planning and pedagogical choices or micro-decisions that we make, and the actions that follow from our decisions. In his foreword to Bolton (2014: xiii), Brookfield (2014) suggests that 'reflecting on the meaning of events and constructing experience from these is as old as human thought and ... central to any attempt to lead a significant life'. Bolton herself argues that reflection involves 'taking ownership of learning' (p. 33).

Unless we want to become mere automatons who follow uncritically the directives of others, we need to reflect on what we do and why we do it. Reflecting on our practice, then, involves deliberately and systematically looking at what is going on in our day to day work: exploring and analysing incidents that happen and seeking ways, perhaps, of working more efficiently. We ask ourselves lots of 'how' questions and 'when' and 'what' questions – nuts and bolts questions that might result in descriptions of our practice.

Critical reflection

But there are also 'why' questions. *Critical* reflection goes beyond the 'nuts and bolts' of practice and is concerned with explanation. Alhadeff (2003: n/p) suggests that critical reflection is 'the capacity to challenge the assumptions through which one gives meaning to one's own experience following a purpose of emancipation'. Here we see that there is a bigger reason for critical reflection – one that is located in a wider sense of social justice. He cites many authors who write about critical reflection and who all vary in their definitions depending on their own epistemological backgrounds (e.g. Brookfield 1995, 2000; Burbules and Berk 1999; Garrison 1991; Gore 1993; Mezirow 1998; Usher *et al.* 1997).

As we can see, reflection then, can be seen as a tool for, or an approach to, understanding practice. It might also be seen as a skill or competence, evidence of which may be required by teacher education courses. For people like Brookfield (above) it is to do with issues of emancipation and justice. Dewey and Schön might view it as a form of problem-solving and as active learning, and Freire would consider it necessary for 'problematising', again with a social justice perspective. We will take a deeper look at the work of these theorists in later chapters. Greene's work shows that she sees reflection as a means of existential pondering so as to become more wide awake. She argues that, as teachers, we are all influenced by our background and contexts (1984: 58). Reflecting then, might entail, for some of us, examining what our personal experiences of education, schooling and teachers were.

Our understanding of critical reflection

Having looked briefly at what other theorists say about critical reflection, we authors take a broad definition: we consider that critical reflection involves deliberately and purposefully looking at issues and incidents from as many angles as possible, analysing them for their effects on us and on others, and then using our critical faculties to synthesise, evaluate and make informed decisions about them. We can then provide a rationale to ourselves and others for why we work the way we do. This process may even involve challenging our deeply held assumptions about the way things are. It may include asking, as Greene frequently did, why things are as they are and why they can't be imagined otherwise.

Pause and reflect

Now we are going to look at examples of two different sets or types of reflective questions. Both sets of questions are key to reflective practice. (Note: the following are just examples of questions – they may not all be relevant for you.)

Here is the first set: why do I teach the way I do? Am I right or wrong? Why did my efforts to differentiate my assessments not work? Why are some students not engaged? Is it my fault? Why do some students hand in sloppy work?

Here is the second set: why are schools organised the way they are? Why is the curriculum structured in the way it is? Who decides that frequent testing is the answer to school improvement? What influences how a curriculum is formed?

Ask yourself: how is the second set of questions different from the first set? What are they about?

Hint: The first set of questions is located at the micro level of classroom practice; the second relates more to the macro level of education in general. Is it easier or more difficult to answer the second set of questions than the first set? Why?

The point that is being made here is that we cannot really separate what is happening in our own classrooms from the wider world of education. Our schools and our pupils and our work are influenced by complex socio-cultural and policy contexts.

We cannot separate our work from our values either.

Values

Many of the texts written about action research devote space to considering values (Loughran 2006; McNiff and Whitehead 2002, 2006, 2009; Reason and Bradbury 2001, 2008, and many more).

As we said earlier, we might notice that sometimes, when we take a step back from the daily busy-ness of our classrooms, there are aspects of our practice that have a recurrent pattern or a rhythm. We notice that perhaps there are underpinning values to what we do. Identifying these values involves taking time to think things through for ourselves – asking ourselves 'What do I do and why do I do it?' Maybe we can even go a step further and ask 'How can I do it better?' But that begs the question 'Why do I want to improve?' and brings us right back to the notion of values.

Here is a vignette, drawn from my own work, that explains how, when I took time to reflect, I began to identify and articulate my educational values.

Vignette

When I first began to teach I was confronted by very large classes. Much of my school day was spent keeping them conforming and silent. It did not dawn on me to question the justice or fairness of an educational system that put an unprobated teacher in front of a huge class of disadvantaged kindergarteners. For me and, I suspect, for many other young teachers that was simply the way things were: that was how education was 'done'. One 'delivered' the curriculum as best one could in the circumstances. Being largely uncritical, I was unable to form the language to question those circumstances. However, as the years went on and class sizes diminished somewhat, I still felt a sense of unease and concern about my didactic practices that I began to realise were grounded in norms of control and management. I examined my educational values and realised I valued dialogue and enquiry and active learning; I started to look for ways of encouraging more dialogue in my class. As I grew in confidence and grew as a critically reflective practitioner I discovered that it was up to me to change me. I joined a group of like-minded teachers and engaged in professional conversations. I began asking more and more critical questions. I began researching how I might develop more dialogical pedagogies. This has led me to develop an approach called 'Critical Thinking and Book Talk' through which I encourage children to engage in critical thinking through using picturebooks and through providing professional development courses; I encourage teachers to try it for themselves in their classrooms. Four decades after my first teaching experiences I published a book called *Developing Children's Critical Thinking through Picturebooks* (Roche 2015). That book is firmly grounded in my values of dialogical pedagogy and critical thinking.

> But this all began because I identified that I held educational values about creating a democratic classroom where children were invited to talk and think with each other and with me as we created a community of enquiry.

In my case, the process of becoming critical developed slowly for the first two decades of my career and accelerated sharply when I began my postgraduate studies and was obliged to think more critically. I can vividly recall the sense of excitement and discovery as I began to unpack and challenge some hitherto taken-for-granted norms. It was the beginning of a process of personal and professional transformation.

How do we establish that our values are 'good' values?

Brookfield (2012: 14) cautions about the assumptions we make around thinking critically and values. He warns that, as soon as you understand critical thinking to be linked to action, you enter the realm of values because you have to ask the questions 'Action for what?' and 'Whose actions do we want to support?' However, care must be taken, he says, because 'sometimes actions serve the ends of the actor, and if the actor is trying to hoodwink, manipulate, harm or brutalize another, then those actions surely are questionable'.

Given what Brookfield says, then, how do we establish that our values are 'good' values? We could begin by asking ourselves if our values are what Whitehead (2007: n/p) calls 'life affirming'. Are our values likely to endure over time? If they are just focused on, perhaps, getting through our postgraduate degree programme, then they might be too short-lived to be sustainable. Are our values likely to contribute to the common good – are they likely to lead to actions that will ultimately benefit others – our pupils, our colleagues, our institution and even, ultimately, wider educational contexts?

There is no view from nowhere (Nagel 1986). Education, learning, teaching, knowledge are concepts that are all deeply imbued with values and ideologies. Education is never neutral: everyone involved in education has an agenda. It may be very benign – such as wishing to make a difference in children's lives, to help children learn what is going to be useful to them as active participants in the world and so on. The everyday choices we make when planning lessons, in relation to teaching strategies, resources, assessment tools, all draw on our assumptions and values. Sociologists who theorise the socio-cultural bases of education might argue that education policy is influenced by prevailing socio-political agendas.

Critical pedagogues delve into the grander narratives that inform how education policy is formed. They critique the technical rational or neo-liberal agendas at work in our world. We will examine more closely the work of some critical pedagogues in Chapter 2. For each of us teachers, though, uncovering the values base that informs what *we* do is often the starting point for critical reflection. Greene (1988: 134) suggests that, in the classroom, we must be able to uncover 'those ideologies that masquerade as neutral frameworks'. She argued that 'teachers ... have to learn to love the questions'. Reflection then, for Greene, involves trying to become critically conscious of what is involved in the complex business of teaching and learning. It involves trying 'to come awake and find new visions, new ways of living in the fragile human world' (Greene 2001: 207).

What Greene suggests requires a great deal of highly critical and informed reflection and may not be easy for people beginning the process. So let's break the process down and begin to articulate some of the underpinning values we hold about teaching and learning.

Stepping back and looking at what you value in education: beginning the process

In the next few pages we will interrupt your reading quite often with some reflective questions. We begin with what you value about your teaching life. We start with some guiding questions. They are in no particular order and you may think up new ones for yourself as you go on.

Pause and reflect

What led you to become a teacher? What were the deciding factors for you? Were you guided by pragmatic or economic factors such as the teacher education college being near you and thus saving on accommodation and travelling costs or that teaching suits childcare? If so, take heart. Maxine Greene admits that she got into education because the course hours matched her child-minding needs.

Did you have a particular teacher you admired and whom you wanted to emulate? Nel Noddings (1997) stated that her professional and academic life developed largely as a result of 'various accidents and awareness of opportunity' (p. 166), and that the chance of moving schools and being taught by a passionate and caring maths teacher led her into maths education and subsequently into writing about care. A famous study by Dan Lortie (1975) showed that many people are drawn into teaching and have (often misguided) preconceived ideas of what teaching involves because of the many years they spent in school observing teachers.

Did you always want to be a teacher? Were you the kind of child who played 'school'? When asked to write a personal philosophy of teaching, many education students and teachers admit that this was the case.

Did you become a teacher because your parent, grandparent or cousin was a teacher? This could be very helpful to you because it means you have a fair enough grasp of the trials and tribulations of a teacher's life. It means too that you already have a vocabulary with which to express your ideas, or one that allows you to access the discourses of education.

Are you animated by a sense of justice and equity? Do you want to make a difference in the lives of children and help them to become active agents in their own learning and in their world? These too are valid reasons for becoming a teacher.

What do you think each of these often taken-for-granted words mean – education, intelligence, teaching, learning, knowledge?

Aspects of reflective practice and some theorists of reflective practice

Definitions of reflection vary but all agree that reflection is about learning. For example, Moon (2001b: 2) says that 'Reflection is a form of mental processing – like a form of thinking – that we use to fulfil a purpose or to achieve some anticipated outcome.' She also says (p. 10) that while 'Reflection can be superficial and little more than descriptive', it can also be 'deep and transformative (and involved in the transformative stage of learning)'; she outlines how difficult the process may be for those who do not understand why reflection is necessary and how to do it.

Di Stefano *et al.* (2015: 1) draw on literatures of cognitive psychology and neuroscience to propose that they also consider reflection to be 'one of the critical components of learning'. Drawing on a field experiment and from literatures of cognitive psychology they argue that 'purposeful reflection on one's accumulated experience leads to greater learning than the accumulation of additional experience' and they suggest that 'reflection builds confidence in the ability to achieve a goal, which in turn translates into higher rates of learning' (ibid.).

Brookfield (1995: 1) considers teaching to be an extremely moral and ethical undertaking. He considers critical reflection crucial for ensuring that educators act in ethical and moral ways. Once again, you might need to unpack statements like this and examine how you might ascertain that you are acting ethically and morally. Brookfield (ibid.) provides lots of examples that might support your exploration as he examines all kinds of assumptions about teaching and learning. We authors believe that Brookfield's work resonates strongly with the educational values we hold. For example, he suggests that what we think are democratic, respectful ways of treating people can be experienced by them as oppressive and constraining. 'One of the hardest things teachers learn', he says, is that 'the sincerity of their intentions does not guarantee the purity of their practice' (ibid.).

'Every teaching event', says Brookfield (ibid.), 'takes place in a social setting that involves the subjectivities of others, usually our learners.' He bids us remember that each of *them* must also be using *their* beliefs, values and assumptions to interpret the teaching events and settings.

Brookfield (2012: 1-2) also suggests that the basis of critical reflection is 'the basic process of critical thinking'. He argues that if practitioners cannot think critically their survival is 'in peril':

> If you can't think critically you have no chance of recognizing, let alone pushing back on, those times you are being manipulated. And if you can't think critically you will behave in ways that have less chance of achieving the results you want. So critical thinking is not just an academic process... It is a way of living that helps you stay intact when any number of organizations (corporate, political, educational, and cultural) are trying to get you to think and act in ways that serve their purposes. (Ibid.)

In his earlier book, Brookfield (1995) lists six benefits of critical reflection. The first pair are to do with making informed decisions and providing a rationale for practice; the second pair are about caring for oneself – avoiding self-laceration and see-sawing emotions; the final pair deal with enlivening the classroom and providing a more democratic learning environment.

We have already referred to how critical reflection provides us with ways of explaining our practice. We have also spoken about the social justice aspects of engaging in critical reflection. What we haven't mentioned is that, sometimes, critical reflection can unearth uncomfortable or stressful aspects of practice. Brookfield's (ibid.) second pair of benefits can be very reassuring. Here is a vignette from my current practice setting.

Vignette

I teach in an initial teacher education context. When my student teachers read Brook-field's piece on 'avoiding self-laceration' as they reflected on perceived 'disasters' while on school placement experience, they often felt comforted. They came to realise that if they planned and prepared and did their level best to teach in ways that were just and fair, differentiating their teaching, resources and assessments to the best of their ability, treating all children with respect, then any 'disaster' may not be their fault. The reasons for such 'disasters' may lie outside their control and may require a whole-school or community-based solution.

Arguing from a socio-cultural standpoint, Ballantine and Spade (2015: 9) state that 'Educa-tion is one of the major structural parts, or *institutions* in society... [and exists] in a larger framework of interconnected institutions found in every society, including family, religion, politics, economics and health, in addition to education' (emphasis in original). All educa-tion systems involve people in community, interacting with each other. Education systems involve processes and policies also. These are premised on value bases about knowledge and learning, and how and why people should be educated. This provides another standpoint for reflection.

Coghlan and Brannick (2014) suggest that reflection is a process of 'interiority' – a term they use to describe how action researchers move between the realms of theory and practi-cal knowing, valuing both while recognising the different contributions that each makes.

> The challenge is to turn from the outer world of practical knowing and theory to appro-priation of oneself as a knower i.e. one's own interiority. Interiority involves shifting from *what* we know to *how* we know, a process of intellectual self-awareness. (Ibid.: 52, emphases in original)

Citing Mezirow (1991), Coghlan and Brannick (2014: 13) identify three forms of reflection and argue that all three are crucial: content reflection – where you think about the issues, what you think is happening; process reflection – where you think about strategies and pro-cedures, and how things are being done; premise reflection – where you critique underlying assumptions and perspectives

A key feature of most of the theorists outlined is that a reflective teacher is aware of and questions the assumptions and values they bring to teaching. Rudduck (1991: 324) argues that many experienced teachers do not see the 'capacity for analysis and reflection as part of their mainstream image of professional practice'. Critical reflection is a robust activity and Rudduck asserts that reflection is active and developmental – not 'a flabby, armchair aspiration' (ibid.).

Examining values and attitudes or assumptions and beliefs

Now we interrupt again to help you try to examine the values and attitudes or assumptions and beliefs that you hold about teaching and learning. Answering the questions below will help you to begin to identify your values about knowledge and about your pedagogical rela-tionship with learners. This involves another active session of reflection.

Pause and reflect

What do you think constitutes effective teaching? What kind of teacher is an effective teacher? What are the characteristics or traits of an effective teacher? What is your role as a teacher? Do you see yourself as master, guide, coach, facilitator, evangelist, 'edutainer', social worker, deliverer of a syllabus, transmitter of knowledge and so on? Do you see your role as including more than one of these? What kinds of teaching strategies might you be most likely to use? Are there areas of concern to you? What are they? Jot them down in your research journal. Try to zone in on what, exactly, is causing you disquiet. What possible steps could you take to improve?

What do you think learning means? What would an effective learning situation look like? Who is likely to be a 'good' learner? Do you have an idea of how your ideal pupil behaves? Is your ideal pupil most likely male or female? How would you know that learning has happened? What methods would you use to determine this? Are any of these areas causing you to feel that you could do better? How will you go about it?

The answers you gave to these questions will assist you now in identifying your values about teaching and learning. These values will inform your methodology – how you teach. If, on the one hand, you see your role as deliverer of a syllabus and of facts and knowledge, then you will have a particular style of teaching that may be didactic and teacher-centred. You will focus on measurable outcomes and will use assessments in a particular way. You will have strong views on how pupils should behave and what a classroom should look like. You will plan well, be well prepared for lessons and will brook no laziness or lack of attention on the part of students. Your classroom management style will be firm and as fair as you can make it. You could be an extremely diligent, hardworking and conscientious teacher. But there may be aspects of your practice with which you are less than happy. You may need to examine these further so as to form a plan of action as you seek to improve. An action research approach may help.

If, on the other hand, you see your role as a guide and a facilitator of learning, then you will also have a particular style of teaching that will be grounded in developing a good peda-gogical relationship with your pupils so that you can help each one learn to the best of their ability. Your teaching would be considered as learner-centred. You will plan equally well and you will focus on differentiation as you tailor content, teaching strategies, resources and assessment to match learners. You may have a busy and buzzy classroom with a more laid-back approach to discipline as long as children appear to be participating and engaging. You too could be an extremely diligent, hardworking and conscientious teacher. Again, maybe you feel you could improve and, again, an action research approach may help you formulate a plan. The rest of this book will guide you through that process.

So, reflection, especially critical reflection, is complex: it is not easy, or for sissies; it is pur-poseful action with an intention of learning more about, or improving one's understanding of, one's practice, but it is rewarding because it can help us to understand our practice and our contexts and the values that inform us, as we seek to improve what we do so as to maximise the learning opportunities for our pupils. Most importantly, remember that Dewey (1933: 78) said 'We do not learn from experience ... we learn from reflecting on experience.'

Conclusion

One of our aims in writing this book is to try to help you create and develop the habit of critical thinking and critical reflection. Quinlan (2014) states that 'habits can be incredibly powerful, and forming the right ones can make a huge difference to the way you teach' (p. 61). However, making habits is one thing – breaking bad habits is another. If we have been 'proceeding unthinkingly' (Greene 1984: 55) throughout all our teaching lives, it will take a huge effort to begin to change that. Thinking is *hard* work. Students will often reach for Google or Bing to find someone else's thinking rather than sit and drill down into their own thought processes. To transform our practice into a meaningful exercise will involve the intentional and purposeful *action* of reflection and critical reflection.

> Transformative learning is the process by which we call into question our taken for granted frames of reference... to make them more inclusive, discriminating, open, and reflective so that they may generate beliefs and opinions that will prove more true or justified to guide action. (Mezirow 2000: 5-8, cited in Kasl and Yorks 2002: 1)

Transformative learning often involves deep, powerful emotions or beliefs and is evidenced in action. 'We experience a sense of surprise oftentimes, an acute sense that things may look otherwise, feel otherwise, be otherwise than we have assumed' and suddenly the world seems new, with possibilities still to be explored (Greene 2001: 116).

We end this chapter with a quote from Larrivee (2000) that we feel is apt: 'Unless teachers engage in critical reflection and ongoing discovery they stay trapped in unexamined judgments, interpretations, assumptions, and expectations' (p. 294).

In this chapter:

- You have been introduced you to the idea that before you can carry out any kind of systematic evaluation of your practice as a teacher you must first understand what reflection is and its relevance for carrying out an action research enquiry into what you do and why you do it as you go about your daily teaching life.
- You have seen that values are a core aspect of reflective practice and you have had your awareness of some of the complexity of education raised.
- You have begun to reflect on your life as a teacher and you have identified some of the values you hold about teaching, learning and education.
- You may have begun the process of identifying some concern you have about your work as a teacher.

Recommended reading and resources

Educational Action Research Ireland website www.eari.ie has the authors' publications.

McDonagh, C., Roche, M., Sullivan, B. and Glenn, M. (2012) *Enhancing Practice through Classroom Research: A Teacher's Guide to Professional Development* (Abingdon: Routledge) provides a good foundational text for those wishing to carry out classroom research.

Jack Whitehead's homepage offers a cornucopia of action research-related material: http://www.actionresearch.net/

Jean McNiff's website www.jeanmcniff.com has examples of theses and her own writing.

Stephen Brookfield shares several resources on his website: http://www.stephenbrookfield.com/Dr._Stephen_D._Brookfield/Home.html

Maxine Greene's (1988) *The Dialectic of Freedom*, New York: Teachers College Press, Chapter 1, pp. 1-23.

Video: *The Call to Teach*: William Ayers speaks with a group of educators at the Museum of Education at the University of South Carolina: https://www.youtube.com/watch?v=xQlEcXS5uQw

Video: *Inner Work and the Life of a Teacher*: Dr Debbie Stanley on the way inner work can change the outer world – for all ages: https://www.youtube.com/watch?v=pf2dcNmjd2I

2 What is action research?

Introduction

Before we can begin to understand what action research entails, we need to examine what we mean by research, specifically research in education, after which we explore what is meant by self-study action research. You will see, we hope, why we began this book with a chapter on reflection – because reflection plays a central role in all forms of action research. Self-study action research, however, depends on the researcher's ability to be critically reflective.

Research

According to the *Oxford Dictionary Online*, research is considered to be 'the systematic investigation into and study of materials and sources in order to establish facts and reach new conclusions'. Bassey (1990: 35) defined research as 'systematic, critical and self-critical enquiry which aims to contribute to the advancement of knowledge'. At its most basic, then, research is about searching for and gathering information so as to answer a question or solve some kind of problem.

Research in education

Morrison (2007) suggests that educational research is both 'a distinctive way of thinking about educational phenomena, that is, an *attitude*, and of investigating them, that is, an action or *activity*' (cited in Briggs and Coleman 2007: 13, emphases in original).

For a complete beginner trying to come to terms with the complex sets of ideas about what constitutes research and the different types of educational research, Bassey (1990) provides a concise overview. Suggesting that there are three main paradigms of research, Bassey begins by defining a research paradigm as 'a network of coherent ideas about the nature of the world and of the functions of researchers, which adhered to by a group of researchers, conditions the patterns of their thinking and underpins their research actions' (ibid., cited in Pollard 2002: 37). This is an important point: each paradigm of research is grounded in different values – beliefs about the nature of reality, and beliefs about the nature of education (see also Bassey 1999). In Chapter 1 we discussed how each of us is influenced by our beliefs and values and the assumptions we make about important aspects of education such as teaching, learning, intelligence, knowledge. We discussed how we often allow such important concepts to go largely unexplored because we assume that our understanding is the correct one. Morrison (2007) suggests that, as researchers make sense of research data, they draw both implicitly or explicitly upon a set of beliefs about how their analysis might be understood.

> Researchers who adhere to a specific paradigm will hold a kind of consensus about what does or should count as 'normal' research. (The term 'normal' is set in inverted commas deliberately; a range of practitioners, researchers, and policy makers may hold rather different perceptions about what constitutes 'normal' research.) (Morrison 2007, in Briggs and Coleman 2007: 23)

In this chapter:

- We discuss action research and self-study as appropriate approaches to reflecting on practice.
- We invite you to consider how you might experience critical pedagogy in your everyday work as we explore the ideas of some key critical pedagogues and examine the relevance of their work for challenging norms and assumptions around teaching and learning.

So, what exactly is action research?

Action research embraces the idea that each researcher is informed by their own values, norms and assumptions. Action researchers work in different ways in different contexts and settings and the action research approach provides practitioner researchers with a way of studying their own work so as to understand it better as they begin to try to make some systematic improvement to it. For the teacher researcher, action research can constitute a living, authentic form of continuing professional development (CPD) that has the potential to change both the practice and the practitioner irrevocably. McNiff (2002a: n/p) emphasises the centrality of self-reflection to action research – because, she argues, 'Action research is an enquiry conducted by the self into the self.' Each practitioner (teacher) using this research approach thinks about their own life and work, asking themselves why they do the things that they do, and why they are the way that they are (ibid.). Schulte (2002: 101) defines that transformation as a 'continuous evolution of one's own understanding and perspectives'. She argues that the transformation requires teachers to think critically about the world and to challenge how power and control are constructed and 'mapped onto them'. She warns too that engaging in such critical reflection may result in a 'disruption of values or cultural beliefs'. Perhaps you can see now why, in Chapter 1, we asked you to begin the process of challenging some norms about the world of education.

Kemmis (2009: 463) suggests that 'action research has the potential to change people's practices, their understandings of their practices, and the conditions under which they practice'. Action research, he says, can change people's patterns of 'saying', 'doing' and 'relating' so as to form new patterns, new ways of life. In other words, Kemmis argues, action research can be 'a meta-practice: a practice that changes other practices'.

When we study our own work we, too, are seeking knowledge about our practice, perhaps with a view to transforming it. We are doing so in order to make meaning of it and, thereby, to learn more about our professional lives. Mezirow (1990: 1) makes strong links between reflection and learning when he suggests that we reflect in order to 'make meaning'. To make 'meaning', he says, means to make sense of an experience – that is, we make an interpretation of it. Mezirow goes on to say that when we subsequently use this interpretation to guide decision-making or action, then making meaning becomes learning. Reflection, argues Mezirow, 'enables us to correct distortions in our beliefs and errors in problem-solving'. Because we are interpreting our own actions, Mezirow argues that reflection and meaning-making are intensely subjective and informed by our own beliefs, values and assumptions. 'What we perceive and fail to perceive, and what we think and fail to think are powerfully influenced by habits of expectation that constitute our frame of reference, that is, a set of assumptions that structure the way we interpret our experiences' (ibid.). He goes on, then, to suggest that the role of critical reflection is to unpack and challenge these assumptions. Here is further evidence that values matter in educational research, which is why we asked you to begin the process of identifying and articulating your educational values earlier. Reflection is key to this process and key to researching our practice to see if it matches our values.

Early work by McNiff *et al.* (e.g. 1996: 13) suggested that action research is 'systematic, critical enquiry made public', that it entails 'informed committed action' and has a 'worthwhile purpose'. By 2002 this stance had evolved considerably when McNiff (with Whitehead) stated that she began to see 'worthwhile purpose' as contributing to a 'good social order; a form of living in which people are free to make choices about creating their own identities and to recognise the need to negotiate these identities with others' (McNiff with Whitehead 2002: 13).

In (2011: 3) McNiff and Whitehead write:

> 'How to do action research' turns into 'Why do action research?' and 'What can you achieve for social good?'... how your action can transform into the grounds for your own and other people's new learning, and what the implications for your work may be.

This contrasts sharply with other definitions and discourses of action research. *The Glossary of Educational Reform* (http://edglossary.org/) provides an overview of action research as 'a cycle of action or cycle of inquiry, since it typically follows a predefined process that is repeated over time' (n/p). However, in this simplistic description of action research, the deeply reflective nature of the process is not mentioned at all, nor is there any reference to values or critical thinking.

Like McNiff and Whitehead, both Elliott and Riel emphasise the reflective nature of action research. Elliott (1978) suggests that action research is a self-reflective process in which teachers examine the themes implicit in their everyday practice; Riel (2010: n/p) suggests that:

> Action research provides a path of learning from and through one's practice... Over time, action researchers develop a deep understanding of the ways in which a variety of social and environmental forces interact to create complex patterns.

Koshy (2010: 4) states that 'research is about generating knowledge' saying, 'the purpose of action research is to learn through action leading to personal or professional development'.

As a teacher researcher you will come across a wide range of terms to describe practitioner research. In McDonagh *et al*. (2012: 3) we outline many of these, including self-study action research, critical action research and living educational theory (Whitehead 1989), which all share similar features.

From even the few theorists we have cited, perhaps you can see already that educational research seems to be about trying to gain a deeper understanding of some aspect of education, and action research can be viewed as a means for examining, through reflection and action, your own piece of the wider educational context.

It is worth noting that, referring to the positivist and interpretative traditions, McNiff and Whitehead (2011: 47) state that the stance of researchers working in these traditions remains external and that 'reality, and ideas about reality, are turned into free-standing things which can be studied, taken apart, and put back together again in new ways'. Disagreeing with such a stance, they suggest that 'this tendency has been exported also into many forms of action research. People talk about action research, but do not always see themselves as living participants doing action research.' It could be said that this does not fully address the critical theoretic framework of action research. 'Action research', according to McNiff and Whitehead,

> emerged from critical theory, and went beyond it. Critical theory asked, 'How can this situation be understood in order to change it?' but aimed only for understanding, not for action. Action research went into action and asked 'How can it be changed?' Some researchers, however, still like to locate action research within a broad framework of critical theory, emphasising its participatory nature to combat relations of power. (Ibid.)

In McDonagh *et al*. (2012) we also examine how one might begin the reflective process of uncovering and articulating one's own educational values. This brings us back to self-study action research. We suggest that as a teacher researcher you begin by examining the underpinning assumptions and values that inform your practice, through rigorous reflection; we have outlined the rationale for this process in some detail in Chapter 1.

Self-study action research

Lassonde *et al*. (2009) provide a historical account of the development of the self-study action research movement, suggesting that research in the area of reflection and reflective practice has strongly influenced the development of self-study as an approach to practitioner action research. They argue that this developing focus on reflective practice and practitioners led to a form of research that focused on the teacher as researcher of his or her own practice. 'Researchers found that teachers could examine and problematize their teaching by reflecting on their practice and by becoming reflective practitioners' (ibid.: 4) and they suggest, as we do, that Schön's and Dewey's influences were considerable.

Lassonde *et al*. (ibid.) further argue that self-study action researchers have particular characteristics: for example, they suggest that they must have a disposition that is open to ideas from others, and be willing to collaborate. This resonates with Dewey's thoughts about the characteristics of reflective practitioners of which we spoke in Chapter 1. Lassonde *et al*. (ibid.) suggest that self-study action research involves collaboration and dialogue, where one shares one's experience with critical friends who provide support as well as constructive challenge and critique. We fully support this view and you will be guided through this process in later chapters.

Pause and reflect

If you were to examine your own teaching, why might self-study action research be a suitable methodology?

Can you give a brief rationale?

As we try to process and summarise all of the information above, we might conclude that self-study action research is a deeply values-based approach to critical reflection on one's own work. It is basically about you studying you (in collaboration with others such as your pupils and colleagues), with a view to becoming a better practitioner. You can then provide a rationale for your actions along with evidence for your claim to any new knowledge. Like Schulte (2002: 104) you might find that reflecting on your teaching practice will assist you in seeing the connections between your personal self and your professional self. However, this kind of insight does not come about overnight.

I will now show you, through a vignette drawn from my own practice, how difficult it was for me to get on the inside of the idea that I was the focus of my research. I continually slipped into an externalist perspective.

Vignette

When I first started on self-study action research for my PhD I wanted to try to establish a more dialogical pedagogical practice. I set about trying various approaches and strategies and writing up with zeal my accounts of what happened. I researched literatures of children's oral development, children's thinking, classroom dialogue and dialogical pedagogy; I devoured texts about emancipatory education and critical pedagogy; I downloaded journal papers about critical thinking: and I wrote long polemics. One day, my supervisor asked me: 'What exactly are you researching?' and I burbled on and on about children and classrooms and teaching and education and got more and more perplexed as she shook her head after each one. She suggested I reflect on why she might be disagreeing with me and left me to it. 'Don't write another word until you can answer that question,' she added. I pondered and reflected and was still baffled. I discussed it with my adult daughter and as we teased it out; finally, the penny dropped. I saw what my supervisor meant. She had seen what I hadn't: that I was so busy focusing on pedagogical concepts and the actions of others, I had neglected to show evidence that I was the focus of the research. I needed to demonstrate more critical reflection on my own actions and decisions.

Let's assume that your area of concern is the low reading scores of your pupils. Let's look at two possible wordings of a research topic.

- I am researching my class of twenty-seven eight- and nine-year-olds in order to improve reading scores.
- I am researching my teaching of my class of twenty-seven eight- and nine-year-olds in order to improve as a reading teacher.

The first statement implies that you are doing research on your pupils. You are adopting an externalist or outsider stance, studying them and their reading test scores. In the second scenario you are looking at what you, as a teacher, are doing. Here, the stance is that of an insider and is subjective. In the second situation you are engaging in self-study action research.

Given the two scenarios above, now, perhaps, you can see why my supervisor was concerned (in the vignette). In my case, I was focusing on the class group, trying to improve or change them. In fact, what needed improving and changing was me. My focus had to change from looking at what others were or were not doing to what I was doing. My pupils could be the mirror in which I saw my practice reflected, but I needed to see that I was researching 'me': my thoughts, my ideas, my solutions to problems, my actions, decisions and plans.

I discovered throughout my own studies that it is really difficult to absorb these concepts and hold on to them. I frequently thought I 'got it', but I slipped constantly and needed my group of critical friends and my supervisor to keep me on track. Researching one's own *actions* is not the difficult part: researching one's rationale *for* that practice and *for* those actions is difficult; researching one's ideas, thoughts, assumptions and values is difficult too. I felt it would probably be far easier to research others. I could simply collect a lot of observational data, read a lot of literatures, analyse and synthesise and evaluate it, see where a lacuna existed, perhaps, and endeavour to fill it and create useful educational knowledge. Researching my own practice was far less linear and straightforward. It was like nailing jelly to a tree at times. Schön says:

> There is a high, hard ground where practitioners can make effective use of research-based theory and technique, and there is a swampy lowland where situations are confusing 'messes' incapable of technical solution... in the swamp are the problems of greatest human concern. (1983: 42)

When you begin to research your own practice you may feel that you are like someone slogging through a wet bog of opportunities, questions and advice. And, according to Mellor (2015: n/p) 'problems start to appear when we try to see new things we haven't seen before'. 'Self-study action research involves reflecting on and analysing your own practice with a view to improving it' sounds fine and good, but where do you begin? Neither reflecting alone nor reflection alone is enough.

Mellor (1998) speaks of the search for a methodology as a most confusing process:

> I have toyed with the metaphors of a journey, a garden, 'buying the thingamygig' and 'hunting the snark', but that which most closely embodies the development of this undertaking, with its dead ends, confusions, shifts in focus and occasional fruits of publication, is the unusual, but nonetheless extremely successful growth of the banyan tree. (p. 467)

In Roche (2007) I explain that, for much of my study, I had 'no research question and no clear method' and, like Mellor, I was 'working without rules in order to find out the rules of what

[I]'ve done' (Mellor 2001: 465). Initially, I found the situation destabilising because I could find no definitive 'method' for self-study action research. Being largely uncritical at that time, I desperately craved certainty: I wanted definition, clear answers, even a 'right' procedure to follow. For a long time, I floundered in the methodological freedom I had. It was all very unsettling. What saved me was the supportive and collegial nature of my PhD peers. We each brought our concerns and questions and tentative 'current best thinking' to our tutorial seminars and teased out together the more tangled knots.

This social and collegial aspect of professional conversations around one's self-study is crucial. My colleagues and I had regular face-to-face meetings in the university, but in between times there was always email or phone support. As we said earlier, self-study action research is definitely not for wimps: it requires deep critical reflection about our practice and we may uncover uncomfortable 'truths' from time to time. At these times we need affective nurturing as well as cognitive challenging. As one of my colleagues stated,

> self-study action research is not just about researching your working life: it becomes a *way of being*: you go to bed with it, your dream about it, you wake up with it, eat with it. It is everywhere in your world. (Conversation with MG August 2015)

The language of self-study action research

Perhaps you are beginning to see that there is a particular kind of language and discourse with self-study action research. It is not 'Dear Agony Aunt' confessional discourse; neither is it the detached language of the objective scientist. It is not mere description and anecdote and solipsism. It is careful and deliberate language derived from deep reflection and scrutiny of one's values and the actions that derive from holding these values. For example, here is a short vignette from the beginning of my own research account (Roche 2007).

Vignette

[This] is the narrative account of my self-study action research as I deliberately transformed myself from being a propositional thinker into a critical thinker. It is therefore a story of my own epistemological journey, and tells of what I now know and how I came to know it (Whitehead and McNiff 2006). My claim throughout is that I have come to know how I think and why I think as I do.... I now understand my pedagogical practice at a new level, in ways that I did not appreciate before. I can offer descriptions and explanations for my work with young children, and these descriptions and explanations constitute my living theory of critical practice. (Roche 2007: 1-2)

Articulating ontological and epistemological values

We said earlier that self-study action research begins with the articulation of one's values. We also need to show how these values then act as the explanation for how and why we act as we do (Whitehead and McNiff 2006). In my case, I began by examining my epistemological and ontological values. We looked at what these terms mean in Chapter 1, but let's remind ourselves here. Epistemological values are to do with how we view knowledge; ontological values are to do with being and how we see ourselves in relation with others. I stated in my thesis that my research was grounded in the values I held about research, education and my relationships with others. To make this accessible to others, I needed to show how these values acted as the explanatory principles for my work and for how I wrote my research account (Whitehead 2005a; McNiff and Whitehead 2006). I endeavoured to show how, as a self-study action researcher, I held myself morally accountable for the actions I took within my practice by explaining the reasons and purposes for those actions.

I explained how my practice was shaped by who I was/am, and how my identity was rooted in the ontological values I held. The scrutiny of my values as the grounds for practice enabled me to understand and justify my choice of research methodology. I explained that I had deliberately chosen a self-study action research methodology for my enquiry because I believed it to be one in which my educational commitments and my educational values would be in harmony. Whitehead and McNiff (2006: 86) describe how, in a living approach to educational action research, the researcher's ontological values can transform into an educational commitment. Similarly, Bullough and Pinnegar (2004: 319) suggest that issues of ontology, as 'one's being in and towards the world should be a central feature of any discussion of the value of self-study research'.

Values can transform into action

Raz (2001, cited in Whitehead and McNiff 2006: 85; Roche 2007: 3) explains how values remain as abstract concepts until they are transformed into living practices and thus have the potential for creating meaning. Here is an example from my own work that illustrates this point. I had stated that I valued dialogical pedagogy grounded in the concepts of care, justice and freedom. I needed to see these values in action in my everyday work.

Vignette

Drawing on (Roche 2007) here are some of the questions that I asked myself:
How do I live my values of care, freedom and justice in my practice?
How can I encourage my students to exercise their critical faculties and think for themselves?
How can I resist being prescriptive or didactic and instead seek to provide greater opportunities for my students to learn about their world through their own capacity for enquiry?

In my written account, I explained that this list was far from exhaustive: it simply provided some examples of the kinds of questions I asked of my practice and that you could ask of yours. In addressing these kinds of issues, I aimed to show how my descriptions and explanations of my critical and dialogical pedagogies demonstrated how I tried to live in the direction of my values as the grounds for my original claim to research-based knowledge. My understanding emerged both from the doing and from the reflection on doing. As I started to try to live more closely to the values I claimed to hold, my practice actually changed into a more dialogical form of pedagogy. As I went on to reflect on and scrutinise the various sets of values that informed how and who I was as I went about my daily work, I realised, as Lassonde *et al.* (2009) said, that as I actually did self-study action research I began to understand the process better.

I soon realised that I had learned to problematise. To explain my use of the term 'problematise', I draw on the literatures of critical pedagogy (for example, Darder *et al.*, 2003; Freire 1972; Kincheloe 2004). I began to understand problematising as looking at a situation from all sides so that, rather than accepting normative understandings, one draws back from a situation in order to look at it again from a more critical perspective.

This capacity for problematising led me to important new insights about the nature of my work. I learned that 'being a critical thinker' is not the same as 'doing critical thinking' or 'having critical thinking skills'. My examination of the processes of becoming a more critically aware person informed and transformed how I thought and taught, and now influences my approach to encouraging my students to be critically aware.

This brings us to a brief look at some of the proponents of critical pedagogy whose work has been influential in helping me to understand how my practice is located in broader narratives about education and the world.

Critical pedagogy and reflection

I believe that the reason it took me so long to see the contradictions in my thinking as I began my postgraduate studies may have had something to do with my own school experiences of being taught to think about knowledge as information 'out there' rather than something that I could generate for myself. Perhaps, too, the form of pre-service teacher-education I had received had led me to see myself as an implementer of others' theory. It also probably had to do with my lack of critical development to the extent that I had accepted both of these situations for so many years.

Whatever the case may be, as I became aware of the existence of critical pedagogy literatures, I began to ask myself more questions. I wondered why, for example, student teachers at undergraduate level seemed not to be encouraged to read literatures of critical pedagogy and when I began teaching in an ITE context I ensured that I introduced my students to the work of people like Freire, Greene, Kincheloe and Brookfield. I had no personal experience of being exposed to any critical literatures of education when I was in college and a survey I carried out during my postgraduate studies showed that my experience was not singular.

So who are the critical pedagogues you should read? Let's begin with Freire.

Paulo Freire

'Critical reflection is also action,' according to Freire (1972: 99). The work of Freire also resonates with the ontological perspectives of self-study action research.

> Education as the practice of freedom – as opposed to education as the practice of domination – denies that man [sic] is abstract, isolated, independent, and unattached

to the world; it also denies that the world exists as a reality apart from men. Authentic reflection considers neither abstract man nor the world without men, but men in their relations with the world. (Ibid.: 54)

Freire described teaching as a way of inviting others to share in knowledge generation through dialogue. He critiqued the dominant transmission method of teaching and used his now famous 'banking metaphor' to explain what he meant: teachers deposit information into children's heads from which it is withdrawn at exam time. Instead, Freire argued for a humanising form of pedagogy where problematising, enquiry and collaborative relationships are the norm.

Pause and reflect

Does Freire's 'banking metaphor' raise any questions for you?

How does your philosophy of education contrast or match with Freire's?

Do any of Freire's ideas resonate with your educational values?

Maxine Greene

Greene's work, as we pointed out in Chapter 1, is very relevant for the reflective practitioner. Greene (1995) suggests that each person's reality must be understood as interpreted experience, and that the mode of interpretation depends on his or her situation and location in the world. It depends as well, she says, on the number of vantage points a person is able or enabled to take: the number of perspectives that will 'disclose multiple aspects of a contingent (not a self-existent) world' (p. 19). Didactic teaching mostly involves one perspective – that of the didact – either the teacher or the textbook. In my case, I sought pedagogies that embody my values of care, freedom and justice – pedagogies that would allow my students to think for themselves and go beyond the commonplace and glimpse what could be.

> It is to see beyond what the imaginer has called normal or 'commonsense' and to carve out new orders in experience. Doing so, a person may become freed to glimpse what might be, to form notions of what should be, and what is not yet. And the same person may, at the same time, remain in touch with what presumably is. (Ibid.: 17)

I was deeply influenced by Greene's ideas. When I first read her work (Greene 1978) in 2002, I was instantly enthralled by her belief in the potential of each person and her assertion that we must educate so as to encourage the development of this capacity and to 'transcend passivity' (ibid.: 2). She argued that, unless educators engaged in their own quests for meaning, they would be unlikely to be able to influence or encourage others to do so. This made sense to me. So, also, does her statement that teachers must be ongoing questioners and, through questioning, learners.

Greene (1988) led me to try to come to an understanding for myself of what an education for freedom entailed. Educating for freedom means, for me, that I must do what I can to encourage myself (alongside, and in relation with, my students) to come to an awareness of the many points of view there can be, and the multiple ways that exist for interpreting our worlds. To be free, I believe, is to be able to think and speak for oneself; to be able to engage the world in an ongoing conversation; and to value the power and meaning that new points of view bring to the collective search for fulfilment. I was enabled by Greene (1978, 1988) to understand that freedom requires a refusal to accede to the given, that it entails a reaching for new possibilities and potentials and a resistance to the objectification of people.

Greene's work led me to revisit Dewey (1933): he too emphasised the dangers of passivity and 'complete uniformity' the 'routine and the mechanical' (ibid.: 272). Greene, like Dewey, advocates that education should be aesthetic, encouraging 'wide-awakeness' (Greene 1988: 125) rather than 'anaesthetic' (Dewey 1933: 272). Anaesthetic education, she argues, numbs people and prevents them from reaching out and enquiring. Greene often drew on Dewey's ideas of growth and of 'aesthetic' education and active, enquiry-based learning. She urged teachers to break through what Virginia Woolf called the 'cotton wool' of daily existence and experience life more fully.

Pause and reflect

In your research journal note the main educational values that you see in Greene's work.

How might Greene's work have relevance for you?

Joe Kincheloe

> For the naïve thinker, education involves moulding oneself and others to the normal-ized past. For the critically conscious thinker, education involves engaging in the con-scious improvement and transformation of self and reality.
>
> (Kincheloe 2004: 72)

Kincheloe was a devoted follower of Freire. In a tribute following his untimely death, his part-ner, Shirley Steinberg explained (in the introduction to Hayes *et al.* 2011: xii) how, in founding the Paulo and Nita Freire International Project for Critical Pedagogy, Kincheloe wanted to 'support an evolving critical pedagogy that encounters new discourses, new peoples, with new ideas, and continues to move forward in the 21st Century'. The project is now under-stood, she said, as continued evolution of the work of Paulo Freire. She stated that Joe's passion 'fueled his struggles against inequality, oppression in all of its varied forms, and the stupidification of education'. (Steinberg, in Hayes *et al.* 2011: xii).

Kincheloe was a strong believer in practitioner research. For example, writing posthu-mously about Kincheloe's work, Tobin (in Hayes *et al.* 2011: xvii–xviii) said that, for Kincheloe, enacting practitioner research effectively means looking anew and in different ways, at edu-cation and the places in which it is conducted. In order to come to some understanding of what teaching and learning in schools is all about, a deeper understanding of the people that schools serve and the communities in which schools are embedded is needed. This means getting to know their histories, their real histories – 'not only as they are portrayed through the voices of the mainstream, but also those histories as they are expressed in the voices and lives of those who are oppressed and represent minorities'. Tobin suggests that, in the same way as Stenhouse advocates teachers as researchers as a hedge against the domineering effects of positivism (Stenhouse, 1975), Kincheloe views teachers as practitioner researchers as a hedge against the 'perpetuation of oppression through the well-intentioned efforts of educators' (Kincheloe, 1991). 'Joe', says Tobin, 'regarded practitioner research as a priority... and [he] embraced the necessity for researchers to inform their intellectual work with rich theoretical frameworks' (Tobin, in Hayes *et al.* 2011: xvii–xviii). It would appear, then, that Kincheloe was a strong advocate of teachers critically reflecting on their practice and on the context in which those practices are located so as to challenge the oppression and deprofessionalisation that he saw as being endemic in western education systems.

Kincheloe, along with Berry (2004), has strong ideas too, about how some forms of research can be reductionist. They refer to what they call 'researching things-in-themselves' separated from the 'real' and complex world. They suggest that, as reductionists 'abstract such phenomena from the contexts and process that give them life and meaning, they destroy them... entities are not simply things-in-themselves. They are embedded in the world, existing in multiple horizons, in multiple, parallel, and intersecting universes' (ibid.: xi). They suggest that researchers need to explore the ontological view of 'being-in-the-world', both for themselves, others and the phenomena they set out to study. For Kincheloe and Berry, an ontological concept is a 'pragmatic scholarly assertion that holds the power to change the way we research and perceive both ourselves and the world around us' (ibid.).

As I read works like these, and viewed them from a self-study action research perspective, what they said made sense to me. They became transformational in the sense that I could not go back to 'not-knowing'. I began to think far more critically about many hitherto taken-for-granted aspects of education, as illustrated by the following vignette.

Vignette

Initially, I took action in my context, without critically reflecting on what I was doing or why I was taking action. However, some new understanding began to emerge as I engaged with the literatures of critical theory and critical pedagogy. This too became a form of action because reading critical literatures (such as Freire 1972, Greene 1995 and Kincheloe 2004) raised more questions for me than answers. I often found the process quite destabilising, as my faith in the hitherto unshakable foundations of the education system of which I was a part had begun to crumble. Now I began to look with new eyes at education and question many of the assumptions around current educational policies. I began to rethink and critique the notion of a standardised curriculum, the breaking up of knowledge into discrete curricular areas, the dominance of didactic pedagogies and standardised assessment processes and the ensuing labelling of children. Now, with raised critical consciousness, I began to look again at what I understood by intelligence and interrogate how I had made assumptions about children in the past. I also began to question my own logics. It was only then, as I began to deconstruct concepts and my own mental models, that I began to realise that, although I thought I was teaching children to think critically, I needed, first, to engage in the idea of what critique meant. In order to do that, I first needed to examine the contextual frameworks of my study – critical thinking, the primary school curriculum and the research contexts around teaching children to think critically.

Pause and reflect

If you were to examine critically your educational context, what might be the starting point for your critique?

What might be some of the conceptual frameworks in which your study might be located?

How are these related to your educational values?

Are you beginning to form an embryonic research question?

Experiencing myself as a living contradiction: engaging with critical pedagogy literatures

I realised that – to address the problems I had identified in my teaching, in order to live more closely to my values, to avoid being what Whitehead (1989) calls a 'living contradiction' – I needed to develop a wider range of dialogic pedagogies. The idea of 'living contradiction' comes from the work of Whitehead (ibid.) and will be explored further in later chapters.

I began to see that didactic lessons are reifiable 'things' that can be 'planned', 'executed' and 'assessed' within a given timeframe, especially if the only voice is that of the teacher and the children passively follow her plans. Such a lesson could be considered a product. A dialogic lesson is a process: it is about opportunity, conversation, flow, engagement, being: the process can be 'planned for' but there can be no guarantees around 'outcomes' or about what happens when children and teachers explore and create new knowledge together. Dialogic pedagogies could be seen as square pegs that resist being pounded into the round holes of timetables and schedules. Evaluating such activities can also be problematic, as I will demonstrate below.

The following vignette shows how these realisations came about very slowly, but were scaffolded and supported by reading the work of people like Greene, Freire and Kincheloe.

Vignette

Prior to embarking on my study I never knew any of this 'stuff' – I simply did not have any of the tools of critique. I had not read widely enough, or thought deeply enough about what I had read. I felt a sense of dissonance about my practice, but thought that the solution would have to come from 'out there' somewhere. Thus I was the kind of teacher who often went along to in-service courses convinced that there would be some magic bullet – some new approach or strategy or set of handouts that would be an instant 'fix' for my teaching concerns. These new approaches and teaching resources were often advocated by teachers for whom they had 'worked'. I thought that they would 'work' in my class too and was often deeply frustrated when they didn't. I had not got the critical experience to realise that contexts vary and teachers vary and children vary and that what works for one may not work for another. I had not yet reflected critically enough to realise that change would have to begin with me. This realisation came about through embarking on self-study action research.

I had to do some serious critical thinking so as to try to live my educational values out in my everyday teaching life in order to avoid being what Whitehead (1989) calls 'a living contradiction'. The realisation that I was a living contradiction came about slowly. I believe now that I have always been a reflective practitioner (Schön 1983) and have always tried to teach with integrity, but now I realise, too, that reflection alone is insufficient for bringing about methodological change in one's practice. In my case, a further element was needed: that of becoming more critically aware.

When I looked at my own practice I saw that, although I could challenge pedagogical issues in relation to the curriculum, I could not unilaterally decide to jettison any part of the curriculum, or decide, for example, that the concepts of division or fractions should be left until fourth class rather than be taught in third class. To do so would have to involve whole-school policy and negotiation with the inspectorate.

I could, however, change my pedagogy, and, perhaps challenge pedagogical norms by introducing new forms of pedagogy that seemed to carry more hope for the realisation of my values than traditional didactic pedagogies. This is what I decided to do. I began critically to reflect on and generate insights about what I was doing. I began to move from description to explanation.

Conclusion

Perhaps, as you read some of my account of how I gradually transformed my own practice, you had some thoughts about where you could begin to make some changes in yours. I taught in a school where staff were genuinely committed to trying to be the best they could be so that their pupils could learn to the best of their ability. Yet, even in that supportive context, I saw room for how I could improve. This then, could be a good time to take another timeout, so that you can critically examine some areas of your practice.

Pause and reflect

Choose an area of education that you might now examine. It may be an area that, up to this point, you have felt needed no critique. This could be to do with organisation, classroom management, classroom talk, questioning, assessment, teaching activities, workbooks, norms and practices in your classroom.

Here are some questions. Feel free to change them or add some more. Maybe something will strike a chord:

- Think over the past week in your classroom: who did most of the talking? How much voice did children have in the day-to-day school experience? If there were behaviour issues, who were the children involved and are certain children always in trouble?
- If you could change some aspect of school practice what might that be? Could changing your own practice be the first step on that ladder?

In this chapter:

- You have been introduced to some of the theories around educational research, in particular, action research and self-study action research.
- You have been made aware of the importance of being critically reflective about your own practice.
- You have examined some of the ontological and epistemological values that inform self-study action research.
- You have been acquainted (or perhaps reacquainted) with the work of Paulo Freire, Maxine Greene and Joe Kincheloe – key figures in the field of critical pedagogy.
- You have seen how engaging with such theories of critical pedagogy may help you to become more critically reflective about some of the wider assumptions around education.

Recommended reading and resources

Pinnegar, S. (1998) Introduction, in M. L. Hamilton (ed.), *Reconceptualizing Teaching Practice: Selfstudy in Teacher Education*, London: Falmer Press.

Video clip: In this video Jack Whitehead explains *how* values animate and give meaning and purpose to our lives: https://www.youtube.com/watch?v=XIAYiE_weql

SECTION II

Putting your research in context

Máirín Glenn

Section II will explore further how you might practically reflect on and develop a better understanding of your practice and begin the process of preparing for your action research project.

In Chapter 3, you will explore the idea of critical thinking as a key element of reflective practice and self-study action research. As you aspire to gaining insight into your work practices, you learn to ask 'Why do I do what I do?', as this question is a good launch-pad for engaging in critical thinking and reflection. Keeping a reflective diary and using it to ascertain both your educational values and the key areas that are causing you concern can be very helpful when trying to improve your practice.

In Chapter 4, you will learn how, sometimes, we do not act in the direction of our values and we experience ourselves as a 'living contradiction', an idea developed by Whitehead (1989). This experience often gives you an opportunity to focus on particular areas of your practice that might need attention.

As you develop an understanding of your work practices through reflection, you will explore some of the 'reconnaissance' or preparatory stages of an action research cycle.

3 Thinking critically

Introduction

Good teaching needs good decision-making, and good decision-making, according to Brookfield (1995), calls for critical thinking. The links between good practice, good understanding of one's practice, reflective practice, self-study action research, living theory and critical thinking have been widely discussed (see McDonagh *et al*. 2012; McIntosh 2010; Reason and Bradbury 2013; and Whitehead and McNiff 2006, for example), and, very often, the boundaries between them are blurred. Elliott (1991) even goes so far as to say action research and reflective practice are one and the same (McIntosh 2010: 34), but we must see action and reflective practice as intertwined, as reflection without action is meaningless. Similarly, working in an educational setting – teaching children, lecturing undergraduates or designing postgraduate programmes – without critical thinking about what is happening in your practice is also inadequate. Action without understanding is blind (Reason and Bradbury 2013) because practitioners need to know not only why they do what they do in their everyday practice, but also the purpose of it.

Throughout this text, you will see how reflection, critical thinking and self-study action research are interdependent pieces of the 'puzzle' of the journey of an educator who seeks to improve their practice, or their understanding of their practice, as they generate an educational theory from that process.

> In this chapter:
>
> - You are invited to ask 'Why do I do what I do?', as this question is a practical starting point for linking critical thinking, reflection and taking action to change things.
> - You explore critical thinking as a key element of reflective practice, in terms of using different perspectives; being able to be 'wrong'; finding it difficult to reflect critically and establishing the practice of critical thinking.
> - You are introduced to cycles of reflection and action, how you might collaborate with colleagues, the concept of praxis and the idea of keeping a reflective diary.

Asking 'Why do I do what I do?': linking critical thinking, reflection and taking action

As we explore how we might think about and develop a better understanding of our practice as educators engaging in action research, we look at the idea of reflective practice. We examine how keeping a reflective journal can enhance the reflective process and explore the importance of critical thinking. As you engage in reflective practice, you develop a sense of 'stepping back' from your work and developing a new awareness of what is happening in your everyday work.

As you have already seen in Chapter 2, you can take the time to pause and to take more control of your professional life right now, by developing a keener sense of awareness, and becoming more questioning and more reflective. Remember that Greene asks us to stop and think and to interrupt ordinary activities: to pause and make the effort 'to shake free of what Virginia Woolf called "the nondescript cotton wool" of daily life' (Greene 1984: 55).

Perhaps this is the moment for you to stop rushing around, to reflect and to think about how you might make your practice a little more meaningful. Try making a space for a pause each day and try to think about your practice. Ask yourself 'Why do I do what I do?' and reflect on your work.

As a teacher, I tend to be a practical person. As a teaching principal, I tend to be a *very* practical person. If I see something wrong in school, or something that needs fixing, then I simply take action and fix it. This works well for activities like non-functioning heating systems and intermittent WiFi. For these practical problems, the sooner the action is taken, the better. But, when it comes to issues relating to human beings, their teaching and learning, and how they might interact with one another, then a much more sedate and reflective approach is generally needed. Reflection helps educators to 'better understand what they know and do' by placing an 'emphasis on learning through questioning and investigating' (Loughran 2002: 34). As you engage with the ideas of action research, self-study or living theory, remember that you are investigating your practice with a view to improving it. You are also seeking to explore how to improve your workplace by improving learning, as well as trying to influence the education of social formations (McNiff and Whitehead 2011), by realising that your work (even though it may only be small in scale) may have the potential to influence policy both locally and at national level.

Pause and reflect

In earlier chapters, you already explored what attracted you into teaching. When do you feel career satisfaction?

What have been the 'best' times so far in your teaching career and why?

What factors might make you feel discontented? Why?

Why do we do what we do?

Education is surely one of the most important influences in people's lives. How a student experiences education often has a long-lasting and, perhaps, life-changing influence on the life choices they make. For this reason, we educators need to take our work very seriously and see education as a life-enhancing and life-long journey.

Chomsky (2013: n/p) reminds us that 'Education is really aimed at helping students get to the point where they can learn on their own', so, as educators, we aim to equip our students with the skills they need, and enable and influence them to become self-directed learners. While we hope that our influence is a positive and life-enhancing process for all involved, we have to acknowledge that, sometimes, the activities in which we engage as educators are not as stimulating or life-enhancing as they should be. Because our work is so important and because it can have such a far-reaching influence, we need to be very mindful of our practice and to ensure that it is of an excellent standard. We need to take stock of our work on a regular basis, and establish that the work we are doing is, in fact, enhancing our students' learning. We need to reflect on our work and think critically about it. We need to ask ourselves questions like 'Why do I do what I do?' in our everyday practice. Before we can ask ourselves 'Why do I do what I do?' and think critically about our work, we must establish clearly for ourselves:

- What we are meant to be doing?
- What we are contractually obliged to do?
- How we might position these obligations alongside the demands of our own education values?

The following is an excerpt from my own reflective journal, which gives a flavour of my dilemma as I interrogate my difficulties with contractual obligations and my own values.

Vignette

I have a problem with teaching poetry and, in fact, for a long time I actively disliked poetry. I know that it stemmed from my inability to learn things off by heart when I was at school myself, and how being 'good' at poetry traditionally meant being able to recite it by heart. It also meant being able to reproduce prescriptive interpretations of what the poet meant.

So now that I am a teacher, how exactly am I meant to teach poetry?

The Primary School Curriculum of Ireland suggests:

> Poetry should have a special place in listening and reading experience. The heightened and often compressed expression of thought and feeling and the music, rhythm and rhyme in the language can provide unique and striking glimpses into aspects of the human experience. Through it the child's enjoyment of language can be fostered and his/her aesthetic response and sense of beauty awakened.
>
> (Ireland, Department of Education and Science 1999: 78)

I agree with this. My own gut feeling is that poetry should be treated very similarly to responding to art or music, and that pupils' responses to the poetry should supersede all other actions. However, I have a difficulty with the demand that students be able to recite one new poem every two weeks, as suggested by Department of Education and Science officials.

My dilemma is: how should I teach poetry? I find it difficult to demand that pupils learn verses by heart, especially when I cannot do it myself. I wonder if I am generating a new generation of poetry-haters? Or should I just go with my instinct, and allow the students to listen to it, read it and then respond? (Reflective diary 12 May 2011)

Now let's look at how I could take each one of the critical questions in the bullet points above and explain my thinking around them.

What we are meant to be doing?

While ideas around the purpose of education have clearly evolved over time, some resonate more strongly than others. For example, when I think about what I am meant to be doing in my classroom, I am drawn to Russell's ideas (1971). He believes the purpose of education is 'to provide opportunities of growth and to remove hampering influences... to give culture to the individual and develop his [sic] capacities to the utmost and... to train useful citizens' (ibid.: 18). Even though these ideas originally date from 1932, they are not unlike Chomsky's ideas (see above) from 2013. Both see the educator as someone who enables the student to learn and who has the ability to remove shackles which diminish learning opportunities.

What we are contractually obliged to do?

As an educator, I lay down my contractual obligations as the foundations of my work, and I look to the teaching contract and curriculum to establish what I am contracted to do. Here in Ireland, the Education Act (1998) specifies, as one of its primary functions, 'the Principal and teachers shall – (a) encourage and foster learning in students' (ibid.: 23). Again, this is commensurate with my own thinking on education. According to the Introduction to the Primary School Curriculum (Ireland, Department of Education and Science 1999), the three general aims of primary education are:

> to enable the child to live a full life as a child and to realise his or her potential as a unique individual, to enable the child to develop as a social being through living and cooperating with others and so contribute to the good of society and to prepare the child for further education and lifelong learning. (p. 34)

How we might position these obligations alongside the demands of our own education values?

I know that as I begin to engage with the question 'Why do I do what I do?' I need to foster conditions to fulfil these obligations. I need to examine my everyday routines, responses and actions critically and see how well I am meeting the requirements of my job. Thinking critically about my practice, I then look to my own educational values and see how well I live those out in my everyday interactions with students, colleagues and parents. I need to keep a reflective diary and record my interactions and reflections on interactions. Asking the question 'Why do I do what I do?' requires a type of 'stepping outside' oneself and viewing oneself and one's practice as an outsider would. As Sartre (1966: 155) says, 'to know is to make oneself other'.

When we think about the purpose of our work as educators, we subscribe to Palmer's ideas (1993) about a spirituality in education that assumes that there exists a 'hidden wholeness on which all life depends' (ibid.: xix). He perceives 'that intellect and spirit would be one, teachers and learners and subjects would be in vital community with one another, and a world in need of healing would be well served' (ibid.). As we search for this 'vital community' between teachers and learners and subject areas, we need to try to give this amazingly powerful job that we do as educators our very best attention and focus. And sometimes, giving our work our best attention demands that we need to tweak, change or improve some aspects of our practice, both in *what* we do and how we *understand* what we do. To tweak or improve our practice, we must first look at it critically, reflect on it and then take action towards improving those aspects that need adjustment. These ideas are kernel to action research and the desire to improve practice and our understanding of it.

Frequently, when we ask 'Why do I do what I do?' we find areas of our practice or our understanding of it that are a little rusty and need improvement. Sometimes, however, we make more complex discoveries and we find that the areas that need improvement are outside our control and are in the area of school policy or national educational policy. Working towards changing policy at any level can be exceedingly difficult and, while success with changing policy can be hugely rewarding, you have to decide if this is what you want to do.

Engaging in reflective practice can be one of the most powerful tools in any practitioner's professional kitbag because it can initiate and sustain powerful change in thinking and practice. It helps us dislodge those taken-for-granted assumptions that may hamper the quality of our practice (Loughran 2002). As we read in Chapters 1 and 2, the term 'reflective practice' implies not only thinking retrospectively about how an event went, examining it critically – examining the factors that influenced it internally and externally – it also implies a desire for a better, more productive experience for the next occasion. When reflecting as an action researcher, it implies taking action. When reflecting as an action researcher for academic purposes, it implies taking action and generating theory.

Pause and reflect

Ask yourself:

Is there any area of my practice where I have difficulty fulfilling my contractual obligations?

Can I describe this difficulty and articulate why this is a difficulty?

Critical thinking as a key element of reflective practice and self-study action research

Preparing for any event, and reflecting on our prior knowledge to help and enhance our preparation, is an innate part of our being. Asking 'Why do I do what I do?' is one of the initial steps that any educator can take as they begin on a journey of discovering a somewhat better version of themselves as practitioners, as thinkers and as researchers. It can help dislodge any stale, out-of-date or mindless work practices while encouraging fresh new questions (see Chapter 2). It can help a practitioner take those first tentative steps towards problematising work practices and encourage them to think about how they might then plan some form of action to enhance their own understanding or their methods.

The following vignette is taken from my reflections on a summer programme we provided for teachers; it shows how problematising their thinking and exploring ideas critically can draw different responses from different people.

Vignette

Our critical thinking skills are developed as we take our everyday habits and interrogate them critically. We ask ourselves why we do what we do. Questioning the 'given' and accepted practices of everyday life in school can be quite difficult. Noam Chomsky warns us that 'once you are educated, you have already been socialized in ways that support the power structure' (2000: 3) and your ability to think critically about the education system and other systems has already been modified unbeknown to you. Chomsky (ibid.) is critical of educators who have already subscribed to a non-critical form of thinking.

In an in-service online course that we ran for teachers and which was entitled 'Enhancing Practice for Self-Evaluation' we asked participants if they agreed with Chomsky's views. Some replied positively, as SK does here:

> Agree absolutely with Noam Chomsky. Many teachers (most teachers) have been steeped in middle class values and CANNOT (or WILL NOT) entertain the notion that any other value system is legitimate too. How often have we heard 'Well I know BUT…' when trying to explain for example why something like the quality of homework takes a back seat in a home when there is a question about whether or not there's food on the table? Many (even young) teachers seem to feel the need to make everyone conform to their standard.

Others disagreed, as BM does here:

> Although I understand where Noam Chomsky (2000) is coming from, as a teacher I fundamentally disagree with what he says. If we don't set out with the belief, at the very least, that we can actually effect positive change on the system then what is the point of going into school everyday? While Chomsky's (2000) opinion is logically sound, it is based on a defeatist premise that will not benefit any of our pupils.

Regardless of whether you agree or disagree, it is the process of critical thinking that is important for all educators wishing to engage in meaningful practice.

Pause and reflect

Can you see areas in your work that need some attention?

Do you sometimes make demands on your students or fellow workers that cause them (and their families) an unhealthy amount of stress?

Do you give your students opportunities to be self-directed in their learning?

How can you help your students engage more positively with their studies?

Examining practice from different perspectives: using Brookfield's lenses

One of the key aspects of doing critical thinking as part of an action research cycle is taking everyday actions, putting them under the microscope of critique and problematising them. Taking Brookfield's (1995) four sets of lenses to scrutinise practice can enrich the critically reflective process. Brookfield (ibid.) recommends using (i) the lens of our own autobiographies as learners, (ii) the lens of students' eyes, (iii) the lens of colleagues' perceptions and (iv) the lens of educational literature to dissect our practice. As we examine our work lives through these lenses, it is important to be aware of the values we hold and to see how we live them out in our practice. These lenses can provide us with huge amounts of data, so, if you are undertaking an action research project, it is a good idea to keep a record of all the observations you make (through all lenses) from the outset of your project. It is important that appropriate permission is sought and all ethical procedures are followed before collating any data, especially with regard to children. See Chapter 6 for more details.

In using (i) the lens of our own autobiographies as learners, we can examine our practice using reflective journals and using our own intuition. Keeping a reflective journal can enhance the process of critical thinking about practice because it heightens your awareness of what is actually happening for you in your place of work, as teaching and learning are taking place. Writing in your journal will also call you to re-examine everyday occurrences or incidents of interest to you with fresh eyes after the event. This writing can be revisited again at a later date as you bring your own new ideas, ideas from the literature you are reading and ideas from dialogue, to your original journal entries in a reflexive manner. We examine reflective journaling later in this chapter. This re-examining, metacognitive process is kernel to reflective practice and self-study action research.

Intuition is part of the human condition and human interaction. Parents often develop a sense of intuition about their children and just *know* when their children need something. Intuition is a component of that gut instinct that many teachers develop when they sense that something is wrong with a student without being able to say how or why they know this. This innate sense of knowing is difficult to define, but most people have it. Hocking *et al.* (2001) use the term 'embodiment' in the context of education and explain that: 'Embodiment moves us away from the Cartesian legacy of how we view knowing and knowledge not as concrete things that reside in the body or mind but that emerge through our interactions with/in the world' (ibid.: xviii).

Intuition and innate knowledge are tied in with personal ways of knowing. As you engage with your action research project, you will be doing research on yourself and your work. Your thinking and learning will be key to the process. Researchers involved in self-study action research frequently put 'I' in their research question to show how important *their* thinking and learning is in the research process. This makes your action research project quite different to traditional, technicist approaches to research, where an external perspective is valued.

Using (ii) the lens of students' eyes can help to inform our ability to think critically about our work. It is a good idea to listen to your students, whether they are young or old, because their stories will tell you about their reality. Remember, there is nothing like the honesty of a young child. Students' understanding of an event can be quite different to yours at any age, and giving students an opportunity to voice their learning, their ideas and their understanding can illuminate your own thinking. Students' perceptions can be collated through conversations; written documents; blogs; video/audio recordings; email; and art work, for example.

Using (iii) the lens of colleagues' perceptions can also help you question the assumptions you make about your daily routines and work practices. It is a good idea to develop a habit of engaging in professional conversations with all colleagues, regardless of whether you are engaging in reflective practice, critical thinking or action research. If you can invite a colleague into your classroom; or have a classroom assistant; or are involved in shared teaching programmes, then you already have another set of lenses in your classroom. Their perceptions about students are valuable; but their perceptions about your work and interaction with the class may be invaluable. You should try to schedule a time to talk to such colleagues and seek their insights into teaching and learning in your place of work. It is a good idea to establish the assistance of at least one critical friend who will not only support your endeavours, but will also unpick any inaccurate assumptions you may make.

If no other adult works with you and your students in your workplace, other educators with whom you work may see your students in other situations, for other subjects or at recreation periods and give you ideas about them. Often their insights are important because they see your students in a different light. Their input can enhance your critical thinking greatly. If you have sought permission from these colleagues, you may keep your records of such conversations as data as they may be useful for your research. Whenever you get the opportunity to learn with colleagues, Pollard *et al.* 2008 remind us that 'reflective discussion capitalizes on the social nature of learning... and is as significant for adults as it is for children' (ibid.: 24).

The use of video or audio recordings of your practice can enhance your perception of what is happening in your class also. It can highlight aspects of your practice of which you were unaware. You should ensure that all aspects of your school's policy on recording children are met, as well as all guidelines on child protection, before you begin to record. We explore the ethics aspects of action research in greater detail in Chapter 5.

Using (iv) the lens of educational literature to help us peel back the more fixed views we hold is kernel to the process of critical thinking. While there is some evidence to support the idea that teachers are neglectful of professional reading (see Cremin 2011 and Roche 2011, for example), huge numbers of teachers actually do engage, productively, in reading literature in education. It is important to keep your critical thinking processes flowing when engaging in professional reading. Ask yourself if you agree with what is being said or not. Do not be afraid to disagree with the author. After all, you are the professional working in your educational setting and you probably know as much as any other adult about it. If you disagree with what you are reading, ask yourself why you disagree. Sometimes, reading articles with which you disagree can be a very productive learning experience for you.

It is a good idea to try to see things from as many perspectives as possible so as to get a more accurate sense of what is happening. As your research project progresses, and if you have ethical permissions in place, you can use the data you collate from the various lenses to triangulate data for validation purposes. You can read more about validation in Chapters 5 and 6.

Be prepared to be wrong

As we engage in critical reflection on our practice, we need to acknowledge, right through-out the action research process, that we may be wrong or mistaken. As Brydon-Millar *et al.* (2003: 21) say, 'You have to be willing to be wrong... This comes hard to those of us who have been trained to believe that we are smarter than everyone else.' Because action research is an emergent process, and the theory we generate is generated in the process of our learning, we need to be aware that our thinking or even the values we hold can actually change over time.

Why do we find it difficult to reflect critically?

We have established that critical thinking, reflection and asking questions like 'Why do I do what I do?' are kernel to the process of self-study action research and we are aware of the enormous influence educators can have on people's lives. Wilcox *et al.* (2004: 307) explain self-study thus: 'self-study is vital to professional practice. Self-study allows practitioners to engage in inquiry that contributes to their own capacity for expert and caring professional practice while also contributing to the growth of their profession.' Yet, despite this awareness, large numbers of educators are not terribly enthusiastic about reflective practice. We will have a look here at the main pitfalls that constrain us from engaging in productive critical thinking.

Becoming stuck

One of the most dangerous practices in which educators can engage is complacency. It is easy to develop a sense of self-righteousness around teaching a lesson that goes well. It is important, of course, for educators to have a sense of job satisfaction, but when job satisfaction turns into complacency, a laziness in thinking can occur and the educator can neglect to examine their practice critically. One good lesson, or one good day's work, or even one good week of work in education should not dissuade an educator from trying for an even better lesson the next day. The critical examination of one's work should be an ongoing daily routine that runs for the lifetime of a career in education.

Repetition and reliance on the past

As educators, a good deal of our energy in everyday practice and thinking is tied up in repetitious actions, especially if we teach younger children. We can easily fall into the trap of repeating our everyday routines on a regular basis, without giving much thought or attention to what we are actually doing. While the repetition of key messages is an inherent element of a teacher's work, it can lull us educators into a false belief that what we are doing is productive and educational (see Brookfield 2009). We can begin to become lazy in our thinking and believe that what we are doing, in our everyday work, is of a good standard, simply because we did it yesterday, last week or last year.

Frequently, how we teach and how we think about teaching is linked with how we ourselves were taught as children and teenagers. hooks (2003) reminds us that 'Teachers who are wedded to using the same teaching style every day, who fear any digression from the concrete lesson plan, miss the opportunity for full engagement in the learning process' (ibid.: 134), and teachers should avoid missing opportunities for full engagement in learning processes. While many prior educational experiences may have been positive, and indeed they influence our chosen teaching methodologies greatly, it is important for us to problematise our practice in light of our current experience. Reflection on practice and critical thinking about our work can help rejuvenate any practices or thinking that might have become stale.

Compulsory self-evaluation and reflection

Somehow, some reflective practice has got itself a bad name over the last number of years. We have noticed that many of our students (especially on postgraduate programmes) sigh heavily and roll their eyes at the mention of 'reflective practice'. We believe that this is due, to a certain extent, to the fact that reflective practice has become a compulsory module or aspect of many undergraduate/postgraduate programmes, continuing professional development (CPD) programmes and self-evaluation programmes. Boud and Walker (1998) are critical of the way that reflection can become a set of checklists 'which students work through in a mechanical fashion without regard to their own uncertainties, questions and meanings' (ibid.: 193). Somehow, reflective practice seems to have evolved from being a fairly innovative, powerful and potentially life-changing process to a nasty chore that has to be done to fulfil the criteria of a particular programme. Boud (2010) says one of the current problems with reflective practice is when educators perceive 'reflection as recipe following, reflection without learning, over intellectualising reflection and uncritical acceptance of learners' experience' (ibid.: 3). If there is a disconnect between reflection and the lived practice of the practitioner, then the exercise of meaningless 'reflection' is fairly worthless.

Ennui, exhaustion and external factors

Sometimes teachers who are exhausted and have overstretched themselves, find it difficult to reinvigorate themselves and to hold that natural enthusiasm for teaching and learning that is at the heart of good education. Family life or factors both within and outside their educational setting can overwhelm people for a time. Sometimes educators are bullied in their workplace and are so stressed that they are unable to think for themselves (Whitehead and McNiff 2006). The thought of engaging in reflective practice is, frequently and understandably, very difficult for such people.

Power relations

Freire (2003) stipulated that critical reflection on one's practice should not be confined to questions about teaching methodologies or practical issues alone. He said that it is important for teachers to develop their awareness of issues of power, oppression and culture in the different aspects of education also. Brookfield (2009) echoes these ideas and suggests that 'critical reflection calls into question the power relationships that allow, or promote, one particular set of practices over others' (ibid.: 294). He also proposes that critical reflection should aim to unearth hegemonic aspects of practice. The idea of hegemony was developed by Gramsci (1971) and it pertains to 'those assumptions we embrace as being in our best interests when in fact they are working against us' (Brookfield 2009: 298). Frequently, when teachers begin to examine their practice closely, they begin to realise that the source of many of the difficulties that they experience is embedded in the system of which they themselves are part; a system wherein certain assumptions are made and are not questioned. Brookfield suggests that such ideologies are difficult to penetrate. Some teachers who try to engage in critical reflection find these ideas frustrating, and they begin to develop a sense of their own powerlessness as they see examples of oppression in many aspects of their work.

Moving beyond the constraints and establishing the practice of critical thinking

Any of these constraints (and more besides) can keep us from thinking critically about our work. However, the very act of engaging in reflective practice, thinking critically about one's work and reconnecting with one's educational values can help to dislodge that sense of being stuck in one's non-reflective practice and help kick-start a new vision of one's work. As outlined in earlier chapters, Dewey (1933) identified three main qualities that reflective practitioners need: whole-heartedness, open-mindedness and intellectual responsibility; we must keep these in our hearts as we engage in any educational practice.

The principles of self-evaluation and reflective practice – and, indeed, self-study – have merged to such an extent that there is little difference between them. We are convinced of the power and potential of self-study action research, but we are equally convinced of the importance of basing all such learning journeys on our educational values as they provide us not only with the base-line for our research, but also give us the overarching goals and purposes of our everyday work (see Chapter 1).

It is important for us also to problematise and ask critical questions about our own reflective practice. Moon (1999: 57) reminds us thus: 'Copeland, Birmimgham and Lewin… ask a critical question: "Do students of highly reflective teachers learn more or better or even differently?"' While we may not be able to answer such a question easily, it can provide us with an opportunity to critique how we ourselves engage in reflective practice and critical thinking about our work.

Pause and reflect

Take some time now and ask yourself:

What, are the constraints that might hold me back from engaging in critically reflective practice?

Make a list of them and explore their underpinning issues.

Cycles of reflection and action; the concept of praxis; collaboration with colleagues; and keeping a reflective diary

The reflection/action cycle

Being a reflective practitioner is very different to being a passive worker or technician (Zeichner and Liston, 1996) in that reflection on one's practice takes into account the thoughts, emotions, reactions and questions the practitioner has, based on their thoughts about their work. Many practitioners claim to be reflective about their work because they think about incidents that have occurred at work, after the event. However, reflective practice is not just thinking about things in a haphazard manner, nor is it about lying awake at night worrying about work-related issues. Reflection on one's practice is a structured, deliberate process, which calls for time for reflection on a regular basis; dialogue with others; involves writing a reflective journal; and requires critical thinking.

Action research embraces the idea of articulating your educational values and using them not only as the overarching principles that guide how you teach and learn, but also to help you gauge that your everyday practice is as it should be. The idea of self-reflection, therefore, is central. McNiff (2002b) reminds us:

> In traditional forms of research – empirical research – researchers do research on other people. In action research, researchers do research on themselves. Empirical researchers enquire into other people's lives. Action researchers enquire into their own. Action research is an enquiry conducted by the self into the self. You, a practitioner, think about your own life and work, and this involves you asking yourself why you do the things that you do, and why you are the way that you are. (n/p)

Reflection-in-action and reflection-on-action

There are many models of reflection/action in the literature. We will look at some basic models here and, then, you can use them or tweak them for your own purpose. Dick (2002) reminds us that the basic process of most activities is that we do something and we check that it went well. We review it and try it again: 'act – review – act – review ...' (n/p). Gibbs's (1988) model takes the practitioner's feelings and emotions into account and suggests the following model: description; feelings; evaluation; analysis; conclusions; and action plan. Pollard *et al.* (2008: 18) suggest the following as the key stages of the reflective process: reflect; plan; make provision; act; collect evidence; analyse evidence; evaluate evidence; and reflect again, which brings the reflective process into the realm of taking action. McTaggart (1997) suggests the following action research cycle: planning; acting; observing; and reflecting. This particular model has become widely used and modified throughout many fields of reflective practice. You can see the striking similarities here between reflective practice and self-study action research.

However, these models are all quite similar and are cyclical in nature; many are based on the writings of Schön (1983). Schön was one of the key thinkers on reflective practice and is credited with creating the ideas of different kinds of reflection – 'reflection-IN-action' and 'reflection-ON-action'. His ideas have been widely used throughout many professions where practitioners are actively encouraged to be reflective practitioners. He describes *reflection-in-action* as the kind of split-second 'thinking on our feet' type of reflection that educators do all the time. If, for example, a teacher is teaching a lesson and they notice that a child is not paying attention, they may continue with the lesson, but move nearer that child, while momentarily recognising that something is amiss. Reflection-in-action allows educators to mentally acknowledge that something has briefly caught their attention as they work.

Reflection-on-action is what we do later. As educators we formally set time aside; examine the events of the day; ask ourselves what worked and what didn't, and how we might do better tomorrow. The act of reflecting-on-action enables us to spend time exploring why we acted as we did, what was happening in a group, why, despite our repeated explanations, some children simply did not understand what we intended from the lesson, for example. Reflecting-on-action can also be based on something we have read; a conversation we have had with someone or something we have written in our reflective journal. We examine how we hold particular perspectives on various issues. In so doing, we develop sets of questions and ideas about our activities, thoughts and practice (see Chapter 1). Schön also encourages practitioners to utilise their intuition or tacit knowledge and describes practitioner knowledge as a 'kind of knowing-in-practice, most of which is tacit' (1983: viii).

Dialogue with critical friends

We know, nearly intuitively, that chatting to a friend about our concerns and worries is good for us, not only because it helps to relieve some of the stress we might be experiencing, but also because it helps to put our problems into perspective. In the more formal setting of your learning, dialogue can be one of the best ways of clarifying your thinking, developing understanding and generating the new questions you need to become a critical thinker. As with writing, 'it is through finding the right words that an understanding occurs' (McIntosh 2010: 47). Bohm (2004) talks about dialogue in terms of the flow of understanding that emerges between and through people.

Roche (2011) outlines how her dialogue with her primary school students aided her critical thinking processes:

> I think there's two kinds of laughing: it's an instinct to laugh when something is funny but it's mean to come along just to see it.
>
> I'm wondering... is there some kind of relation between McDonald's and Disney cos Happy Meal toys are usually from films?
>
> What's so good about straight lines anyway?
>
> Why do they throw girls in their underwear on the bonnet of a car just to sell the car [in ads]? (p. 333)

Roche (ibid.) continues to explain how her own thinking was influenced by her dialogue with the children:

> After discussions I would type up the transcript or save the video onto my computer and I would reflect on what had transpired and ponder some of the questions raised. I found myself wondering, like Charlie in my Infant class (21 November 2001), why 'we all had to wear the

same colour uniforms'; 'why we had to line up patiently for everything'; 'why we had to ask to go to the toilet'; 'why we had to keep going to school after we had learned to read'... (Roche 2007, 89). In Greene's (1978) terms, I was becoming more wide-awake. (Roche 2011: 333)

Dialogue is also considered to be a key element of the action research process. While you are doing research on your own practice, it is important to remember that you are not working alone or generating monologues in your head. You need to establish some critical friends who will listen to your emergent ideas and query them in a questioning but supportive manner. Professional conversations with critical friends can help dislodge any fixed assumptions you have around your practice and see it through 'new eyes'. Critical friends can also help to dispel any unfair or weak assumptions you make yourself, too. Reflective conversations are not about argument or winning debates; they are by their nature dialogic (McIntosh 2010). So while your critical friends should be able to question your ideas thoroughly, they should also be supportive and collegiate. They should also be aware that your ideas are merely forming in the process of your research.

Dialogue with colleagues, as outlined above, is important at your place of work. It can also be healthy to have critical friends who are not at your workplace, but have an understanding of the work you do and the habitus of your place of work. Sometimes these 'external' critical friends can cut through workplace politics and see issues with a clarity that those involved may not. Dialogue can take place by talking, writing, email, Skype or whatever means of communication suits your needs.

Pause and reflect

As in Chapter 1, can you now name two or three people who are open to your work and your ideas, yet who have a questioning, critical mind, and who could be invited to act as your critical friends?

Praxis

Often, as educators, we see our practice as something practical that we do. However, once we begin to think in a questioning manner about our practice, and improve our practice as result of our critical thinking, then we are beginning to engage in *praxis*. When we ask ourselves *why* we do what we do, seek explanations and try to establish an understanding of what we are doing and why we do it, then we are undertaking praxis.

We see praxis as an action that is taken as a result of reflection: *an informed action* (Carr and Kemmis 1986). The action is then reflected upon and this reflection then influences the original thinking that informed the action so that future actions may be altered accordingly. Further action may be modified in light of the new thinking. We see that action, as part of a living theory/action research cycle, takes the form of praxis.

Often action researchers insert the word 'critically' before 'informed' (see Kemmis and McTaggart 1988) and so imply that critical engagement with the issues has taken place alongside a commitment to an improved form of practice or praxis. When you think critically about your practice, it is important to remember that the practice in which you engage as a result of this reflection and critical thought may change. For many, one of the aims of doing self-study action research is to engage in praxis.

Writing a reflective journal

As you begin to engage in reflection on your practice, you need to decide that you are going to devote some time to this process. We recommend keeping a reflective journal. Our suggestions are loosely based on Progoff's (1992) ideas and the following sections outline how we like to write up a reflective journal.

Drawing on Schön's reflection-on-action, it is a good idea to have a sticky pad or a notebook and pen to hand throughout your day at work. As little incidents occur that cause you concern or cause you to wonder about something that is happening in your workplace (reflection-in-action), jot it down briefly. If you are in the middle of a hectic class, then one word is all you need. If you have a little more time, then you may write a sentence or two. These jottings will act as an aide-memoire for your reflection-on-action.

Then, later on – perhaps in the evening – do your reflection-on-action. It might be a good idea to think about this time as 'me time', or time that you are going to devote to your own well-being and professional development. Use a dedicated journal for this. I like to use a notebook and a good-quality pen. You may like to begin your session with a few moments of mindfulness or some gentle music. Perhaps you might like to take a 'pause' as Greene (1984: 55) suggests.

As you take this 'pause', as you become more attentive to the present moment and as your mind clears, you can revisit the notes made earlier in the day/week. Open up your reflective journal. Some people like to divide their journal into columns for the different parts of the reflective process; it is a good idea to date your work. Others like to write in paragraphs, boxes or write up their journal on their tablets or computers. You choose the method that suits you best.

Begin by rewriting the phrase or word from earlier, in the first column, paragraph or box. Then, as the second step of your reflection-on-action, write your recollection of the event or incident as a detached account of the sequence of events. It is, generally, a good idea to write it as though you were presenting evidence in court.

Then, in the next column or box, write why this caused you concern or sparked your interest.

In the fourth step of your journaling, describe your feelings and reactions to the best of your ability and the feelings and reactions of those around you at that time. Try to ask yourself why the incident occurred and why it caused you concern. Examine your ideas critically. Leave a space blank for writing further thoughts later.

Then move onto your second jotted note from reflection-in-action and proceed in the same way. As you take time to write, you will begin to formulate ideas around what to do about these initial incidents, concerns or events. You should write these down too. It is important to keep thinking critically and to 'interrogate those previously taken-for-granted assumptions' (Taylor and White 2000: 198).

Sometimes, the very process of writing down your thoughts can help clarify them. As you write, you may begin to see why a student is inattentive, or why a colleague is dismissive.

You can develop an insight into the actions of others. Sometimes, if you feel you need to take action, you can begin to plan it now. In either case, you are beginning to move your thinking about your practice on. You are also beginning to track your own learning formally and this can provide huge amounts of data for your action research project, when you begin to tell the story of your learning.

Moon (2004) draws on the work of Hatton and Smith (1995) and suggests that there are four levels of reflection: descriptive writing; descriptive reflection; dialogic reflection; and critical reflection. She suggests that all four levels of reflection should be included in the reflective process and reminds the reader that 'Logically, there is no "end-point" of deep reflection – it can go on and on examining issues in a wider and wider context' (Moon 2004: 98). For practitioner researchers, critical reflection is only one step of an action research cycle. Schön reminds us that 'the proper test of a round of inquiry is not only "Have I solved this problem?" but "Do I like the new problems I've created?"' (Hatton and Smith 1995: 31).

Pause and reflect

Start taking notes at work of incidents that catch your attention, as your reflection-in-action. Make notes of conversations you have had, and articles that you have read that pique your interest too.

Then, begin the process of reflecting on your work in your reflective journal.

Conclusion

In this chapter, we explored the question 'Why do I do what I do?' and examined the links between reflective practice and crtitical thinking. We looked at how we might use Brookfield's 'lenses' to explore different perspectives to our work. For some practitioners, there are constraints which deter them from critical reflection and we looked at how we might overcome such constraints. In examining different reflective cycles, we saw how Schön's (1995) thinking on reflection-in-action and reflection-on-action can be helpful as we write up a reflective journal.

In this chapter:

- We have looked at the cycle of reflection and action.
- We have examined how to link critical thinking and reflection.
- We have explored the concept of praxis.
- We have looked at how you might collaborate.
- We have explored the idea of a reflective diary.

Recommended reading and resources

Brookfield, S. (1995) *Becoming a Critically Reflective Teacher*, San Francisco: Jossey-Bass.

Carr, W. and Kemmis, S. (1986) *Becoming Critical: Education, Knowledge and Action Research*, London: RoutledgeFarmer. While this is a dated text now, it still poses questions for educators and stimulates critical thinking.

McNiff, J. (2002) *Action Research for Professional Development*. http://jeanmcniff.com/ar-booklet.asp. Accessed 31 July 2015. This booklet is a concise and accessible introduction to action research and the importance of reflection and critical thinking.

Video: Robinson, K. (2006) *Do Schools Kill Creativity?* http://www.ted.com/talks/ken_robinson_says_schools_kill_creativity?quote=83 Accessed 31 July 2015. This video gives much food for thought to educators and educational leaders as it poses the question 'Do schools kill creativity?'

Smith, M. K. (2001, 2011) 'Donald Schön: Learning, Reflection and Change', *The Encyclopedia of Informal Education*. www.infed.org/thinkers/et-schon.htm. Accessed 31 July 2015. This web document gives a brief synopsis of the work of Donald Schön.

4 Experiencing oneself as a living contradiction

Introduction

In this chapter we explore in detail Jack Whitehead's concept of experiencing oneself as a 'living contradiction' (1989) and see how this ties in closely with our values and critical reflections, and perhaps offers us a good launch-pad for our research. We look at how you might establish a period of reconnaissance (Waters-Adams 2006) as you begin your research journey and as you put the preparations for your action research project in place.

In this chapter:

- You will explore the concept of 'experiencing oneself as a living contradiction' (Whitehead 1989) in terms of launching a research project, exploring 'living theory', identifying your values and asking questions like 'How do I improve my practice?'
- You will examine some of the key elements of preparing for an action research project and getting the groundwork done for the reconnaissance period.

Launching your research project

When you begin the learning journey that is self-study action research, you will need to find a focus for your research. As with all forms of practitioner research, it is important that your project be small, do-able and manageable. The focus of your research should be something that is meaningful for you, your students and/or the people in your workplace. It will come from within yourself, your thoughts, reflections and concerns. We, action researchers, are seen as people who take action to improve our personal and social situations and offer explanations for why we do it (McNiff and Whitehead 2011). While our purpose is to develop new understandings, knowledge and practices, we also wish to generate new living theory (ibid.) as educational action research is widely seen as a 'methodology for real-world social change' (p. 15). Some action researchers work towards a more peaceful world while others are interested in ecological, environmental and sustainable issues (see Marshall *et al.* 2011, for example). Many teacher researchers work towards improving their practice or their understanding of their practice in a small way, but have a bigger aim of improving the quality of education in general, not only in terms of methodology, but also in terms of social justice and fairness.

The research project you are undertaking now may only be small in scale, but it could have the potential not only to change your perspective on your practice, but also to change policy at your workplace as well as influence educational policy on a wider scale (Whitehead 2015b). Reason and Bradbury remind us:

> While it is true that we cannot make large-scale change on the basis of small cases, neither can we build truly effective and liberating political networks of inquiry without developing significant capacities for critical inquiry in the individuals and small communities that constitute them. (2013: xii)

In Chapter 3, we looked at different models of reflective practice and, in Chapter 5, we will look at different models of action research, which are helpful for us as we learn about the action research process, but we need to remember that these are only models. These are ideas or suggestions to help us structure our critical reflection and our research projects. Many researchers design their own action plans to suit their own specific situation. While action research projects, when presented in written form, often appear to consist of a logical set of steps, with a clear beginning and end, the reality of engaging in self-study action research can be somewhat different. It can be difficult to begin or to find a focus for your project and, once you do find a starting point, your learning journey may take you down a different path to what you had anticipated at the outset. This is a natural process for people who are beginning to engage with action research, as we already discussed in earlier chapters. Mellor talks about the 'messy method' of practitioner research. He says:

> I know I have a goal, which is that I want to look at my job but I don't know what the questions are to ask but I will know when I get there... It is only by getting stuck in and... being confused and asking questions: What am I doing? Why am I doing it? that it becomes clear. (1998: 454)

Sometimes, when practitioner researchers begin to engage in living theory/self-study action research, they begin to see multitudinous problems emanating from their practice, all of which they want to resolve there and then, as they seek to change the world for the better. Needless to say, this is an impossible task and the selection of a research focus needs careful thought and reflection. Sometimes consultation with critical friends or a research supervisor at the initial stages of a research project can avert that sense of being overwhelmed by too many concerns. Brydon-Miller *et al.* (2003) talk about the chaos of action research and say that action researchers seem to be almost drawn to messes, even though they have no quick-fix solutions; they feel the need to 'do something to improve the situation' (p. 21). Be prepared for a complex but enriching journey when you undertake a living theory/action research project.

It is important also to remember that an action research project is cyclical and, very often, rather than having a nice neat solution at the end of the project, a whole new set of questions has emerged instead. Self-study action research is about your learning (along with others) and, because you are learning in the process of your research, your thinking may change. As a result, the original focus of your project may also shift slightly. For example, what began in your mind initially as a project on your understanding of oral language development in your classroom may subsequently develop into a project on bullying. This transformation of ideas is an inherent part of the process of living theory/self-study action research. This preparatory stage of your project should be an opportunity for you to experiment and play with new ideas and literatures, live with them for a while and see how they play out in your practice and in your thinking. It is also a time for you to get an idea of what you would like to have as a focus for your research project.

However, once you move on from this reconnaissance stage (Waters-Adams 2006) of your research, and start the more formal stage of your research with data-gathering, taking action, gaining ethical permission and so on, it is a good idea to try to hold the focus of your research fairly tightly, for purely practical reasons. Lots of avenues of potential exploration will open up for you as you do your research project, but, if you are studying in a formal pro-gramme, you will probably be under time constraints and academic constraints too. You have to do your everyday work, as well as do your research at the same time, so keeping your research question to the forefront of your research will help keep your workload manageable. This is not to say your thinking will not change in the course of your research, it most prob-ably will and all changes in your thinking should be tracked as part of your learning. You should, however, make a record of the avenues that you did not get an opportunity to explore, as you may get the chance to examine them at a later date. Very often those 'waiting to be explored ideas' can provide the action researcher with the most fertile of locations for explo-ration and the richest sources for critical examination, and should be kept for exploration at a later date.

Pause and reflect

Ask yourself:

Can I name some areas in my practice that I would like to investigate?

(Let your ideas emerge from within yourself; your thoughts; reflections; and concerns.)

Living theory

Throughout this text we refer to action research, living theory and self-study action research almost interchangeably, as many of the ideas that underpin them are quite similar. We explored many of these ideas in Chapter 2. When we use the term 'living theory' we are referring specifically to a concept which has evolved from the writings of Jack Whitehead. He believes that theory developed from one's own practice is of a living form, drawn from the lived experiences of the practitioner researcher. He first published these ideas in 1985 and has continued to write about and develop them up to the present day. He believes that educational theory should not be constrained by the propositional theory that is held in high regard by many academics (Whitehead 1989) and encourages practitioner researchers to use their 'first-person voice' in their research accounts (Whitehead 2015a). He believes (while acknowledging the importance of propositional forms of understanding) that such propositional forms can mask the *living* form of educational theory and, therefore, an adequately whole or holistic story of learning is not produced. He suggests (ibid.) that a *living theory*, which offers descriptions and explanations of the lived practices of live practitioners, is more appropriate for many research settings, especially educational settings. Whitehead is committed to working towards a good social order. He is of the opinion that educational theory is a form of dialogue which has 'profound implications for the future of humanity because of the values it holds and because it is embodied in our practical lives' (Whitehead 1993: 6).

We agree with Whitehead's views as outlined in Chapter 2. We feel that, while much research that has been carried out using propositional forms of theory is useful for informing educational practice, the theory generated from an educator's lived experience in their classroom or work situation is extremely valuable because of the insight and illumination of the practitioner's own learning. Whitehead says:

> educational researchers generate explanations of their educational influences in their own learning, in the learning of others and in the learning of the social formations within which the practice is located. I call these explanations living-educational-theories. (Whitehead 2015b: n/p)

As you commence your action research project, remember that as you generate your educational theory from your practice, you will be telling the story of your learning, giving a description of what has happened and why it happened, and offering explanations of your claim to knowledge and explanations around why you believe your story is valid, as outlined in later chapters here.

Whitehead (along with many other self-study action researchers) recommends that researchers use 'I' when speaking about their first-person accounts of their living theory and finds that, sometimes, researchers are pressurised by institutions to revert to the more traditional, objective, third-person accounts of practice. He says 'When I use "I", I am not referring to an egotistical "I", I am referring to relational "I" of infinite conversations, described by Buber (1970)' (Whitehead 2015a: 246).

Values

As outlined earlier, the values we hold as educators are kernel not only to how we practice, but also to the research process itself. They provide us with the basic structure for our expectations for ourselves, and also with the overarching principles towards which we strive in our practice. The values we hold as educators imbue every action and interaction of our day, and colour the observations and perceptions we make. Once educators are aware of what values they hold, they can look to their everyday practice and check that they are working and living in the direction of those values.

Whitehead (2005b: 1) talks about 'embodied values' as being key to the action research/ living theory process. As we discussed earlier, the idea of 'embodiment' is explored by Hocking *et al.* (2001), who want us to acknowledge the role of an educator's intuition and tacit knowledge in their work.

Many practitioners are already aware of the values they hold, and they can name and explain them to others. They may hold values such as social justice or care, for example, and show how they live towards these values in their everyday work. Some practitioners find it difficult to know what their values are or how to articulate them. Frequently, if you give yourself time to think about and acknowledge what inspires your everyday practice, the qualities of your work that are valuable for you and the interactions with others that are important for you, then you are beginning to discover the values you hold. If you discuss your ideas with critical friends and write about them yourself in your reflective journal, the values you hold will eventually become clearer and you may then begin to articulate them with confidence (Glenn 2011). You may find that when you notice that some topics crop up frequently, both in your diary and in conversation, they will signpost the values you hold and also tap into areas of concern for you. Whitehead (2005b: 18) describes how values are the 'living energies of action that give meaning and purpose to life and whose meanings are clarified in the course of their emergence in educational enquiry'. Frequently, we look to our existing practice and how we live our lives to tell us what our values are. The following vignette outlines the struggle I experienced myself as I worked towards being able to articulate my values.

Vignette

As I began to reflect on my educational values, I came to realise that if my work was to be the enactment of my educational values, then my values must lie in the areas of engaging with the wholeness of the person. In Pat's case, I valued the amazing person he was, even though his test scores were miserable. I was drawn to Buber's (see Yoshida 2002) ideas around 'I-Thou' relationships as opposed to 'I-It' relationships. Buber speaks of the importance of developing an awareness and being totally present to others in all engagement. I was trying to engage with others in an 'I-Thou' manner and to see the wholeness and human-ness of those around me. I also valued respect and held that reciprocal respect was a kernel to all productive work. I was also drawn to Noddings's writings on care in education and seeking of a better self. Noddings (1984) echoes Buber's thinking and suggests that educators should be totally and non-selectively present to each student. (Glenn 2011: 495)

The pivotal role values hold in the research process will be discussed again at later stages in the book, as we see how these same values help you to establish the validity of your research claim.

Pause and reflect

Ask yourself:

Can I name some values I hold around my work in education?

Am I able to give practical examples and instances of how I live these values out in my practice?

Experiencing oneself as a living contradiction

In earlier chapters, in the context of critical pedagogy, we referred to Whitehead's (1989) concept of 'experiencing oneself as a living contradiction'. In this chapter, we examine this concept again, in relation to practice. Whitehead has written extensively on the development of this idea, as part of the living theory/action research process (see Whitehead 1985, 1989, 2005b and 2015a, for examples). He has drawn on the works of philosophers such as Ilyenkov (1977), who suggests that 'living experience... [is] full of contradiction and this awareness should be factored into the generation of theory' (Whitehead and McNiff 2006: 32). Whitehead suggests that sometimes we do not live to the values we claim to espouse. Even though we may think we are working according to our values, we find, when we examine our practice closely, that we are not, in fact, doing this. Sometimes, we may be doing the opposite. Whitehead (1989) calls this 'experiencing oneself as a living contradiction'.

Vanassche and Kelchtermans (2015) describe Whitehead's concept of experiencing oneself as a living contradiction as 'acknowledging and analysing the difference between one's normative beliefs and aspirations on the one hand; and one's actual teaching practice on the other hand' (ibid.: 513). Brookfield seems to be thinking in a similar manner as he says 'People's capacity for holding assumptions that contradict each other, and that are contradicted by events and experiences, knows no bounds' (Brookfield 2009: 294). Frequently, it is within these areas of confusion, and contesting and conflicting ideas, that the most powerful, richest and most meaningful research projects are born. Somehow, out of the gloom of confusion, and 'experiencing of oneself as a living contradiction', a little glimmer of understanding begins to emerge, which can grow to illuminate and improve the most complex of situations.

As you have already read, you use your values as the gauge by which you evaluate your everyday work and check to see if you are, in fact, living in the direction of the values to which you aspire. Whitehead (2010b) speaks with refreshing honesty about his own initial inability to think critically about his practice as a science teacher in the 1970s, in a YouTube video (https://www.youtube.com/watch?v=DzXHp9M39BM). He explains how he valued and placed huge importance on enquiry learning and his students' ability to question. Whitehead describes his discomfort when, on being given a video camera to use in his classroom, he discovered that he was not giving his students the opportunity to ask questions at all. In the video clip, he describes how he uses this moment, this discovery of how he was not living in the direction of his educational values, to explain how he engaged in critical thought about his practice and generated a whole school of thought around the idea of 'experiencing oneself as a living contradiction' (Whitehead 2010b).

The process of this 'experience' can be very helpful for a practitioner researcher because it can provide them with a good starting point for their research. It can also give the researcher an opportunity to think critically about their practice and to question the underpinning assumptions they make about it. Above all else, it can give the researcher the framework or outline for their research journey as they examine the issues underpinning how they are 'experiencing [themselves] as a living contradiction' and as they design and undertake an action plan that will enhance their practice so that it will be more commensurate with the values they hold.

The idea of experiencing oneself as a living contradiction is now embedded into the action research/living theory process (see Bradbury 2015). Some educational researchers find the process of examining the parts of their practice that are not commensurate with their values a little daunting. Many of us like to think that we are doing our work fairly well, but holding our work up to the scrutiny of our values and actively looking for occasions when we do not live according to our values can make the most confident practitioner feel a little uncomfortable. This is understandable, especially when we find that our practice reflects that we are doing the exact opposite to what our values would require from us. However, we are careful not to position ourselves as 'victims' of policy-driven imperatives (Day 2012: 7). Instead, the action researcher likes to perceive the experiencing of oneself as a living contradiction as a positive, as a good opportunity for new learning and an inspiration. We believe that the discovery that one is not living closely in the direction of one's values, can be an opportunity for progression and renewal (McDonagh *et al.* 2012); for new learning; for beginning the action research/living theory process; for stimulating 'the imagination about action plans that are intended to enable the values to be lived more fully in practice' (Whitehead 2005b: 4) and for reinvigorating our practice.

Carr and Kemmis (1986: 84) differentiate between contradiction and paradox, a distinction that is helpful for action researchers. When we speak about contradiction, we know that a possibility of reconciliation exists. When we speak of 'paradox', no compromise will ever be reached. As action researchers, we seek to reduce the area of contradiction and reduce the differences between our values and our practice. We remind ourselves that we are only human and that, at most, we can only enable ourselves to work to the best of our ability.

How might we identify the areas of our practice that are not commensurate with our values?

When we go about seeking the areas of our practice that are not commensurate with the values we hold, the exercise seems quite simple on paper. You might feel that all you have to do is to examine your practice and see where there may be a discrepancy between the values you hold and the way you work. However, to carry out this process in the reality of your place of work can be quite complex. You need to be explicitly aware of your values: to be able to examine your practice critically and reflectively and then identify the areas of your practice where you may not be acting out your values as clearly as you might be. Sometimes, it is difficult to juggle the processes of reflection, dialogue, values and critical thinking/reading as well as do your everyday work. Beginner researchers sometimes freeze and do not know how to begin. It takes a leap of faith to just jump into the living theory/self-study action research process and let the story emerge. This is a messy method; sometimes the messiness is the method (Mellor 1998). However, it is worth the effort and it is important to remember that the theory that emerges from your learning is something that develops as your project progresses and your learning unfolds. Be patient and allow patterns to develop and your thinking to clarify. Tenacity, according to Brydon-Miller *et al.* (2003), is a quality common to nearly all action researchers.

Sometimes using Brookfield's four lenses can help us locate occasions in our practice that are not in keeping with the values we hold. As we saw in Chapter 3, Brookfield suggests we use: (i) the lens of our own autobiographies as learners, (ii) the lens of students' eyes, (iii) the lens of colleagues' perceptions and (iv) the lens of educational literature to dissect our practice. Like Whitehead, we can use video or audio recordings of ourselves at work to enhance this process also, once we have all necessary permissions in place (see Chapter 5 and 6).

Sometimes, as teachers, we get a sense that something is 'just not right'. We see something happening and we feel uncomfortable about it. While we may not be able to describe or explain the sensation accurately, it may be an indicator that we are experiencing ourselves as 'living contradiction' and thus may be worthy of closer investigation. The following vignette outlines an occasion when I was using a camera to video some work that my young students were doing and I inadvertently noticed that I was acting in a way that was almost directly opposite to the values I held.

Vignette

Some years ago I was doing a project with my class of six- to eight-year-olds. It involved writing up short accounts about themselves, doing some artwork and emailing the finished product to a partner school. As part of the project, I recorded sections of it on video, using a camera on a tripod.

The project went well, but when I subsequently watched the video footage, I got a shock. Laura, one of the children, had experienced some difficulty with something she was doing on a computer and called me to help her. The video footage shows me walking towards her, bending down and listening. I can then be seen to grab the computer mouse from her and do whatever needed to be done to get her back on track.

The 'grabbing' of the mouse shocked me because of its suddenness and apparent rudeness, I think. My intent had been to listen to Laura respectfully and assist her with her problem. I did listen, but my 'assistance' looked more like swooping down and taking over than helping her. As I reflected on the video clip, I knew I had not been angry with her, but I may have been pressed for time, or I may have just been delighted that I knew how to solve her dilemma. However, no excuses can be made for suddenness, speed and lack of empathy and absolute authority with which I grabbed the mouse from her.

Looking back on this incident, I know now that when I watched that video, my sense of horror at my behaviour was located in how, at an innate level, I was experiencing myself as a living contradiction. I valued care and respect for my pupils and expected that every action and interaction in my class would be imbued with care. The video clip showed me acting in a manner that was lacking in respect and care (albeit unintentionally) and it rankled with me. As I gradually became more aware of my values and my attempts to enact them in my daily practice, I grew to understand my sense of shock at my behaviour as a clear example of experiencing myself as a living contradiction.

Pause and reflect

Ask yourself:

Can I think of an area in my practice where I am experiencing myself as a 'living contradiction'?

Can I name and describe the value I hold in this area?

Am I able to give an example of an occasion when I did not live/work according to my value?

Asking questions of the kind 'How do I improve my practice?'

Whitehead (1989) suggests that living theory be explained by the logic of question and answer, of the form 'How do I improve my practice?' As action researchers, we are not aiming to improve someone else's practice, nor are we trying to change anyone else. We are simply trying to improve the quality of our own work or our thinking about our work to enable others to learn or work together in a better way. We suggest that the wording 'How do I improve my practice?' should be interpreted fairly fluidly, in a way that is meaningful to your own living practice while, at the same time, maintaining the essence of the question.

For example, we suggest that asking yourself 'How do I improve my understanding of my practice?' is a very closely related question, and is a worthwhile route of exploration (see Glenn 2006, 2011; McDonagh *et al.* 2012). Often practitioners engage in practices and methodologies that are fairly successful, but they have no idea why they use them or what purpose they serve. We believe that asking questions like 'How do I understand better what I am doing?' is an interpretation of 'How do I improve my practice?' and can develop the thinking and understanding of the practitioner in a way that can eventually enhance their practice and improve the learning experience for all involved.

We authors also feel that asking 'How do I share my passion about what I am doing?' (or words to that effect) is also a valid interpretation of 'How do I improve my practice?' Practitioners frequently engage in practices and use teaching methodologies that are innovative or very successful in their own educational setting. Such innovation is always worth scrutiny and sharing with other educators, and examining the values that bring the practitioner to practice in this way can unearth valuable insights, not only for themselves, but for others too. The following vignette shows how I began my research for my PhD by wanting to share my passion for my work with others.

Vignette

In my PhD research (Glenn 2006), I began by wanting to celebrate what I thought was fairly innovative work with internet projects with my primary school class, and to share my ideas with others. As I began to reflect critically on my work, I began to realise that, initially, I had little understanding around why I chose to work with these projects. So, while I could describe what was involved in doing these projects, I could not explain why

I did them. After a fairly long struggle, I developed an understanding of my emergent values around developing connections between different aspects of education and establishing a more holistic curriculum with my class. I gradually came to realise that this sense of holism and connection was at the heart of all my internet-based projects.

I still have not succeeded in formally investigating 'How do I celebrate what I am doing?' but I think it might be a project for the future.

Preparing for your research process: the reconnaissance period

In this part of this chapter, we examine some of the key elements of preparing for an action research project. This reconnaissance (Waters-Adams 2006) period of your research process begins with yourself. Begin in your own mind and body by developing your sense of awareness of yourself and your environment. Take the 'pause' that Maxine Greene suggests (see Chapter 1) and breathe. Take some 'quiet' time for yourself and just give yourself time to reflect and to think. Become more aware of those with whom you work; the atmosphere of your work environment; and your interactions with others. Watch keenly and listen carefully. Try to develop that 'I-Thou' sense of relationship Buber advocates: Buber (1958) saw a difference between 'I-It' relationships (wherein one person sees the other as a separate entity) and 'I-Thou' relationships (wherein each person sees the other as a whole being, deserving of the utmost awareness, attention and respect). Developing 'I-Thou' relationships can make for healthier and more wholesome connections with others.

When undertaking a self-study action research project, there are no correct first steps or second steps or specific guidelines: all the steps come from within yourself and your interactions. Dadds and Hart (2001: 166) remind us that 'for some practitioner researchers, creating their own unique way through their research may be as important as their self-chosen research focus'. However, the following is a list of 'ingredients' or strategies that, in our experience, are important to the reconnaissance period in the research process. Many of them have already been discussed, and those that have not, will be discussed in greater detail below. Pick any one or two of these ideas and strategies below and try them. If you are comfortable with them, then add another strategy or two to your process and so on, until you have the whole reconnaissance process 'simmering'. Many of the ideas below are interdependent and intertwined and, in general, they lead almost naturally into one another.

Remember that, right now, you are preparing for your living theory action research project. If you build a good foundation for your project, then the project itself will be sturdier and more robust. You are preparing to plan your action; take action; collate data; ascertain to see if you are living more to your values; improve your practice or your understanding of it; present evidence to support your claim; and share the story of your learning with others. For now, you are putting the groundwork in place.

Some key elements of the reconnaissance phase of the research

Writing a reflective journal

If you have not begun writing a reflective journal, begin now. Even if you never undertake an action research project, it will hopefully enhance your learning (see Chapter 3). Remember to have somewhere to jot down notes or 'reflections-in-action' on your person at nearly all times. Bear in mind that journals 'can be an effective medium for facilitating deep reflection' (Dyment and O'Connell, 2011: 82) and for clarifying your thinking. Try to read widely and discuss your ideas with others as you reflect.

Values

Think about your values; talk about your values; read about the values others hold (see Whitehead's extensive collection of papers on values at http://www.actionresearch.net); and write in your journal about them. Play with the ideas, discuss them with critical friends and read critically around the ideas. Let your values emerge in the course of your research (see Chapter 1 and above).

Passion

As you prepare for your action research project, you will be thinking about improving your practice (or similar ideas). Nias (1996) reminds us that there are two main factors that influence teachers' sense of success or failure: 'One is the exercise of professional skill' and the other occurs 'when they feel that they are acting consistently with their beliefs and values' (ibid.: 4). As practitioners, we can enhance our sense of self-esteem when we act in the direction of the values we hold and we work towards tapping into and harnessing the passion we have for our work.

Think about how your enthusiasm for education inspires you or inspired you at some stage. Teachers who hold a passion for education are committed, enthusiastic, intellectually and emotionally energetic and hold a clear moral purpose (Day 2004). They hold a certain sense of joy for their work and spend an amount of time preparing for the day's work and evaluating it. Nias reminds us of the role that emotions can play in educators' lives:

> Behind the ordered control and professional calm of all the teachers [whose voices are reported here] bubble deep, potentially explosive passions, emotions bringing despair, elation, anger and joy of a kind not normally associated in the public mind with work.
> (1996: 3)

Try to unlock your inner passion for education and capture its essence by writing about it. If you feel your passion needs rekindling, try writing about a time when you were passionate about your work to help reconnect with your enthusiasm.

What are my concerns and why am I concerned?

In Chapter 5, we will explore different models or structures for designing an action research project. One of the most widely used models is Whitehead's model, which generally begins with the questions 'What are my concerns?' and 'Why am I concerned?' (see Whitehead 2015a). These are key questions for initiating an action research living theory project and we will explore them in further detail in the next chapter. For now, it is enough to ask yourself 'What is my concern?'; 'What am I worried about?'; 'What am I interested in?'; or 'What would I like to know more about?' As you begin to outline your concerns or area of interest, you should also engage your critical thinking processes and ask why you are concerned or why you are interested in this area. Remember, too, that you will be evaluating these concerns in light of the values you hold. Sometimes, when researchers address these questions, they frequently find the focus for their research project and their research question.

Experiencing oneself as a living contradiction

As outlined above, we authors find that one of the most powerful ways to kick-start a living theory action research project, is to engage in some critical reflection about practice and to identify areas that are not in keeping with the values we hold.

Action research: a risky business

Be ready to jump into the unknown

McNiff and Whitehead (2011) remind us that action researchers are always standing on the edge and ready to step out into the unknown. Traditional forms of research begin with a hypothesis, which the researcher sets out to prove. In self-study action research, the emphasis is different. The researcher begins with a question about their practice or their understanding of it. As the researcher works through the project, the theory and their claim to new knowledge emerge. As you prepare for your research project, you do not know what you are about to learn; for many, that is a risky prospect. In the process of the research, you will, hopefully, learn more about your practice and develop new understandings around it, but you may also encounter some unforeseen learning curves.

For example, Pip Bruce Ferguson (2015) recalls her unanticipated learning when she encountered communication problems arising from cultural misunderstandings while working with Māori people, despite her best efforts to anticipate them. She says:

> While I was shocked at the time, I appreciated the action of the Pakeha man and the Māori woman in contributing to expanding my knowledge... When I teach now, I strive to find out the cultural backgrounds of my students. (p. 58)

When Bernie Sullivan realised that she had inadvertently caused a pupil to stay away from school, even though she was actually trying to encourage her student to attend more regularly, she also experienced some unanticipated learning:

> The realisation that I had some responsibility for what had occurred came as a shock to me, but it also represented significant learning for me around the necessity for greater accountability for my actions, as well as greater awareness of the effect that my actions could have on a powerless, voiceless pupil. (McDonagh *et al.* 2012: 199)

As you work through your action research project, you will be opening yourself up to new possibilities and new questions. Be ready to commit to the 'risk of creating a new future' (McNiff and Whitehead 2011: 35) as you encounter new learning and gain new insights into your work.

Victory narratives

It is tempting for some action researchers to relay only the positive parts of the project and neglect to tell the negative aspects of it. You should avoid this practice because it is dishonest, in the sense that negative experiences are excised from the account, and honesty is an inherent requirement of living theory action research (see Chapter 5). Such misleading stories are called 'victory narratives' (MacLure 1996: 293) and have no part to play in any robust piece of research. They are annoying, misleading and off-putting for colleagues and other teachers to read. Even teachers who only have little experience of teaching will recognise that they may be inaccurate and will disregard them. In an academic setting, a victory narrative will receive lower marks or perhaps even be failed by academic supervisors.

Your aim is to avoid victory narratives and to tell the honest and accurate, 'warts and all' story of your learning. For example, let's say that you have decided to use a pre-test and a post-test as part of your data gathering strategy, to show improved learning and that your practice is now becoming more aligned to your values. Let us imagine that the post-test results are no higher than your pre-test results – that is, your students' maths scores may be no better than before you began your project – and you feel your research project has been a failure. However, this is not the case. Despite the apparently less-than-positive test results, you will have gained insight into your practice and extended your learning in the process of the project. You will be telling the story of your insights and learning, and perhaps the growth in your learning, in your research account. It will form the basis for your claim to knowledge. It may involve telling unfavourable stories about yourself, but it will be honest and your account will be trustworthy and accurate.

Action research may be for life, not just for a project

As you begin to prepare for your project, you will probably develop a sense of awareness around yourself and your teaching environment. You will learn to become more critical in your reflections and question the assumptions that you, and others, hold about your area of practice. You will possibly work towards articulating your values and see how you are living them out in your everyday practice. You may seek to improve your practice or your understanding of it and you will probably aim to generate your theory from the story of your learning. You will, perhaps, develop an understanding of the significance of your work and maybe share your story with others. And then your project is finished. Or is it?

Many action researchers find that, even when the project is over, the action researcherly disposition that was adopted throughout the project continues. Lingard and Renshaw (2009) advocate that all education practitioners, policy-makers and teachers should have a researcherly disposition, while we advocate an 'action researcherly disposition'. We find that, even though there is no academic compulsion for us to behave or think in an action researcherly manner, we continue to critically reflect on our practice, seek to live to our values and so on. On completion of his doctorate, Sankaran wrote 'My emancipatory spirit had been awakened and I started feeling restless after I finished my doctorate. My world had been changed and I was looking at it from different eyes' (n/d, cited in Brydon-Miller *et al.* 2003: 17). Developing an action researcherly disposition is quite similar to Cochran-Smith and Lytle's notion of 'inquiry as stance' (Cochran-Smith and Lytle 2009a: 44). They claim that action research is not just an academic project, but also a:

> larger epistemological stance, or a way of knowing about teaching, learning and school-ing, that is neither topic- nor project-dependent... Taking an inquiry as stance means teacher and student teachers working within a community to generate local knowl-edge, envision and theorize their practice, and interpret and interrogate the theory and research of others. (Ibid.)

We, action researchers, are 'bitten by the bug' and are overwhelmed with a new thirst and passion for learning that never leaves us. We live our lives in a way that is guided by the values we hold and we endeavour to live and work in the direction of those values in our practice. We read widely and engage in dialogue and reflect critically on our work and on our lives. We see the world with new eyes and we want to enhance it.

Conclusion

In this chapter, we examined the concept of experiencing oneself as a 'living contradiction' (Whitehead 1989) and we saw how we might use this process as a positive place from which to launch our research. We also looked at some of the elements needed for the preparatory or reconnaissance stage of an action research project.

In the next section, we will move on to how we might to develop an action plan, make a research claim, explore ethical issues, learn how to collect data and present evidence to sup-port our claim to knowledge.

In this chapter:

- You looked at the concept of 'experiencing oneself as a living contradiction' (White-head 1989) in terms of launching a research project, exploring 'living theory', identifying your values, and asking questions like 'How do I improve my practice?'
- You explored some of the key aspects of preparing for an action research project and getting the groundwork done for the reconnaissance period.

Recommended reading and resources

Whitehead, J. (1989) 'Creating a Living Educational Theory from Questions of the Kind, "How Do I Improve My Practice?"', *Cambridge Journal of Education*, 19(1), 137–53. http://www.actionresearch .net/writings/livtheory.html. This is Whitehead's seminal work and one of his first papers, outlining his thinking on values, practice and experiencing oneself as a living contradiction.

Whitehead, J. (2010b) *How did you Develop your Living Theory Approach? Jack Whitehead Inter-viewed.* https://www.youtube.com/watch?v=DzXHp9M39BM. This YouTube video captures Whitehead being interviewed in Bergen, Norway, September 2010. Whitehead gave a lecture to the Pestalozzi conference arranged by the Bergen University College (HiB). Here he explains his own first awareness of how he experienced himself as a 'living contradiction'.

Whitehead J. (2015a) 'The Practice of Helping Students to Find Their First Person Voice in Creating Living Theories for Education', in H. Bradbury (ed.), *The Sage Handbook of Action Research*, 3rd edn, London and Thousand Oaks, CA: Sage, pp. 246–54. Here Whitehead outlines the processes his students undertake as they generate their living theories.

SECTION III

How do I evaluate changes I make?

Caitriona McDonagh

This section is about helping you to clarify what actions you might take and how to assess these in a researcherly way. We offer a number of action plan approaches from literature (McNiff 2013; Mills 2011; Whitehead 2015a) for you to consider. After thinking critically about these, we invite you to develop an action plan that will suit your context and your reflections on your current practice and values. Once you have devised a research plan, the next question to ask is, 'How do I know that my research plan is working?'

To be of assistance with that question, this section is also about gathering information, making a research claim and the ethical issues you need to consider especially when working with minors. From our experiences as teacher researchers, from supporting others in conducting classroom research and from assessing teachers' research projects, we know what quality teacher research requires. We feel we can now offer a critical perspective on how you might ensure the quality of your research.

Chapter 5 considers ways to plan your research project and what forms of information-gathering (data) might best show the changes you are making. We invite you to consider which forms of data might be most relevant in your specific context. We next investigate how to use the information you have gathered to construct and explain a valid research claim. This requires providing evidence. We explain our understanding of the difference between data and evidence in action research. By the end of the chapter you will have examined each step of that process, so that you may confidently answer the question 'how do I evaluate in a researcherly way any changes I have made?'

In Chapter 6 we consider two important aspects of conducting quality teacher research. Because this usually involves working with children and young people, we think about the ethical issues that arise, such as whether we need permission for the children to take part and who we approach for this consent. We encourage you to question why you particularly need to refer to your ethical standards in action research. We look at what influences the ethical choices you make and how this might look in your research report. Finally, we explore the thorny question of how we can show that our research is of good quality. We invite you to consider various requirements for rigour and validity in the process of conducting action research within your learning contexts. We suggest possibilities to ensure reliability and credibility in your research.

5 Generating data

Introduction

We have deliberately left this chapter towards the centre of the book because, as you have worked your way through the earlier chapters, you have reflected on and articulated the important reasons for conducting your research. In Chapters 1 and 2 you have thought about what is important to you in terms of education and critical pedagogy and these will impact on what you plan to do as well as how you evaluate your actions. In Chapters 3 and 4 you have thought about 'Why do I do what I do?' and found tensions in your practice that help you to select a research topic; these will also impact on what you plan to do. Because you have already critically considered all the 'why' questions about your research, it is time to formulate an action plan by addressing the practical what, where and when questions such as 'What will I do? Where will I do it? With whom and for how long?' You will also be asking, 'How can I find research methods that support my critical thinking and reflections on my practice?'

In this chapter, we address the following questions:

- Can I find research methods that support my critical reflections on my practice?
- How do I draw up an action plan?

Collecting data to show that my plan is working

- Why do I collect data?
- What kinds of data can I collect?
- How can I show others what is happening?

How I generate evidence to support a research claim

- How can I give a valid research account of any changes I make?

Can I find research methods that support my critical reflections on my practice?

Just as there are clothes and image designers and wedding designers/planners, you may come across research designers. When I first did, I thought that they could answer my question 'How do I draw up an action plan?' I also expected that they could provide me with a variety of useful research tools and examples of their use. But they could not help with my more personal and context-based question, 'How do I draw up an action plan when research-ing something specific to my practice?' So, again, there can be no 'one size fits all' to design-ing a research plan.

Policy-makers often use terms such as 'integration', 'innovation', 'improvement' and 'impact' to show the thinking behind the policies they design (Ó Ruairc 2014; Ireland, Depart-ment of Education and Skills 2014; US Department of Education n/d; UK Department for Education 2005) and I suggest that thinking about these keywords can help in drawing up a research plan.

1   Integration may mean that your plan is based in your specific context and in the con-cepts of education that are important to you. These will have been informed by the literature, policies and practices in your context.
2   Innovation, in terms of a research plan, may mean that you are willing to risk trying methods or inventing your own in order to achieve your research aims.
3   Improvement means looking for improvement in all aspects of your practice. This will include finding ways to show new learning for pupils as well as for yourself.
4   Impact means finding ways to include the potential influence of your research within the learning community around you.

Beginning with the first two keywords, we introduce you to some action planning (Glenn 2015; Mills 2011; McNiff 2013; McDonagh *et al.* 2015; Whitehead 2015a) so you can decide on an integrated plan. Next, we help you draw up an innovative plan that allows for the fluid situa-tion in teaching contexts. There are as many models of action plan as there are researchers. Browse through those below, remembering that a research cycle involves action, reflection and evaluation, and see which one suits you best. When you come to finalising your decision you may use any model provided here, or you may modify them to suit your own needs or devise your own.

Action research, as explained in earlier chapters, involves the following actions: plan, act, observe, reflect, construct a revised plan, act, observe, reflect. These are repeated to form cycles of action and reflection. Below are a variety of action plans for you to consider criti-cally. Mills (2011: n/p) describes his approach to planning an action research process as follows:

- Write an area of focus statement.
- Define the variables (e.g. the curriculum, school setting, student outcomes, instructional strategies).
- Develop research questions.
- Describe the intervention or innovation.
- Describe the membership of the action research group.
- Describe negotiations that need to be undertaken.
- Develop a timeline.
- Develop a statement of resources.
- Develop data collection ideas.
- Put the plan into action.

Rather than posing a list of instructions McNiff (2013: 91) suggests questions to help you move your research plan from descriptions to explanations:

- What do I wish to investigate?
- Why do I wish to investigate it?
- How do I show and describe the current situation as it is?
- What do I think I can do about it? What will I do about it?
- How do I show and explain the situation as it develops?
- How will I ensure that any conclusions I draw are reasonably fair and accurate by inviting the critical responses of others and myself?
- How do I communicate the significance of what I am doing?
- How will I modify my practices and thinking in light of the evaluation?

Whitehead (2015a: 4) offers a further plan which moves into evidence-based explanations of what you are doing:

- What do I want to improve? What is my concern? Why am I concerned?
- Imagine possibilities and choose one of them to act on in an action plan.
- As I am acting, what data will I collect to enable me to judge my educational influence in my professional context as I answer my question?
- Evaluate the influence of the actions in terms of values and understandings.
- Modify concerns, ideas and actions in the light of evaluations.
- Produce a validated, evidence-based explanation of educational influences in learning.

Pause and reflect

What appeals to you in the action plans above?

Take time to recap on where you stand with your project.

Ask yourself:
Have I a research topic?
Why is this topic important to me?
Can I compose an I-focused research question?
Have I imagined possibilities and selected one of them to act on in an action plan?
As I act, what data will I collect to enable me to judge my educational influence in my professional context?
How might I evaluate the influence of the actions in terms of my values?
How might I make public a validated explanation of this educational influence?

How do I draw up an action plan?

We now offer you our action plan to consider based on Glenn (2015) and McDonagh *et al.* (2015). This action plan requires both critical reflections and action. In supporting teacher researchers in a variety of educational settings, we have found a need to add a further critically reflective and practical edge. We have found that the following practical approach appeals to many teachers. They find it helpful because it links an action research methodology to a traditional format for writing up research reports; this is discussed in Chapter 8. We present our plan in six groups of actions that are loosely linked to a traditional format. We use action words or verbs to frame our plan.

1. Reflect on what is happening, think critically and identify values. Record your thinking
2. Read critically, discuss, think critically and record your thinking
3. Find a focus, make a plan, take action, be aware of your values and record everything
4. Reflect on your work, evaluate your actions, review how you see your values in your practice and record everything
5. Make a claim of your learning, establish criteria, present evidence, show rigour and validity
6. Tell the story of your research to others, explain your new educational theory, show the potential significance of your work – and begin again.

We will now take a more detailed look at each of these points in turn.

1. Our research plan above invites you to look back (reflect) with the purpose of planning (think forward) for your work. As outlined in previous chapters, it is important to remember to record and track your thinking in your reflective journal. It is a good idea to gather some data at the outset of your research journey, to show the situation as it is at the beginning, to show what your concern is and why you are concerned. Remember that you are aiming to work in the direction of your values, and this initial stage of your research is usually closely linked to the values you hold.
2. Read literatures related to all aspects of your research and discuss your thoughts with a critical friend. Record your ideas and any critique that arose in your discussions. As action researchers, we aim to engage critically with the ideas and assumptions that make up our everyday lives. We try to explore the ideas that underpin our practice. Reading the literature about your work and about your area of interest may help to illuminate your thinking and assist you in questioning your assumptions. It may provide you with specific language and a more academic voice. It furthers your understanding of your work. Having conversations with critical friends, who support your work but will not be swayed by your rhetoric, can likewise help the critical process.
3. In this context the word 'focus' means looking for an area in your practice that you feel needs investigation. You may seek areas of your practice where you experience yourself as a 'living contradiction' (Whitehead 1989), as outlined in previous chapters, or you may wish to celebrate an area of work where your values are explicit. This is an opportunity to firm up your research question. Make a plan and outline the practicalities of who will take part, how you will invite them and get their consent to take part in your research, how long your project will last and what resources you may need. This is about justifying your research methods and methodology. Act on your plan and find ways to record what happens. Reflect on this.
4. Evaluate your actions by thinking about how your values may have been realised in what has happened. Review this by monitoring any new learning for you personally and for other participants. Record this and reflect on this.

5   Make a claim to knowledge about what you have learned. You need to establish the rigour and validity of your claim. Later in this chapter, we will provide examples of how this might be achieved.

6   Tell the story of your research to others. These others may be participants who are spoken to informally or in prearranged meetings. They may be work colleagues who are told informally at staff meetings or through teach meets. They may be other researchers who hear your story through refereed journals and conferences. All of this will help you reflect on and recognise the significance of your research as we discuss in Chapter 7. The telling of your story is part of adding validity to your research and we will explain this and how to generate a theory later in this chapter and those that follow.

Pause and reflect

What aspects of the planning above might be practical, manageable and relevant for you?

Collecting data to show that my plan is working

Now that you have devised a research plan and are beginning to enact your plan, the next questions to ask are, 'How do I know how my research plan is working?' and 'How can I show this to others?' In answering these questions, you are explaining why you collect data. Data has to do with gathering information.

We want to show how you might gather information in ways that are sensible, practical and relevant to your research and practice. This information provides descriptions of your practice as you research it. In a self-study research approach, we need to show why, and for what purpose, we are carrying out our actions (McNiff and Whitehead 2011). For this reason we are inviting you to cast a crtitical eye on data-gathering. The *Oxford Dictionary* (2010: 2167) tells us that data comes from the Latin word 'datum', meaning something given, and that the word data has been used in philosophy since the seventeenth century to mean things known, or assumed as facts, making the basis of reasoning or calculation. We explain not only why you collect data – things known – but also how to consider critically which forms of data are most relevant to your research question and context. Next, we consider how to make this data the basis of an authentic research account so that you can make a valid research claim.

Why do I collect data?

Here are some reasons why we may collect data:

- For ourselves, to ascertain the veracity of our thinking about our practice (which we have discussed in previous chapters)
- For evidence of the changes we make to our practice – or in our learning
- To check how closely we are living to our values (as discussed in previous chapters). We can collect data to show what is our concern at the outset. We can collect data again as we take action to improve our practice and act in the direction of our values
- To generate evidence to support our claim to knowledge and show what is true.

What kinds of data can I collect?

There are many data sources in a classroom; some are statistical and some are not. Statistical analysis from the forms of testing commonly in use in classrooms may be of use in describing how some aspects of your research are working, but this analysis alone will not give your research reader the full picture about the processes of learning and teaching that may have occurred. In self-study action research you are looking at the bigger picture. To help you keep a broad research lens, the examples in the next pages show how we authors gathered information from a variety of perspectives and also show how our pupils, ourselves and others can have a part in this process.

The classroom-based examples demonstrate rigorous ways for you to make explicit things that you know, or assume as facts, about teaching and learning in your setting. Often teachers look at their students for evidence of improvement. Teacher researchers, however, need to focus their research lens on their own teaching and practice as well (McDonagh *et al.* 2012). To do so they find the following useful: the school journal or diary, yearly and short-term plans or reviews.

How can I show others what is happening?

Over the next pages we will look at gathering information from:

1   yourself – using reflective journals, video, planning and assessment review documents
2   pupils – using photographs, students' journals, students' work, audio files, student questionnaires, digital camera and assessment results
3   other educationalists – from critical colleague(s) and triangulation.

We invite you to consider these data-gathering methods and to evaluate if they are relevant to your work. In deciding how to gather data, be creative and seek out ways that are relevant and valid in your own context.

Gathering information from oneself – our experiences

When we are gathering information from ourselves, we are looking at our actions/work, interactions and thoughts and understandings. Reflective journals, videos and digital storyboards offer ways of showing how we collect data in terms of our reflections on our teaching and thinking, as well as ongoing evaluation of what is happening. Here are some of our personal experiences of using these approaches.

A reflective diary or learning journal can provide data about changes in how you think, about your work and how you go about it. These changes are important because they track the story of one's learning, which is at the heart of generating theory from practice. See Chapter 3 for more on reflective journals. For example, Glenn (2006) says,

> When I first set out to examine my practice, I found it very difficult to articulate my understanding of my work. I have found that it is a good idea to keep a reflective journal by your side at all times to enable you to record events and your reflections on them, almost as they occur. It is a good idea to jot down these reflections whenever you get

a brief moment during the day. Frequently, reflection-in-action (Schön 1983) occurs in your mind as you respond to events in your practice. These may be fleeting thoughts but often they can inform your thinking about your work when you get an opportunity to reflect more deeply. You can then revisit these jottings in a more tranquil frame of mind after work and try to reflect on them and perhaps rewrite them more coherently. (p. 49)

Your reflective journal or video diary is like a tracking device (assuming you have all necessary permissions in place – see Chapter 6). It will help you follow the process of your thinking and learning. Your claim to knowledge will be drawn from the stories of your learning throughout the research process. Your reflective journal or video diary will also help you to see a timeline in your work. You might notice, for example, where you digressed in order to investigate a new aspect of your topic; or when a new idea dawned on you; or when a few words from a pupil or colleague influenced what you were doing. Whitehead (2010a) explains how, through the use of video, we can clarify and communicate the 'energy-flowing values we use to give meaning and purpose to our lives', our teaching and our research. In one of his many videos on http://www.actionresearch.net, he uses the term 'empathetic resonance', where you can slide the cursor over the same section of a video, to show the authenticity that words alone cannot capture. His website gives examples, from accredited theses up to doctoral level, of the use of video for capturing and evaluating practice.

Pause and reflect

How might you gather information about your teaching from your own writing, records, videos or observers?

Why might this data be important?

Our experiences of gathering information from students

Data can be collected from students copybooks, homework, projects, conversations with students, comments from parents, questionnaires to students, interviews and so on. Below are some ways in which teacher researchers have used pictures and video as data, once they have ensured all necessary permissions are in place. Always ensure that you comply with child protection guidelines in relation to permissions and be aware of your particular institution's policy on photographs and videos. This will be discussed in detail in Chapter 6.

Picture and video recordings may be taken by the students, by the teacher researcher or by an observer and may show the progress in diverse learning activities such as:

- The engagement of students while recording the results of their discussions
- A film clip showing the strategies and stages in a learning process – for example, computing, reasoning, applying and engaging
- Students' digital storyboarding that shows the planning and construction of board games to test their new learning
- Video clip of tentative and developing thinking when engaging in group activities

- Film clips of the choices students make when dividing tasks according to each student's strengths
- Scans of pupils' hand-written journals of their learning in which they may retell, relate and reflect on what happened and their understanding of it.

From these examples you will note that, when you are examining your teaching, your pupils are part of the process. Your students' voices can provide valuable data. Pupils involved as participants in your research may influence the directions you take and how you might evaluate your research. These developmental interactions can be a rich data source, as in the following examples.

Vignette

Glenn (2006) was interested in encouraging creative use of technology and wrote: 'My pupils were using a digital camera to record something from their homes related to history. A pupil, aged 10, surprised me with additional pictures which he took on his way to school the following morning. He was struck by the beauty of the icy dawn at a lakeside, and asked his mother to stop the car while he took some more photographs. When he came into the classroom, he wrote the following, which I believe captures what was for him a spiritual moment. "I saw a beautiful sight and decided to capture it on my camera the sun shining down on the ice. It was just amazing and I wanted to show the world how beautiful our environment can be. The waves were frozen they stood perplexed and just waiting for the sun to melt the ice away so it could be free again and no longer be still to crash against the rocks once more. I stood and looked and stared through the ice barrier and slowly looked up and watched the sun slowly move over the horizon. The End."' (ibid.: 13) Here the pupil had taken the teacher researcher's information-gathering tool and created his own use for it. His inventiveness meant that his voice in her research project had added a new focus to her work.

In the second example, I was working with pupils with dyslexia (McDonagh 2007) to help them understand how they might learn more effectively and gain self-confidence. Because of their writing difficulties I invited pupils to draw their feelings about dyslexia and then discuss them, as in this example, where a pupil drew herself on a black swing. Her large smiling face stared from the picture. Beneath her was black foreground and above her a rainbow. The student said that her picture showed how dyslexia made school black and dark at times, but as colourful as a rainbow at other times. She said: 'I am on a swing because I have mood swings – sometimes I'm good and sometimes a failure, up and down, colourful and black, up and down again and again. But when I stop swinging to think, I am in the black' (ibid.: 187). In my research account I explained how the pupil's description of her picture added to my personal understanding of the effects of dyslexia.

As you can see, data from students can include teacher observation, conversations with students, comments in class, samples of students' work and artefacts they have made as data.

Pause and reflect

What kinds of data could you collect from your students?

How might you gather data about how students experience your teaching?

How would this be important for your practice?

Gathering information from others – our experiences

Others can confirm and critique not only what you have done, but also the changes in how you think about your work. We authors have found this process useful and beneficial because dialogues can illuminate our thinking. Below are some examples from teachers' work of how critical colleagues provided data that contributed to triangulation.

Cross-checking your work from different perspectives is triangulation, which can show the accuracy and validity of information you gather. Triangulation can explain more fully the richness and complexity of the changes you have made because they are viewed from more than one standpoint (Cohen *et al.* 2011) and so give a more detailed and balanced picture (Altrichter *et al.* 2008). Documenting what a critical friend says is a useful data-gathering tool. We authors have sometimes called our critical friend a 'learning partner'. So this partner should be someone you have confidence in as a person who could critique your actions and be honest with you (see McDonagh *et al.* 2012: 57–9). By including their comments in your research report you are adding another perspective that can validate your work. Again, it is important that you have their permission to use their words.

Below is an example of how Roche (2007) used triangulation by taking one research event and checking what happened from a variety of perspectives: pupils (research participants); her own stance (teacher researcher); teacher observers (professional critical friends who had knowledge of her research topic and setting); and her tutor (external professional), who had expertise in the research methodology. Roche was interested in helping pupils to become critical thinkers and used the event below to evaluate her teaching from multi perspectives. The pupils (aged nine to ten years) were seated in their circle to discuss what they found interesting in the novel, *The Indian in the Cupboard* (Reid Banks 1982). The vignette below provides multiple sources of data, as you will now see.

Vignette

In her journal, Roche wrote: 'In keeping with my democratic values, all the teachers sat in the circle as equal participants with the children and only spoke when it was our turn to do so.'

In the discussion, a pupil said: 'Well, I think Omri kind of grew up in the story because at the start he was excited about having a real live Indian toy to play with and then when the Indian chief died he began to see that you can't use people as toys or things. Then when Patrick wanted to get loads of cowboys and Indians to come to life and make them fight, Omri was really terrified of that idea!' Pupil S responded: 'Yeah, I agree with M: I actually think that this book is really kind of important for making us think about the way people get used... like soldiers get used and like we were saying before, beautiful girls... models... they often get used for selling boats and cars and stuff. People aren't things; people shouldn't be treated like objects!'

Roche noted in her diary: 'The children's questions quickly became deeper and more thought-provoking. One of the children raised the idea that Omri, the principal child character in the story, had become very mature as the story evolved.' From the children's contributions to the discussion, Roche described how she could see that the book explores many concepts, among them the idea of objectifying and using people for gratification – in this case as children's toys.

One of the teacher observers commented: 'Those children made me think about issues that I've never thought of before!... I'd be scared to teach that class – they know more than I do!'

The tutor noted that this account would have been strengthened by the use of video. (Roche 2007)

Adding more perspectives to check the accuracy of what you are describing and claiming in your research is triangulation. For example, you could get comments from pupils, parents, others who visit your work setting, teaching colleagues, a teacher outside your school or someone who knows a lot about your topic. We discuss how triangulation provides validity for your research in later chapters.

To conclude this section, consider the relevance to your setting of this list of information-gathering tools which teacher researchers have used in practice: conversations between or with students, colleagues or critical friends; photographs; audio or video clips from your classroom; email conversations; descriptions of interactions in your classroom; artefacts from your classroom; letters; drawings; excerpts from your reflective journal; lesson plans; inspectors' reports; blogs; test scores; scrapbooks; statistics; surveys; interviews; questionnaires; transcripts of phone conversations; samples of pupils' work; quotes from pupils or their parents; and so on. All kinds of data are valuable in action research. You can draw on both qualitative and quantitative approaches.

Pause and reflect

How can others act as a mirror to help me show changes in my work?

Does the information I gather from others tell me more about my teaching?

What other forms of information-gathering could I use?

How do we generate evidence to support a research claim?

As we have seen above, all forms of data that you can gather about your practice have relevance in teacher action research. We believe that it is necessary not only to describe your data-gathering tools, but also to explain why you have chosen to collect this form of data. To establish this, you may address these questions, which are both critical and professionally appropriate:

- Does this data show change in my teaching and/or in my students' learning?
- Was my data collected in ways that fit well with my epistemological and professional values, as explained in earlier chapters? This means that, as an action researcher, you would be collecting data about your own thinking as well as data about student performance.
- Does my data show that my practice is more commensurate with the values I hold?

Here is an example, from my own reflective journal, of a dilemma I experienced in choosing relevant forms of data.

Vignette

I was investigating 'How do I improve my teaching of students who have learning difficulties with the language of maths?' I presumed that if I drew up elaborate profiles of each pupil, I could begin to understand how to change my teaching. As I worked through more and more detailed assessments, I felt I was walking through a forest of data and had lost clarity about what to do next. I was convinced that, by using large numbers of pupils and gathering large amounts of data, over time, my findings, or generalisations, would help other professionals to understand the construct of learning difficulties with the language of maths. Although this is a thorough approach to research, it does not necessarily lead to personal and professional enhancement – which was the aim of my research question: 'How do I support students with language difficulties in my maths classes?'

My supervisor posed a critical question that altered my research dramatically: 'Where are you and where is your teaching in this research?' This question puzzled me because I thought that my thoroughness as a researcher was obvious. But as a teacher, I began to query how could I possibly describe something as complex as students' difficulties with maths language. Often in class I was surprised and enlightened by comments students made or facial expressions they used. Gradually, I started to appreciate that my research question was actually about my relationship with my students. If I did succeed in improving my teaching it would not only be seen in students' improved test results, but also in their attitudes, feelings and inner thoughts. Collecting qualitative data helped me access some of these. My students' ideas and perceptions had already instigated changes in my thinking about my research topic and methods. In this way they were becoming participants in the data-gathering and research process. Because my role as a teacher is to empower my students, my data-gathering as a teacher/researcher should do the same.

I can explain what happened in the research example above as follows. Initially, I had used quantitative data-gathering tools – for example, test scores. When I reflected on my supervisor's question I realised that I also needed to use qualitative tools. We believe that data-gathering in self-study action research doesn't fit neatly into either side of the debates about quantitative and qualitative data. This debate has both philosophical and epistemological underpinnings, which can help you explain your choices of data collection. The philosophical basis of my initial information-gathering was that, by using accurate, analytical methods and by controlling other factors, I could come to a simple, distilled truth. Epistemologically, this places knowledge as information – a box-able set of facts that can be handed from one person to another. It follows the Aristotelian idea that there is only way of knowing, By contrast, when I considered the questions of my supervisor, changes in my data-gathering approaches reflected 'the Platonic search for explanations of his world' (McDonagh 2007: 201) and his view that there is no one 'right' way of knowing (ibid.: 242).

No matter how carefully we try to organise our data-gathering and test our claims to new learning, our reality intrudes and often causes problems. The experience of conducting the action, reflection and evaluation on one's teaching is a living process that can take on a life of its own – increasing the forms and often the amount of information collected. If you are researching your practice for accreditation purposes, you will have to decide for yourself when to stop formally gathering data. Because teaching and learning are continuous processes, often a college deadline or approaching date for meeting with colleagues is what draws a particular research cycle to a close. We authors have found that living theory action research is an ongoing process – in fact, a life-long process of research and professional development. Your project and formal studies may stop, but your action researcherly disposition (Roche 2014) continues because action research can be a transforming and life-changing process. Based on our experiences, our key suggestion, when collecting data in the messiness of the living reality of classrooms, is to trust the untidy reality of action research (Mellor 1998, 2015; Cook 2009).

Ways of collecting qualitative data in research often grow as the actions develop to suit the specific circumstances, location and participants. Recall how Glenn's (2006) student added a new focus to her research earlier in this chapter. Messy methods of data collection are common experiences for teacher researchers (Mellor 2001; Glenn 2006). When the fog gets too thick and you feel overwhelmed, our advice is to look to your values and see how you might live them more fully in your practice. Mess can add to rigour. (Cook 2009: 277) refers to the rigour of gaining accreditation and the mess of actually gathering data as 'strange bedfellows'. Cook argues that the purpose of mess is to help us move our thinking towards new constructions of knowing and that these, in turn, lead to transformations in practice. We authors have found that it is vital to work through the messiness to critically engage with practice-based research.

> It is the place where long-held views shaped by professional knowledge, practical judgement, experience and intuition are seen through other lenses. It is here that reframing takes place and new knowing, which has both theoretical and practical significance, arises. (Ibid.)

We have looked at both quantitative and qualitative data in the previous pages. 'Quantitative' means something that can be measured and written down with numbers, which can be statistically analysed. 'Qualitative' means information that can't actually be measured and is about qualities (observable or innate). For example, students could be described qualitatively as friendly, civic-minded, environmentalists with a positive school spirit, whereas quantitatively there are 72 students, 39 girls, 33 boys, 68 per cent scoring above average in literacy and 15 per cent scoring above average in mathematics. Here is a chance to reflect on how you understand the quantitative and qualitative data that may help you think critically about their relevance in your research.

Pause and reflect

Think over what data collection tools you plan to use and determine for yourself if they are qualitative, quantitative or both.

As teacher researchers we may gather vast amounts of both qualitative and quantitative data and often find it hard to prioritise what is important until we come to the validation process of our research. Begin by putting physical data into a data archive box and digital data into a folder of the same name on your computer. It is by sifting through these that we mine the data relevant for making a valid research claim, as we will now explain.

How to give a valid research account of any change you make in your practice or your understanding of your practice

By this stage in your research you know that there have been changes and improvements in your practice. You know that your thinking has changed, or that you have gained new understanding, or that your teaching has changed and that you have influenced your students' learning. The next question is: how can I make a valid research claim of these intuitive and hard-to-measure changes? Summative student tests, for example, may be a measure of learning, but this cannot capture the 'wow' factor for teachers when, for the first time, a struggling student has achieved something, or an anxious student begins to participate in learning, or when an anxious student smiles for the first time in class. So you are asking: how can I open a door into my setting so that readers of my research can view and evaluate what actually happened? In this section we will explain how you can make a valid research claim to new knowledge about your practice or a new personal theory.

When we, as teacher researchers, believe that we have influenced our situation, we offer this as a research claim. Next, we look through our data for evidence to support our claim. We then state what standards can be used to evaluate our claim. We use these critical living standards of judgement (Whitehead 2005b) to show that our research is quality research in terms of originality, significance and rigour. We show our research claims to others so that they are publicly scrutinised (Winter 1996; McTaggart 1997).

We will now talk you through the process of presenting a rigorous research account. This needs to be a thorough process because classroom action research is about generating valid theory from practice (Hadfield 2014; McDonagh *et al.* 2012; Whitehead 2009). To develop valid theory from practice requires critically reflecting on and assessing the quality of your research with rigour. Through this process you will come to see the need to develop an awareness of how you give your personal and ethical professional values life in your work and your research. These are the values we examined in earlier chapters.

Here is a simple example: let us suppose that you value children's voice. One of your research criteria might be 'that all children have an opportunity to speak in class'. Your concern is that you haven't heard Molly's voice contributing in class. Your research question is: how do I create opportunities for Molly to use her voice in class? You develop a plan and take action to provide opportunities for Molly to talk. You gather data to record what happens. In the data you see examples of Molly contributing in class. Your data now shows evidence of achieving the criterion above. You may present that as evidence of your claim to be living to your value.

We use five questions to signpost our journey:

1   How do I make a research claim?
2   How do I find evidence of my claim to new learning or to support my claim?
3   What standards can I use to test my research claims?
4   How do I use these these critical living standards of judgement (Whitehead 2005b) to show that my research demonstrates integrity?
5   How do I offer my research claims to others for public scrutiny?

We will now examine each question in turn.

How do I make a research claim?

The form of wording of research claims may vary. Here are examples of research claims from across levels of projects, so you can see the links between research questions and claims.

An undergraduate's research into his teaching at Level 7 asked 'How can I teach in a way that ensures no student is left feeling isolated or marginalised in my classroom?' Although the research began by focusing on inequality in education, the student teacher claims that 'this umbrella term incorporated every single aspect of education from equity and equality to differentiation and planning and preparation' (www.eari.ie).

A teacher doing a Level 8 course research project asked 'How can I incorporate peer teaching methodologies into my maths lessons and what effect will this strategy have on student learning?' She claimed through the changes in her teaching that (i) students were more motivated to learn, (ii) students appeared empowered by the fact that they were responsible for their own learning and that of their peers and (iii) there was a small but evident improvement in student academic performance.

At Master's level or postgraduate diploma at Level 9, researching the question 'How can I improve my practice so as to help my pupils to philosophise?', Roche (2000) says that:

> I can claim to have a theory about philosophising in my classroom – a theory that I have generated through my practice. My claim is that now I know how I can best stimulate my pupils to use their higher-order thinking powers. (p. ix)

At PhD, Level 10, Sullivan (2006) started with the questions 'How can I improve the quality of educational provision for children from the Traveller community?', 'How can I ensure that Traveller children's experience of education is a positive and emancipatory one?' and 'How can I model my own practice as demonstrating acceptance and respect for other cultures, for other ways of knowing and of being?' She developed 'A living theory of a practice of social justice: realising the right of Traveller children to educational equality'from her research questions.

Research claims develop from the actions and from the learning that occurred during your research. Your wording of a claim is about you and your learning. It will come from what you wanted to investigate and the values that made you choose these topics. Your claim to developing living theory from practice will include the values you hold – for example, 'How do I improve differentiation (action) in my teaching of maths (who and where) so that I teach in ways that respect (value) the individual capabilities of my students?'

So far, you have gathered data to describe what was happening in your research. Now you need to move this data a step further in order to get evidence of your research claim to new knowledge or to new theory. Anecdotes and descriptions about what happened are not enough.

How do I find evidence of my claim to new learning?

At this stage you are looking for data to show how you are improving your practice, or your understanding of it or living more in the direction of your values. The first step on your journey from gathering data to producing evidence is to make sure that your data is saved and stored correctly – so it is important to label and date all data. Your data is like an audit trail and, usually, teacher researchers collect far more data than they actually use in their final report. Some courses ask teacher researchers to provide appendices of data used in the report. Some courses require researchers to have their data archive ready for inspection by an external examiner. For the beginner action researcher this can seem like a difficult process but Glenn (2006) explains it clearly in the vignettes that follow.

Vignette

I was researching my practice with primary school students during an inter school East/West Joint Curriculum Project using ICT. During my research into my usage of ICT in the classroom, I came to see the interconnectedness of people and their environments as a locus of learning which may be embraced through technology. One of the original claims I make is to have developed a living epistemology of practice that is grounded in dialogical, holistic and creative ways of knowing. Here is an example of how I collected some data

I kept an audit trail so that I will be enabled to 'address the issue of confirmability of results' (Guba and Lincoln 1989: 109). Much of this audit trail can be located in my data archive, in the artefacts my classes have produced, in the web pages they have created and in the evidence I am presenting in this thesis. I have drawn my evidence from the data I have collected. (Vignette based on Glenn 2006: 216)

Similar to our processes of gathering data, we can look again to our pupils, ourselves and others for evidence of our claims to new learning. Here are some critical question you could ask to help identify changes that have ocurred during your research: Do I have pupil work or tests in which I can note any changes in their learning? I can ask about change or examples of what I was aiming towards in my research, such as: 'Where in my class file preparation is...? Where in my teaching is...? Where in my assessment is...? Where in my differentiation is...? Where in my reflections...? I can look for changes noted by critical friends, peers and colleagues and ask if they could see my values in how I was now working with my pupils.

What standards can I use to test my research claims?

By this we mean that, in order to judge the effectiveness of how we are working, we first need to set standards of judgement. Glenn (2006) tells us of critical standards of judgement that she chose to test one of her claims. She values dialogical and inclusive ways of knowing, so these were the standards of judgement she chose for her research. This means that we should be able to see dialogical and inclusive ways of knowing in her practice. You will see, in the vignette that follows, that she examined two pieces of her data – a video clip and a digital slide show – to check if her living epistemological values were realised in her practice and could be transformed into one of her living critical standards of judgement. Here is Glenn's account.

Vignette

I prepared the first video clip for a parents' information evening, at which I communicated the content of the East/West project to the parents of the children with whom I worked. The video contained the project aims and examples of the children's emails to one another, their poetry exchange. First I described the video, and how the pupils were 'responding here to other living members of the human race, not to a text-based lesson from a book. When asked about their thinking around such projects, Student R commented: 'It's really good to do e-pal projects because (a) it's easy to write on the computer and (b) it's really good fun to talk to people you don't know and see what their interests are' while Student A said 'It's not only that I enjoy it [the project] but you get to make new friends and they get to meet your friends' (Data archive). Student A comments, 'You're learning but you don't know you are learning because you are on the computer. You're having great fun... but you're learning while you are having fun' (Data archive). (Glenn 2006: 227)

Glenn explained how the clip represented a piece of data that was now a piece of evidence to support her claim that she encouraged dialogical and inclusive ways of knowing. In self-study action research you too will need to set standards by which your reader can judge your evidence.

How do I use these these critical living standards of judgement (Whitehead 2005b) to show that my research demonstrates integrity?

When we are researching for accreditation purposes there may be two separate forms of standards by which research will be judged. The first are academic or college criteria. These regulations may include evidence of independent enquiry, originality in the methods used and/or in the conclusions drawn and must make an appreciable new contribution to knowledge or thinking in the candidate's field. We authors, drawing on the work of Whitehead and McNiff (2006), established the second set of criteria by which our work could be evaluated in conjunction with our research tutor and colleagues. In these criteria we are checking if our embodied values are being lived in our practice and research. We are also continuously checking that our thinking is of a critical nature, and that we are making a contribution to new knowledge as we share our emergent theories with others. To demonstrate this critical thinking, we need to explain what kinds of knowledge inform the particular values based standards in our research accounts.

How do I offer my research claims to others for public scrutiny?

This is an important phase in the validation process of study action research. When you make your research public others can confirm or challenge the accuracy of your claim. Here is how Glenn (2006) wrote about this process and how she linked her values to the methods of public scrutiny she used.

Vignette

I value dynamic, fluid and inclusional ways of knowing, I have generated my own learning process from a multiplicity of sources, that is, from my practice, from my engagement with the literature, through dialogue with research colleagues, in conversation with my classes and so on. I have then attempted to validate my claim to knowledge in a similar manner, acknowledging multiple ways of knowing also. These values inform my research. (p. 212)

In the following chapters we explain ways of offering a research claim to others for public scrutiny in order to add to the validation of the research.

Pause and reflect

Revisit your data collection choices with these critical questions

List some ways I can collect information about the changes I am making in my practice and about changes in my thinking about my practice?

How can I show others that I reflected critically on my situation?

How do my proposed actions relate to my research question?

Could the data I gather as a teacher researcher differ depending on when, where and with whom I am researching?

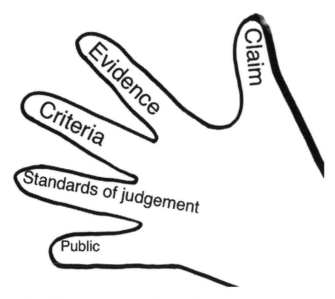

Figure 5.1 A reminder of how we demonstrate quality in our research

Conclusion

I visualise a hand as an aide-memoire for the approach we use to demonstrate quality in our action research. Each finger on that hand represents a section of the process of making a valid research claim for improvement in practice. My thumb extends towards me to show that I have succeeded in drafting a research claim linked to my research concern or question. The first finger points to evidence to back my claim. The tallest and most prominent finger reminds me of the standards by which I evaluate my claim. My ring finger reminds me of how I use critical living standards of judgement (Whitehead 2005b) to demonstrate that my research has integrity. My little finger extends towards my neighbour reminding me of the need to have my research claims scrutinised by other knowers.

In this chapter you have become familiar with key terms in moving from professional practice-based language to the academic language of research. Data are the distinct pieces of information that you collect or observe to examine and analyse. When you state that you have influenced your situation for good, you are making a claim to knowledge. There are a variety of standards by which you can test your claims. We focused on how to develop critical living standards of judgement (McNiff and Whitehead 2011). These standards are 'relationally-dynamic and grounded in both improving practice and generating knowledge' (Whitehead 2008). They are based on how you view and understand your world; your ethical profes-sional values (see Association of American Educators 2014; Teaching Council Ireland 2012; UK, Department of Education 2011). The final part of making a research claim is to have it publicly scrutinised and checked by others; in the next chapters we will examine how to add rigour and validity to your research project.

In this chapter:

- You explored how to plan a research project.
- You looked at ways of collecting data that is relevant to your research setting and topic.
- You developed an understanding of how to generate evidence of a research claim from the data you have collected.
- You examined how to construct a research claim about changes in practice, or understanding of practice.

Recommended reading and resources

Cook, T. (2009) 'The Purpose of Mess in Action Research: Building Rigour through a Messy Turn', *Educational Action Research*, 17(2), 277–91.

Mellor, N. (2001) 'Messy Method: The Unfolding Story', *Educational Action Research*, 9(3), 465–84.

Mellor, N. (2015) *The Untidy Realities of Research* cites Glenn's work (2006) in Mellor podcast for Newcastle University https://sites.google.com/site/nigelsbitsandbobs/Home/messy-method-the-secrets-of-the-doctorate

Whitehead J. (2015a) 'The Practice of Helping Students to Find Their First Person Voice in Creating Living Theories for Education', in H. Bradbury (ed.), *The Sage Handbook of Action Research*, 3rd edn, London and Thousand Oaks, CA: Sage.

Examples of living theory theses: www.eari.ie, jeanmcniff.com, www.action research.net

6 Ethics, rigour and validity

Introduction

When you are researching your practice as a teacher, you are researching within a learning community – yourself, students, professional colleagues and other educators. You are researching your teaching of people who are moving within their ever-changing worlds and understandings of those worlds. Because your research approach involves real live participants, they must be treated ethically. In this chapter we walk you through the consequent ethical issues.

Generally, teachers accept that if it were possible to teach an identical lesson in exactly the same way, it does not follow that each student would learn in exactly the same way or retain the same understanding of the lesson. So when teachers are researching their practice it is difficult, if not impossible, to achieve replicability and generalisability: that is why we will look at other ways of demonstrating rigour and validity in your research.

In this chapter, we consider:
Ethical issues from critical perspectives by asking questions such as:

- Why does my research need a section on ethical standards?
- On what are my ethical standards based?
- Where in my research do I need to refer to ethics?
- What does informed consent of participants look like?

Rigour and validity in the process of self-study action research within learning communities.

- What the literature says with specific reference to Shipman and Habermas
- What do some of those assessing action research say?
- How to demonstrate reliability and credibility in my research.

Ethical issues when conducting self-study action research within learning communities

When you research your practice within your learning communities, you have responsibilities towards your participants – responsibilities that can be compared to those of doctors towards their patients. You can relate an ethical stance to both the thinking behind the Hippocratic Oath, which doctors take, and to your professional ethical values as a teacher (see, for example, Association of American Educators 2014; Teaching Council of Ireland 2012; UK, Department of Education 2011). In a spirit of caring for our participants and respecting them, we invite them to voluntarily participate, and we keep them informed about what we are doing and why. In other research paradigms there can be pressure to get the correct answer, but in self-study the focus is on learning from the process and on explaining the influence of that learning. So, even if our actions fail to achieve what we hoped, we always learn from our failures and we can describe and explain this learning in our research report. A further ethical issue worth remembering is that we cannot use others' ideas without acknowledging the authors. This is called plagiarism and we will look at it in more detail later.

Pause and reflect

What kind of responsibilities do you have to students in your research?

What is the difference between anonymity and confidentiality?

Plagiarism is using someone else's ideas and writings without acknowledging the true author. Is plagiarism illegal or unethical? Or both?

Why does my research need a section on ethical standards?

Here are three reasons why you might be thinking about your ethical standards and considering including an ethical statement in your research report. First, to protect the rights of the participants in your research; second, to ensure accuracy; and, finally, to protect individual and intellectual property rights. We will begin by considering the rights of participants. Most colleges have an ethics committee, often called the institutional review board (IRB), to oversee the process. One must adhere to their guidelines. Here is an ethical dilemma I faced involving my research participants, who were aged nine to 12 years (based on McDonagh 2007: 137–40).

Vignette

Informed pupil consent to voluntarily participate became an issue for both the university Ethics Committee and for me. We differed on our understandings of informed consent. The university required that my ethical statement and consent form be addressed to participants' parents only, signed by parents and co-signed by students. I believed that this withdrew from students their ability to give consent. My decision was to comply with the university requirement. In addition I got both oral and written consent

> from my students using a version of the form that was written in language appropri-
> ate to the student's age and reading levels and signed by both the parent/s and the
> children. Because of my belief in respect for the individual, I felt justified in my ethical
> stance. I was respecting my students as fellow human beings, entitled to 'dignity and
> privacy'. (Bassey 1990: 18)

Subsequently, the ethical requirements of the university were updated to include Child Protection Guidelines (University of Limerick 2010). These are commensurate with the ethical
stance that I adopted at the beginning of my research. The guidelines require that informed
consent is obtained from the parents/guardians of children under 18 and from the children
themselves. Children need to be informed 'in appropriate language so that they understand
the research they are being asked to participate in' (ibid.: 12).

   We will explore the other reasons for including a section on ethics after some critical
thinking on where our ethical standards come from.

On what are my ethical standards based?

Earlier in the book you considered the personal epistemological and ontological values that
underpin and inform your teaching and research decisions. Now we look at some policy, state
guidelines and professional ethical guidelines that may influence your ethical stance and
consequent research decisions. These include an influential work – *The Belmont Report* (USA
Commission for the Protection of Human Subjects 1979) – and more recent ethical research
guidelines from a variety of countries.

   Values permeate policy directives. We know that, as teacher researchers, we may work
with large numbers of students. Our familiarity with them, and our authority, can cause us
to assume that they should automatically become participants in our research. This would
mean that we have taken them for granted and not treated them ethically and with the
respect they deserve as human beings. Historically, such unethical research has had devas-
tating consequences for people – for example, Nazi research on humans. To eliminate future
unethical research the USA's Commission for the Protection of Human Subjects compiled *The
Belmont Report* (1979). It named respect for persons, beneficence and justice as central to
ethical research.

   What, then, are the implications for you as a researcher? Remember, this is research *with*
people, not research *on* people. They are, in fact, your co-participants. With that in mind,
respect for the dignity of the persons in your research must be reflected in the consent
process you design. This process is about how you intend to inform participants about your
study, and ask them if they wish to participate. In *The Belmont Report* 'beneficence' means
that the study will minimise any possible harm and maximise any possible good – physical,
psychological or societal – from the study. The *Belmont* idea of justice is about how the selection of participants should be without bias. For example, a researcher might be tempted to
select only participants whom they consider likely to make their research look good. If you
are conducting your research for a college or institution you must also comply with its guidelines for writing your research proposal and show that your proposed research is ethical.

These guidelines are usually decided by IRBs or ethical review boards (ERBs) within your institution.

We will now consider some international questioning of the ethical issues that have arisen since *The Belmont Report* (1979) and the resultant ethical guidelines and policies that many countries developed. Our critical question is: what can we, as teacher researchers, learn from the concerns they raised? The Southern Cross University (SCU), Australia, suggests that those involved in research with children need to work out how ethical principles apply in this specific context and recommend that researchers receive support to do so. New Zealanders share this concern by stating that: 'Both novice and experienced researchers face ethical issues (Duncan *et al.* 2009) and experience alone is insufficient to anticipate and plan for all relevant factors (MacDonald and Greggans 2008)' (Centre for Children and Young People *et al.* 2013: 96).

A video (*The Research Clinic* 2014) from the USA's Office of Research Integrity (ORI) and the Office for Human Research Protections (OHRP) offers an example of such support. It allows you to experience and discuss practical ethical dilemmas from a variety of perspectives - from the researcher's perspective to that of the IRB chair. Although the video deals with hospital/patients research, it raises some critical questions for all researchers; some might be of relevance to you. What would you do in the following teacher researcher vignettes, which I have chosen to reflect the dilemmas on the video? How would you deal with the pressures - for example, from an employer agency - to manipulate or falsify data?

Vignette

A teacher researcher was advised by her school to adjust the transcripts of student interviews. They were accurately transcribed with many grammatical errors and colloquialisms that, if the report was published, would not reflect well on the school.

How could you ensure that you adhered to all protocols - particularly the difficulties of getting informed consent from all participants?

Vignette

A teacher researcher wanted to engage her whole class in her research; two consent forms were not completed by the college deadline. On investigation, she found that one family did not have English as a first language and the minder of the other student, at that time, was neither the parent nor guardian.

Given that your research aims to enhance teaching and learning, how would you maintain research integrity in a context and culture that is resistant to change?

Vignette

A teacher researcher was laughed at in the staffroom for wasting time on researching practice when nothing would change - as the students in the school came from disadvantaged backgrounds and would always be disadvantaged.

How would you balance participant and research priorities?

> ## Vignette
>
> The agreed research timeline meant that a teacher researcher completed lesson content without ensuring students' learning.

This final question looks at the imbalance of power that may exist between researcher and participants (Dalli and Te One 2012; Welikala and Atkin 2014). In order to avoid these power issues, it is essential for me, as a teacher researcher, to critically analyse my value system and take the students seriously as agents in their own education. The Norwegian researcher Broch, who has conducted research in various parts of the world, says that 'children, like adults, are strategic, narrative-making beings, and should not be investigated as if they were passive receptors' (Broch 2014: 13). The British Education Research Association (BERA 2014) guidelines propose that the best interests and rights of the child should be the primary consideration when designing and conducting research with children and young people. Alderson and Morrow (2011) warn against the potential to cause emotional distress or feelings of embarrassment and impact on participants' self-esteem. As teacher researchers we should also show that we are aware of issues that arise in researching alongside children in specific contexts, such as 'those with special education needs or in a care environment' (Ireland, DCYA 2011: 6). So it is important in writing our research reports that we identify and outline any potential for risk and clearly state how we will manage this (Alderson and Morrow 2011; ESRC 2010).

In Ireland, where currently no one body is responsible for research ethics, we, as teacher researchers, may avoid risks to our young participants by employing a child-centred, inclusive approach according to *Children First: National Guidance for the Protection and Welfare of Children* (Ireland, DCYA 2011). Participating children also have rights under the Data Protection Acts, as do their parents (Government of Ireland 2014). This means we need to be careful about collecting, storing, accessing and the disclosure of personal data we hold. We suggest that you collect and retain only the minimum amount of personal data and implement your guarantees of confidentiality and anonymity (unless child protection issues arise). This could include removing direct identifiers and using pseudonyms. In essence, the values that guide us as professional teachers inform our core ethical research stance. The values of care, respect, integrity and trust are often sited as professional ethical values (Association of American Educators 2014; Teaching Council of Ireland 2012; UK, Department of Education 2011).

Pause and reflect

How do I show care and demonstrate that I work from principles of beneficience?

How do I show respect for the people involved in my research, and for their autonomy?

How do I show integrity?

How do I show justice and trust?

Make a list of particular policies that impact on your research and what you must do to implement them.

Where in my research report do I need to refer to ethics?

Your ethical stance influences all aspects of your research. It can be seen in your research proposal, in your topic selection, in your methodological choice, in the participants you decide to work with, in how you evaluate your new learning from the study and in how you protect intellectual property rights. Some colleges ask for copies of your ethical statement to be included in your appendices or presented to your supervisors. It is usual to include a section on the ethical considerations, and how you deal with them, in the methodology section of your written report. You could begin this by outlining the ethical considerations of your workplace and the college with whom you are studying. Following this, you may detail how you propose to deal with them in your research.

   Here is how you might clearly link your research to professional ethical values of care, integrity, trust and respect for human dignity (Association of American Educators 2014; Teaching Council of Ireland 2012; UK, Department of Education 2011). The suggestions that follow are based on the work of Shamoo and Resnik (2009). You can show care by critically examining all aspects of your work, by providing participants with anonymity, and by keeping accurate data records of all research activities, including research design, and correspondence with supervisor. You can show integrity by aiming to improve the situation you are researching through influencing the situation, by honestly reporting data, methods and procedures – even when they don't go as expected, by acting with sincerity, showing where your ideas and actions diverge. You can show respect for human dignity by maximising benefits for participants; by taking special precautions with vulnerable participants; by making sure you have all necessary permissions. We authors make our research available to participants throughout the process. Sample letters of permission and consent for pupils and adults are usually included in the appendices and referred to in the text of your research report. You can show trust by honouring copyrights and by never plagiarising. In the accuracy of your referencing and your bibliography you show how you ethically protect intellectual property rights. Refer to and comply with the rules of citation that your college recommends. Plagiarism is literary theft, where a writer duplicates the ideas or words of another and then calls the work his or her own. To engage in plagiarism can mean denying key professional values of teaching as well as personal values, and is not accepted by awarding institutions.

Pause and reflect

How do I cite authors and websites in the main text of my research report?

How do I cite authors and websites in the bibliography or reference section of my research report?

What does informed consent of participants look like?

Protecting the rights of the participants in your research includes getting informed consent. The generally accepted criteria for informed consent are information, comprehension and voluntary participation (Bourke and Loveridge 2014; David *et al.* 2001). What might these look like in your research report?

You should provide adequate information about the project's aims, methods and potential outcomes in a student-accessible form. Students' comprehension of your research, and its implications for themselves, may depend on their age and maturity. Similarly, age is relevant to voluntary participation in research, but it may be culture specific. In the USA, the National Commission for the Protection of Human Subjects (1977) recommends that children over the age of seven should be asked for their consent. Once your participants reach 18 years, you no longer need parental consent (Spriggs 2010). As a demonstration of voluntary participation, you need to make it clear how participants can withdraw from your research, if they want to. This should be made clear in your letter of invitation to your research participants. Sometimes, when teachers are implementing creative projects, they may need to include all students in the project but only do research with those who have given permission.

Voluntary participation again raises the issue of power balance within the research relationships. Might students agree to activities, in order to please you, that they might otherwise reject (Morrow and Richards 1996; Roche 2011). We need to avoid situations where students feel that their decisions, to opt in or to opt out, may have consequences for them, such as causing isolation or embarrassment. When conducting classroom-based research you may need to consider alternative arrangements for those who are not participating in the research. Literature reminds us that this disparity in power and status is even more of an issue when dealing with students with learning disabilities or in social care situations, where they may be accustomed to adults making decisions on their behalf, so that they would not consider opting out (Meaux and Bell 2001; Australian Government 2007; Carroll and Gutmann 2011).

Pause and reflect

How can I show that all participants are aware of

The purpose of the research?
What they will be doing and for how long?
Potential benefits to themselves or their class (research setting)?
Potential risks to them?
How privacy is protected?
Who the researcher/s is/are and how they can be reached?
How to withdraw at any time for any reason?
Who to contact if they feel the research is unethical?
How participants might access the research reports?

We began this chapter reminding ourselves that teacher research is conducted within learning communities. Because of our responsibilities as members of these communities, we looked at how you can research in ethical ways within your own context and why this is important. We explain how this might influence both your research and how you report your research. Next, we ask: how can you ensure that your research is rigorous and valid, reliable and creditable and worthy of accreditation if this is part of your aim?

Rigour and validity in the process of self-study action research within learning communities

---

Vignette

Here is a version of an often-told allegorical story, which I found helpful in teasing out what rigour and validity might mean for me as I engage in teacher research.

Visualise an interview where Socrates is helping a doctor to show the validity and rigour of his research process as he examines how he can improve his practice by bleeding sick people with leeches in order to cure them. The literature of the time suggests that, for good health, the four humours need to be in balance and that releasing blood with leeches will redress this balance. The doctor researcher offers statistical validity for improvement by stating that 81 per cent of patients eventually got better and only 17 per cent died. Querying the accuracy of this, Socrates asks what happened to the other 2 per cent. The doctor didn't know because they didn't come back. Socrates considers this is an unethical response because the researcher has responsibility for participants and to find out why and how his claim works. Socrates continues to challenge the credibility of the research because, even if all the participants got better, it has not been shown that the leeches were the cause of their cure. The doctor protests that his findings are based on his experiential knowledge gained over many years, when many more patients died. When Socrates pushes for evidence that the doctor has caused the change in his patients, the doctor provides data showing that 58 per cent of participating patients rated the treatment as positive and that, when the leeches were removed, the patients' blood was in the leeches. Again, Socrates challenges the rigour and validity of the research, by asking what evidence convinced the doctor that bloodletting was effective? The doctor responds by quoting the theory of the day: 'We know that the four humours need to be in balance and so releasing the blood in this way redresses this balance.' At this stage, Socrates gives up in despair, as most research tutors would.

The doctor had not undertaken rigorous and valid research. He had taken a theory from the literature and implemented a practice to try to support it. He did not develop any new knowledge or theory from practice, but accepted the theory in the literature unquestioningly. Arguing for rigour and validity in educational research often resembles this story. How could you deal with a similar form of questioning of your action research? In the story above, Socrates has proposed the following dilemmas for us as we seek to conduct rigorous and valid research, namely: accuracy in reporting all facts; clarity in what we mean by ethics and showing care to all participants; showing our epistemological understandings about knowledge and who are valid knowers; critically evaluating current relevant theories; credibility; and finding relevant data-collection tools to generate evidence of your new learning.

To address these dilemmas, in the remainder of this chapter we will look at ideas around rigour and validity in the process of your action research by next thinking about:

- how literature tells us that Marten Shipman and Jurgen Habermas viewed those issues
- what those assessing teacher action research say.

To help you implement what is important in their ideas, we will go on to walk you through ways of checking the reliability and credibility in documenting your research.

What the literature says about rigour and validity, with specific reference to Shipman and Habermas

Marten Shipman was a sociologist who queried the limitations of social research when he asked: how can we be sure that this is good-quality research? (Shipman 1997, 2014). In 1997, quality research for him was about replicability, reliability, credibility and generalisability. By the time he produced the 4th edition of his work on the limitations of social research, in 2014, he had honed his understanding of these quality criteria. Similarly, we authors, through doing action research and through assessing research projects for accrediting bodies, have enhanced our understanding of what counts as quality research. So we will now discuss Shipman's (2014) understanding of the these criteria using his four critical questions, and refute some of them using research examples.

Shipman's four critical questions to check for quality research

1   To check the replicability of your research, ask, if the investigation is carried out again and again by different researchers using the same methods, would the same results be obtained? (Shipman 2014: ix). Generally replicability, as described here, is not expected in action research for teachers researching their practice. Having thought critically about this issue, we, along with other action researchers, are convinced that replicability is not a relevant, valid criterion for this methodology. However, when I began researching, I, like many educationalists, had developed a mindset that valued replicability. Here is a vignette from McDonagh (2007) to show when my mindset changed.

Vignette

I was investigating how pupils, with specific learning difficulties, learned spellings. In my classroom-based research I recorded the answers of each of eight children to the question: 'How do I learn spellings?' Below I describe how the children became personally aware of how they learn.

During one-to-one sessions with me, their teacher researcher, I encouraged them to speak, but did not suggest any methods. I produced a table showing the various ways in which they learned spellings. The first column had their exact words; in the second column I related these to different learning strategies. The activity above was repeated by a second and third cohort of eight children each. The same question was posed by me in the former case and by another teacher in the case of the latter. The tables of findings differed in that some additional strategies were mentioned by these groups and some pupils also combined two learning strategies at a time (ibid.: 211–12). The information from the three separate tables added nothing to my pupils' understanding of how they learn spellings. The greatest learning came from the process of activating the pupils' metacognitive awareness of their personal learning strategies.

Despite my efforts to achieve replicability I did not succeed. I came to understand that replicability could not be a criterion for quality teacher action research because the pupils and those with whom I am researching are constantly developing and not inanimate objects.

2   To check the reliability of your research, look at the methods used and ask: does the evidence reflect the reality under investigation? Has the researcher found out what he thinks or claims it is about? (Shipman 2014: ix). In this case we agree with Shipman that methodological reliability is an essential criterion. In earlier chapters, we have already emphasised the necessity to explain as well as describe each aspect of your research process.

3   To check the credibility of your research, make it public and ask: is there sufficient detail on the way the evidence was produced for the credibility of the research to be assessed? (ibid.). To answer this, we examine the way the research is conducted, the research expertise of the researcher and his or her familiarity and knowledge of the specific research context.

4   To check the generalisability of your research, ask: what relevance does the new learning have beyond the situation investigated? (ibid.). The idea of generalisability implies that others can take your theory and apply it to their practice. Again, this is not a criterion that is expected in teacher action research on practice. In this methodology, we are developing personal living theories. We are making valid claims to new learning and do not claim that they are directly transferable. Our research is located in a specific moment in time, and involves an identified group of individuals, as Sullivan (2006) explains: 'The participants in my research were children, whose lives are complex, constantly evolving and producing new meanings. My knowledge, too, is continuously reforming as I incorporate my new learning into my system of meaning' (p. 133).

Rather than generalisability, we believe that an important valid criterion is that action research projects 'have an application elsewhere, and that action researchers are able to communicate their insights to others with a useful result' (Lomax 1994: 118). Our experiences as researchers and as assessors of projects convinces us that action research projects should, instead, show that they have significance for others A valid criterion, therefore, is that teacher researchers demonstrate this significance. Winter (2002) suggests that 'persuasiveness' or 'authenticity' might be used as criteria to judge the value of action research reports. He states that: 'a research report has "authenticity"' (epistemological validity and cultural authority) when it gives direct expression to the 'genuine voice', which 'really belongs to those whose life-worlds are being described' (ibid.: 145).

To recap, you, as a teacher researcher, are not expected to engage with gerneralisability and replicability, but reliablity and credibility are key criteria in quality research. Additional criteria are that the authenticity of your voice in the research can persuade others of the significance of your research. Communicating such insights to others is about developing understanding between people. This requires dialogue so that those reading your research can acknowledge the authenticity of the research. This is called social validity (Habermas 1976), which we will now examine.

Can social validity (Habermas 1976) become a criterion for quality research?

Jurgen Habermas was a German teacher, philosopher and sociologist; his work on social validity is helpful in teasing out what reliability and credibility might mean for your research. Many examples of this form of validity can be seen in the MAs and PhDs available on www.eari.ie, www.actionresearch.net and www.jeanmcniff.com. Habermas (1976) begins by examining how understandings between people develop. Understanding happens when what is being said is agreed to be valid. So we use dialogue to come to this consensus of agreement on what is valid. He claims that we convey ideas, experiences and information to other humans through dialogue. Furthermore, it is through dialogue that the validity of your research claims in some educational settings can be challenged, as in a viva voce. According to Habermas, in order for agreement to take place, the speaker (that is you, as teacher researcher) must speak comprehensibly, truthfully, authentically and appropriately. These are his four criteria for social validity. As part of action research, you can speak with colleagues about your work, about your research claims, and this is where the social valid-ity of your research may be tested. We have already spoken, in Chapter 5, about the need to make your research claim public. Now we are explaining the process of doing so in order to obtain valid evaluation of your research actions, reflections and claims. Critical friends may listen, question, suggest improvements and alternatives. A validation group or group of persons who are knowledgeable about your research context, when you meet with them on a number of occasions during your research, may pick holes in your research and give you a hard time questioning every assumption you make. Their agreement will constitute validation of your research claims and demonstrate that you have extended your profes-sional knowledge.

Here is how you might achieve those social validity criteria in practice. In your research you may speak comprehensively, making sure people understand what you say, being clear in your message. You may speak truthfully answering queries and showing reasonable evidence. By providing evidence that you have subjected what you have learned in your research to critique, others can believe your claim – cultural authority (Winter 2002). You may speak authentically, talking about the values you hold as a practitioner and how you upheld these values during your research – epistemological validity (ibid.). This will help authenticate your research claims. You may speak appropriately. This means immersing yourself in journals and research articles to learn academic language and the language of your practice. By following Habermas's theory of social validity (1976) you will be able to have your research validated and the claims you make about improving your practice will be upheld.

Pause and reflect

As a teacher researcher

Do you think that if your research is carried out again and again by different research-ers using the same methods the same results will be obtained? And is research repli-cability important to your teaching and your pupils' learning?

Do you think that your research evidence should reflect the reality under investigation, as accurately as possible – warts and all? And is research reliability important to your teaching and your pupils' learning?

Is generalisability important to your teaching and your pupils' learning?

Do you think that your research should give sufficient detailed evidence to show your research expertise and your familiarity and knowledge of the specific research context? And is the credibility of your research important to your teaching and your pupils' learning?

What do some of those assessing research say about rigour and validity in the process of teacher action research?

Elliott (1990) looks at the dilemmas which confront facilitators of teacher-based action research in schools. He was working in an era when teacher-based action research in the UK was mainly focused on school-based curriculum development initiated by teachers. Over 15 years he tried to reconcile the need for rigour in unpredictable school and classroom con-texts (Elliott 2007). He tried to balance rigour and flexibility, regardless of the type of action research, using the principles of theoretical and methodological robustness, value-for-use and the potential to enable beneficial change as described above.

Here is a brief explanation of what these terms mean.

1   'Theoretically robust' means making a significant contribution to new knowledge and thereby extending the knowledge-base of the teaching profession.
2   'Methodologically robust' means using appropriate tools for data-gathering and analysis.
3   'Value-for-use' means showing new learning for researcher or participants. This is the potential significance which we discuss Chapter 7. Often, when research reports are sub-mitted for accreditation, evidence of this new learning may be put in an appendix for examiners to view.
4   'Potential to enable beneficial change in actions or in understanding' means articulating the potential significance of research in relation to concepts, context, the literature, for yourself, for the participants and for others outside your context.

These criteria can be applied across the wide range of action research methodologies, includ-ing narrative enquiry, self-study, participatory research, auto-ethnography, ethnography, grounded theory, critical theory and case study, as well as various quantitative methods (see www.actionresearch.net).

McMahon and Jefford (2009) discuss a further dilemma, namely 'the competing needs of the action researcher to follow the investigation wherever it leads and the need for the student to meet preset programme criteria' (p. 359). For teacher researchers, achieving rigour and validity are not straightforward because 'action research, by its nature, is much less predictable and predictive than other forms of research' (ibid.: 350). They suggest that, if you are doing a project for academic accreditation and are under strict time constraints, you need to focus on the main *whirls* of the research cycles and return later to the less important whirls.

These assessment criteria are specific and demanding. So let's consider a further research example from Glenn (2006: 31) on how a teacher researcher figured out this difficulty for herself. She based her decisions about validity on the seminal work of Winter (1996), who gives us six theoretically based criteria for assessing rigour and validity in action research.

Vignette

As I share my epistemology of practice with others, I demonstrate how I assess the quality of my work, with rigour, as outlined by Winter (1996), in terms of reflexive critique, dialectical critique, risk, plural structure, collaboration and theory/practice transformation and by referring to the specific standards of judgement that are drawn from my values in education. I support the validity of my claims with substantiated evidence from my practice and I offer my claim to others for public scrutiny. I explain how one's embodied ontological values are transformed through the process of clarification into the living epistemological standards of critical judgement that can be used to test the validity of one's claim to educational knowledge (Whitehead 2005b). Then I continue to explain the personal and social validation processes that I have undertaken in relation to testing my claim to knowledge.

Pause and reflect

How will you explain the methodological robustness of your research?

How do you think your research will have a positive influence in your immediate context?

Will your research have relevance outside your immediate setting?

How to demonstrate reliability and credibility in your research

This section addresses the dilemma of how teacher researchers could avoid being criticised for lacking accuracy and for being too subjective or anecdotal in their research. Whitehead (2010b) explains that 'every question on my practice is socially grounded in that I am working within a professional context with others' (n/p). So accuracy can be tested at both personal and social levels. To demonstrate personal reliability and credibility, we need to first ensure that all our data is dated. Teacher researchers often gather more data than they use in their final reports. Some colleges encourage action researchers to place additional relevant data in appendices to avoid exceeding the required word count.

We can ensure reliability and credibility of our research, by using a variety of social settings to test:

- our process of acting in accordance with the research methodology
- the appropriateness of our tools for data-gathering
- our new learning in relation to the researcher or participants and
- the significance of changes in our thinking and our claims.

Making our research public and open to critique is how we check its reliability and credibility. The sections above explained the theories of social validity and the use of dialogue to support the rigour of the methods we employ. We make our research public and have it critiqued through validation groups, triangulation, submitting our research to journals and conferences. Some may think that this is part of the legitimation process of the research, but what we want to emphasise is how critique can impact on one's thinking. We explain each of these processes of critique, with research examples, in the remainder of this chapter.

Validation group

Setting up a validation group, or a debriefing group (Cohen *et al.* 2007) can provide a check and comment on the accuracy and reliability of both your research approach and practice of conducting it. This is how Glenn (2006) described such a group.

Vignette

My validation was both face to face and online. Other researchers at the university, our tutor and I formed a validation group. Our purpose was to share our claims to knowledge, to critique our thinking. Although generally respectful of the thinking of another, there were also occasions where critique and animated discussion would arise. To extend out time for critique, I created an online private space for the group. We called our space the Half-Baked Site because it was a place for introducing emergent ideas in the safety of an enclosed and private setting and extended our validation processes. (pp. 104-6)

Glenn goes on to show how she engaged with the social criteria of comprehensibility, truth, sincerity and appropriateness which form the basis of Habermas's (1976) theory of communicative action. The discussion below shows part of a validation process and part of the process of testing emergent ideas on the methodology.

Glenn wrote: How do we know we're not wrong in our claims to knowledge? OK so we kinda know in our heads, but how do we prove it to others? How do we check it out?... sorry this question has been rattling around in my head for the past few days... any ideas anyone?
Colleague B: I don't know how we know we're not wrong, but I presume that if we're acting with integrity, with respect for others and allow others their opinions too, then we can be reasonably satisfied that we are doing the right thing. I don't think we can ever be certain that we're not wrong so I think we'll just have to be happy that our efforts are compatible with our values of honesty, integrity, justice etc.

Colleague M: I agree with B's interpretation. I know that if we were to nitpick we could also ask 'how do we know that what we mean by integrity and respect' is what others also mean by these values. This is tricky! But if we were to agonise to the extent that we did nothing in case we were wrong then there would be stasis. Everything we do is linked to action following reflection and reflection following the action.... and if we have informed our conscience and looked at as many views as possible and still feel sure enough that we are right.... what else is there? (Glenn 2006: 240 and 245).

Although the language is informal, the group was finding ways to check the integrity and authority of the research claims by teasing out their understandings of rigour and validity. Frequently, these validation sessions were tape-recorded so they could be reflected on and analysed again. A sample of one such occasion where Glenn's (2006) claim to knowledge is validated by the group as detailed in Whitehead and McNiff (2006). A greater degree of clarity emerged from the discussion, from the disagreement and from the negotiation of inter-subjective agreement with the group. This reflects Webb's (1996) claim (drawing on Habermas's ideas) that speech is a form of communication, 'to test counter positions and to gain understanding' (Webb 1996: 143). Glenn calls this 'picking holes' and says that it was out of mutual respect 'that it was incumbent on us to try to disagree and to critique' (Glenn 2006: 257).

Triangulation

Another method for checking social validity is triangulation. This involves checking our research from multiple perspectives. Some qualitative researchers think that this will provide consistency across data, but we find that in self-study action research it also provides opportunities to open up deeper meaning in the research. Triangulation needs to be planned into the research design and time allocated for it. There are a variety of forms of triangulation – multiple perspectives, methodological triangulation and outside observer triangulation. Here is an example of gathering data about the same topic from different sources.

Vignette

A child with low confidence had been anxious and withdrawn in class and your research actions have led to a change, you could gather information from the child, their parents and from an observer. The teacher researcher observed and noted the child smiling in class. The child's mother said he was much happier in school and the teacher on yard duty observed that he was actively enjoying participating in games with peers.

Methodological triangulation involves comparing the findings from different methodological tools such as quantitative and qualitative data, surveys, interviews and focus groups. Triangulation using outside perspectives means asking professionals external to the context but with expertise in specific aspects of the research topic – for example, by inviting third level lecturers to observe and comment on classroom actions (McDonagh 2007). A variety of triangulation approaches will not only help you to validate the accuracy of your research, but also provides you with innovative ways to analyse your new learning from your action research project and shows openness to critique and challenge.

Reliability and credibility: presenting your work to others

Part of checking the reliability and integrity of your work is making it public to ensure that your claims are up to the scrutiny of other knowers in your field or practice. This is essential because research is a systematic enquiry that is made public (Koshy 2010; McNiff and Whitehead 2011; Skilbeck 1983). You have already read about many opportunities for public critique and challenge within a self-study action methodology – critical reflection, critical friends, validation and triangulation processes. Many teacher researchers offer their work to refereed journals or ejournals where you receive written critique and suggestions usually from anonymous reviewers. Educational conferences are another place where you can open your work for academic critique. There, academics and students become learning communities in which the reliability of your research project can be tested. There are many forms of educational conference. Here is an example of insights I gained, as a teacher researcher, from disseminating my living theory at different styles of conferences – traditional and interactive.

> ## Vignette
>
> Here is how I reported my experiences of opening my claim to pedagogical change to academics at a traditional-style conference (based on McDonagh 2007: 243-7).
>
> I presented a paper about my research reflections on how I teach in a traditional didactic format within a group session of papers and was followed only by some clarification questions from the audience. So the presentation demonstrated the reliability of my work. One question, later, over coffee, remains with me today. It was, 'How did you come to develop theories from your practice?'

This critical question highlights, for me, how community critique can move one's thinking on – a feature that tends not to be present in traditional forms of paper presentations.

Communities or networks of researchers of various genres of research hold conferences that support this form of critique. In action research there is a worldwide network of researchers constantly critiquing each other's work (World Map Action Learning and Action Research Assocation, ALARA 2015).

> ## Vignette
>
> When Sullivan and I presented evidence during a paper presentation at one such conference to show our research claims, we asked those present, 'Has our presentation shown that we have contributed to improved educational practices? How can our work contribute to educational theorising?' Researchers in the discussion that followed identified unhesitatingly and unequivocally that teaching colleagues in my workplace had learned from my pupils' theories of how the pupils learned (McDonagh and Sullivan, 2003). This collaborative discussion (which we recorded) gave us an opportunity to explore our educative influences in our individual contexts (based on McDonagh 2007: 244).

We concluded that this presentation helped us to make credible claims for the significance of our research and contributed to the development and validation of our own living theories.

Interactive symposia offer a method to open up research to constructive, more global critique.

Vignette

Here is an example from McDonagh 2003 (p. 246). In my group there were nine individual presenters of self-study action research projects that spanned all sectors of education from teaching to teacher education and policy-making across many continents. Each participant had multiple links of influence to the others in the group. Their papers were web-accessed in advance to encourage discussion on specific critical and current issues in action research such as validity, forms of theory, voice, legitimation and institutional implications. Discussion circles included presenters, invited key speakers and conference attendees. Due to time constraints, some discussions initiated here were continued through email. At that time, I was a teacher researcher in a small town school in Ireland and discussants were from the USA, Australia, Canada, Israel, England and Wales.

You may ask: is there a way for classroom teachers to present their claims to others? Certainly, they may present them to students, to colleagues at planning meetings, at professional development meetings, in teacher education centres and learning circles or at show and tell sessions and teach meets and seminars. The internet offers lots of educational blogs and websites, such as www.eari.ie, for sharing and validating research.

Having read about teachers disemminating their research in ways that demonstrate reliability and credibility within learning communities that are knowledgeable of the practice and the academic aspects of the research, here are some critical questions to ask yourself.

Pause and reflect

How do I get any critical feedback?

Who may help me to demonstrate the validity of the account of my educational influence in learning?

How might I use internet and recordings to develop validity and rigiour?

What permissions do you need to be able to utilise dialogical data?

Conclusion

In this section we have explained a vital process in conducting rigorous and valid action research. As a teacher/researcher you may support the validity of your research claims with substantiated evidence from your practice and you may offer your claim to others for public scrutiny. We have explained how your embodied values can become standards of critical judgement that can be used to test the validity of your claim to new educational knowledge (Whitehead 2005b). We have demonstrated how this process is grounded in criteria of validity in terms of reflexive critique, dialectical critique, plural structure, collaboration and theory/practice transformation (Winter 1996). This process guarantees personal and social validity (Habermas 1976). Teacher researcher judgement is at the heart of this process and, as Biesta (2014) states, that judgement is 'needed because education is an open and evolving domain, where knowledge from the past, even if it is the outcome of randomised controlled trials, provides no guarantees for what will happen in the future' (p. 25). So in the next section we examine your role as an agent of change in education.

In this chapter:

- You explored the relevance of ethics for your research.
- You looked at what an ethical stance means for you.
- You developed an understanding of ethical participation in research and plagiarism.
- You examined a variety of criteria for validity.
- You considered ways to ensure reliability and credibility in your research.

Recommended reading and resources

Powell, M. A., Fitzgerald, R., Taylor, N. J. and Graham, A. (2012) *International Literature Review: Ethical Issues in Undertaking Research with Children and Young People* (Literature review for the Childwatch International Research Network). Lismore: Southern Cross University, Centre for Children and Young People/Dunedin: University of Otago, Centre for Research on Children and Families.

https://www.youtube.com/watch?v=cDzS6T1k7Zk Cartoon explanation of ethics in research (2012) created on http://goanimate.com/

Video: *The Research Clinic* (2014) The Office of Research Integrity and the Office for Human Research Protections has released an interactive video to train researchers about the importance of protecting research subjects and preventing research misconduct.

World Map Action Learning and Action Research Around the World, ALARA (2015) http://www.alarassociation.org/pages/networks/around-the-world

Whitehead, J. (2000) 'How Do I Improve My Practice? Creating and Legitimating an Epistemology of Practice', *Reflective Practice*, 1(1), 91-104.

SECTION IV

The significance of your research

Bernie Sullivan

In this final section of the book we focus on the significance of undertaking self-study action research for yourself and for others, including your students, your colleagues and the wider educational community. We examine how initiating a process of change leading to improvement in your teaching practice can have far-reaching effects, sometimes even beyond your own intentions or expectations. We discuss how you might begin to recognise your capacity to be an effective agent of change and what this might mean for you in your classroom practice.

In Chapter 7, we examine the idea of the teacher as an agent of change and how this could result in improvement in your educational practice. We focus on how new learning can emerge from the process of undertaking critical self-reflection and action on your practice. We emphasise the significance of your new learning, in terms of influencing yourself, your students, your colleagues in your school setting and educational policy in general. Your new learning may not only influence your educational practice, but may also contribute to the development of a new theory of your practice and to the expansion of the knowledge base of the teaching profession.

In Chapter 8, we introduce you to some ideas for writing up your action research project and provide headings under which you could organise your ideas. We indicate some of the problems facing emergent writers and provide guidance on how you might surmount these problems. We discuss various opportunities for sharing your learning with others, including presenting your research at conferences, writing articles for educational journals and writing a chapter for a book. One of the possibilities for influencing the learning of others is through participating in learning communities, similar to the communities of practice as described by Wenger (1998). Finally, we explore the concept of the sustainability of self-study action research as a method of long-term improvement in practice for teacher researchers.

7 The teacher as an agent of change

Introduction

The idea that teachers can be implementers of change in their classroom practice is a powerful one, and it can lead teachers to a realisation of the immense value of the work that they do in their classrooms on a daily basis. An openness to change can also help teachers to develop an awareness of the beneficial effects that can occur as a result of the changes that they make to their classroom practice. Teachers can evaluate the changes that they implement, and the effects of those changes, through engaging in self-study action research on their practice. However, teachers sometimes have difficulty in viewing themselves as competent and confident researchers. This reductionist stance may occur either because they are unaware of or underestimate their ability to bring about improvement in their practice. Perhaps they lack the confidence or self-belief that would enable them to view themselves as capable and legitimate researchers, who can carry out rigorous and robust enquiry into their educational practice.

How, then, could teachers begin to position themselves as autonomous and influential practitioner researchers with a sense of agency in relation to their teaching practice? Sachs (2003) suggests that professional development through engaging in teacher research would be a good strategy for developing the knowledge base of teaching. We suggest that it would also confirm the status of teacher researchers as powerful and influential agents of change, with the capacity to bring about improvement in their practice and to develop theories from their practice, through a process of critical reflection and action. We can confirm, from an action research project that we undertook, that teacher researchers can add to the knowledge base of their profession, developing both agency and influence by engaging in action research for professional development (Glenn et al. 2008).

In this chapter, then, we examine the following ideas:

- Change begins with you, as teacher, embracing your capacity for critical reflection and self-evaluation that could contribute to improvement in your practice or in the understanding of your practice.
- Evidence of change leading to improvement.
- New learning resulting from changes you have initiated in your practice.
- The significance of your new learning for yourself.
- The significance of your research for others.
- Knowledge creation and theory emanating from improvement in your practice.

Change begins with you, as teacher

As we have said earlier, one of the main purposes of engaging in action research is to improve your practice or your understanding of it. This may require changing some aspect of your teaching practice. However, you may lack the impetus, the knowledge or the opportunity required to take the first step. You may be encouraged to take that first step if you bear in mind that change begins with oneself. O'Donohue (1999: 164), drawing on the ideas of John Henry Newman that to grow is to change and to be perfect is to have changed often, suggests that change 'need not be threatening; it can in fact bring our lives to perfection'. Nelson Mandela made a specific link between education and the idea of change when he described education as the most powerful weapon that we can use to change the world. We suggest that, before you can change the world, you need to change yourself or some aspect of your professional life.

You cannot always change the situation in which you find yourself, nor can you easily bring about significant changes in the thinking or behaviour of others, but you can make a conscious decision to try to change your own approach, or your own attitude, through a process of continuous critical reflection on your practice. This is not something that you can achieve overnight; it will require patience, perseverance and determination. Pine (2009: 236) suggests that 'enacting change is not easy – it requires time, patience and sound planning, communication, and implementation skills'. The desire to change your practice may stem from your experience of feelings of unease or of dissatisfaction with the status quo. This concern, and the wish to do something about it, is often the starting point for an action research project (see, for example, Dadds 1993; McDonagh *et al.* 2012; McNiff and Whitehead 2006; Noffke and Somekh 2009).

You may wish to change the way you have always done something, in order to find a more effective and efficient way of doing it. This could prove difficult to accomplish, especially if colleagues do not share your desire for change, or if there is not a culture of change within your school community. Sometimes people seem to have an innate resistance to change, as Humphreys (2015: 2) indicates: 'People instinctively resist ideas that involve change.' Going against the flow is not a comfortable stance to take, and choosing this option can leave you feeling isolated and unsupported. It is important, therefore, to choose your research topic with care. While it is important to ensure that you try to live to your values, you need to do so in a manner that is as collegiate as possible and that takes account of the fact that others have values also. Ideally, your relationship with other members of staff should be based on cooperation and collaboration, but you need to recognise that there may be competing values (Roche 2000, 2007).

It is also worth noting that your initial action research project should be a small-scale and manageable one, capable of being accommodated within your normal working day, and within the timescale prescribed by your accrediting institution. Taking on a large-scale project could leave you feeling overwhelmed and could severely test your perseverance skills, perhaps even causing you to abandon your research plans altogether. Pine (2009) advises beginning action researchers to aim for simple research plans, rather than more intricate ones, and suggests that by engaging in a number of small projects, an action research tradition can be gradually built up, and that this strategy will prove effective and worthwhile in the long-term.

Through your reflection on your practice, you may discover that your educational values, which we discussed in previous chapters, are not being realised in your practice. For example, you may say that you believe in a democratic and participatory approach to education, in which the voices of all are included: yet you may find yourself continuing to teach in a didactic manner, where your voice, as teacher, is the dominant one in classroom discourses (see Chapter 2). This practice reflects a denial of your values of democracy, participation and inclusion. Whitehead (1989) describes this dilemma as experiencing oneself as a living contradiction (see Chapter 4), a situation that may prove difficult to resolve. As soon as you realise that there is dissonance between the values that you hold around education and what is actually happening in your practice, you will, in all probability, feel a need to change the situation. The necessity to bring about change in one's educational practice is highlighted by Niemi and Kemmis (2012: 66) when they state, 'The evaluation of educational systems and practices is a political issue, not only aiming to interpret the world but also to change it.'

You have already begun the process of critically examining your values: if these values are held dearly and are meaningful for you, you will not wish to abandon them easily. Niemi *et al.* (2012) attest to the importance of values in the lives of teachers when they assert that teachers' work is intrinsically linked to the concept of values. It would seem, then, that whatever change you may wish to bring about will, in all likelihood, be at the level of practice. When you have come to this decision, you can begin to implement a process of change in your practice, and this will act as the impetus to start you on your journey of improvement.

Below is a vignette from my research for my PhD thesis (Sullivan 2006) that illustrates these ideas as I outline how I came to understand that the process of change begins with me, as teacher. In it I describe how I discovered that I was not living to the educational values that I professed to hold. This necessitated a change in approach on my part in order to accommodate my discovery and to enable me to begin living to my espoused values, while simultaneously documenting my personal and professional learning from my critical reflection on the incident.

Vignette

For a period of five years, I worked as a resource teacher for children from the Traveller community, the Irish equivalent of the Gypsy community. As part of that role, I provided learning support in the area of literacy to the Traveller children. During reading lessons, I had a notebook in which I entered any errors made by the children, and would bring these to their attention when they had finished reading, so as not to interrupt the flow in the course of the reading. At that time, I had identified one of my educational values as having respect for the culture and ethnicity of minority groups, and firmly believed that I was living to that value in my practice. On one occasion, when a Traveller child whom I shall call MT was reading from her textbook, she pronounced the word 'told' as 'tould'. I made a note of this in my notebook, and immediately MT said in an indignant tone, 'I knew that word, that is how we say it.' Initially taken aback by this, I quickly said that it was alright, that I would not count it as an error, which seemed to placate MT and she continued with her reading.

Later, when I 'reflected-on-action' (Schön 1983) on the incident, while documenting it in my reflective journal, I began to realise the significance of what had occurred. Despite my stated commitment to respecting Traveller culture and ethnicity, my action in correcting MT's pronunciation of words indicated that I was not living up to that commitment. I was aware of the Traveller propensity to use words such as 'tould', 'hould' and 'bould': therefore, I should not have perceived them as errors. When I analysed the reasons for my stance in correcting their enunciation, I concluded that I had acted out of concern that Traveller children might be seen as different, or perhaps as inferior, to other children if they did not pronounce their words in the same way as the majority of students. I also feared that they might not be considered equal to other students if they did not use Standard English. This thinking led me into the erroneous situation of trying to get Traveller children to conform to the norms and standards of the dominant group in society. I did not realise that, in the process, their own culture could be devalued or even subsumed into the dominant one, a situation that would have seemed untenable to me as someone who had professed to value their culture and identity. My critical reflection on the situation, as well as my engagement with some of the literature on the topic, helped me to bring about a change in my thinking and in my approach to managing such issues and I resolved to be more aware of the impact of my actions on minority groups in the future.

I now elaborate on how I brought about a change in my thinking and in my practice, through critical engagement with the literature, through self-reflection on my practice and through my efforts to live more closely to the values that I claimed to hold.

Vignette continued

In the course of my reading, I discovered that Labov (1973) did not subscribe to the theory that minority groups exhibited verbal deprivation, describing it as a myth, stating:

> Before we impose the middle-class verbal style upon children from other cultural groups, we should find out how much of this is useful for the main work of analysing and generalizing, and how much is merely stylistic – or even dysfunctional. (p. 34)

In agreement with this perspective, I resolved to view Traveller children's pronunciation of words as an expression of their different cultural norms, rather than as evidence of the use of an inferior or restricted language.

I came to a realisation that I had been operating out of a mistaken logic of encouraging Traveller children to conform to the system, instead of trying to change the system in order to accommodate the customs and norms of Traveller children. With this new insight came the understanding that I was misguided in regarding Traveller children's different pronunciation of words as errors. Consequently, I began to concur with the views of Torrey (1973) that they should not be regarded as such, when she said, in relation to black children's use of language:

> Although standard [sic] English serves as the medium of instruction in reading and other subjects and is the only dialect acceptable as 'correct' in the dominant society, the deviations of many black children from standard forms cannot be regarded as errors. (p. 67)

Through critical self-reflection and critical engagement with the relevant literature, I became aware of the need for change in my pedagogic approach to teaching Traveller children. I resolved to focus on their cultural practices and to situate their learning in their own experiences. This would enable me to live to my values around Traveller culture and ethnicity, and at the same time ensure that Traveller children would experience learning as positive and life-enhancing, rather than oppressive and marginalising. Freire summed up succinctly the situation that occurred in my practice in the following conversation with Shor: 'I learned that beauty and creativity could not live with a slavish devotion to correct usage. This understanding taught me that creativity needed freedom. So I changed my pedagogy as a young teacher towards creative freedom' (Shor and Freire 1987: 20).

As you can see from the narrative of this vignette, constant vigilance in reflecting on your practice, to assess whether you are living to your values, can result in change leading to improvement in your practice. This improvement most likely will be reflected in the quality of the learning experiences for your students. It will also have an impact on your own learning and on your personal and professional development. A commitment to creative freedom, as described in the above citation from Shor and Freire, could provide you with the courage and conviction needed to initiate change in your practice. To enable you to begin the process of change resulting in improvement, it may help to consider the following reflective questions.

Pause and reflect

Do you consider it important to be open to the possibility of change? Why? Why not?

What change do you think you could bring about in your approach to your work?

Revisit the area of your practice that you would really like to change. Do you now need to adjust this in any way?

Do you feel that you could implement a process of change leading to improvement in your practice or in your thinking?

What qualities do you think you might need in order to be able to implement change?

Evidence of change in practice leading to improvement

We now focus on how you can examine your practice to determine if there is evidence of a change leading to improvement in your practice or in your understanding of your practice.

This process will provide you with new learning or new knowledge about your practice. Your critical reflection as you undertake self-study action research on your classroom practice will help you to determine whether new learning is emerging from the process. Winter (1996) stresses the importance of reflexivity, or reflecting on your own thinking, as well as on your actions. Practical examples of meta-reflection can be found in McDonagh *et al.* (2012). The new learning from your self-reflection could be a different perspective on your own thinking or a change in your pedagogical approach: equally, it could reflect an improvement in students' attitudes or in their work ethic.

No matter how miniscule the improvement achieved might appear to you, it has the potential to contribute to the corpus of valuable learning resulting from your engagement in your action research project. You may feel that no discernible improvement has occurred in your practice, despite your best efforts. Initially, this may be disappointing for you but you will have accumulated some valuable learning from the process. Another positive outcome, that might only become obvious following your critical reflection on the process, could be that the new learning constitutes an improvement in your understanding of your practice. For example, you may have reached clarity in your understanding of why you adopt a particular approach in your pedagogic practice, and this could be described as new learning around your understanding. You could, then, be said to have experienced an enhancement in your learning or in your understanding of your practice.

As we explained in Chapter 5, you can accumulate a considerable amount of information or data in the course of engaging in reflection on your practice. You have one data archive and you are continuously sifting through this data, each time with a different focus. Here, we are focusing on finding evidence of change in your practice. The evidence can emerge in a number of ways and from a variety of sources. Examples might be:

- Your own reflections, which you may have documented in your reflective journal
- Comments made or views expressed during discussions with colleagues
- Results of various tests administered to students
- Views expressed by students on any changes that you have implemented in your practice
- Feedback from critical friends or observers in your classroom
- Video recordings, film clips, photographs or portfolios of students' work
- Comments from parents on changes they have noticed in students.

We will now discuss how each of these sources of data can be used to track changes that may have occurred and that may become evidence of improvement in your educational practice.

A reflective journal, as we explained earlier, is a useful method of documenting information that you have gathered, including details of changes you might have made to your practice and your reflections on the changes. You will be able to reflect again on issues as you read back over your account of events that have occurred and changes that you have made, at the same time tracking the narrative of your own learning. Such reflection and meta-reflection can provide valuable insights into your practice and could enable you to identify instances of change, and to come to conclusions that may not have been evident to you initially. Schön (1983) describes this activity as reflection-on-action, and suggests that all teachers could become reflective practitioners by including this practice systematically as part of their teaching repertoire.

Your teaching colleagues could be a useful source of information, and a valuable resource for you, as you look for evidence of change. Colleagues who also teach the students with whom you are undertaking your research could be of particular benefit to you, as they could provide information on the occurrence of change in diverse areas such as students' attitudes, attendance rates, work ethic and participation levels. They could challenge you to the extent that you might change your own thinking. They may highlight changes that they perceive in your practice. Their views may corroborate your own views on these issues, or they may make a significant contribution to evidence of change in your practice.

Tests administered to students are a source of quantitative data for the purpose of assessing the effectiveness of your research and can represent evidence of change or lack of change. At a qualitative level, the views of students can provide evidence of changes made or improvements achieved in your practice. Students' views can also challenge your assumptions about change, as students can provide wonderfully frank and honest feedback (Hopkins 2014), particularly when they are regarded as co-researchers and treated with respect and equality (Garvis *et al.* 2015; Rudduck and McIntyre 2007).

We have discussed in earlier chapters the usefulness of having a critical friend who could provide evidence of change, or be a catalyst for change, in your thinking or in your practice. Your critical friend will be involved from the beginning of the process and needs to be informed of the aims and purposes of your research, and of your proposed research plan. It would be appropriate to invite your critical friend to observe some of your classroom practice, so as to be well placed to note changes and improvements in your practice during the course of your research. Pine (2009: 237) describes the benefits of critical friends as follows: 'Critical friends share a commitment to inquiry, offer continuing support during the research process, and nurture a community of intellectual and emotional caring.' The concepts of nurture and caring are particularly relevant in this context, as you may find yourself at some stage in the process at a crisis point, where only the empathy and understanding of a supportive friend can provide the impetus to persevere with your research.

Video recordings and tape recordings can be a reliable source of evidence of change over time in relation to your learning. Other useful resources are photographs and samples of students' work. However, as we mentioned in Chapter 5, care is needed to ensure that proper ethical procedures are followed. When research is undertaken with minors, issues of child protection, confidentiality and anonymity are paramount, and so students should not be identifiable through the data-collecting processes. There are various ways of ensuring this, such as ascribing pseudonyms or numbers to the students involved.

It is easy to overlook the role of parents when undertaking educational research, but they can provide useful and relevant information on changes in your practice. For example, if your research is focused on issues to do with homework, parents may be able to tell you how much time was spent on homework, how enthusiastically it was undertaken and whether students needed help with the homework. They would also be well placed to note any significant changes in attitude or approach on the part of students. This information could be elicited from parents in a casual conversation, through questionnaires, or more formally at parent/teacher meetings. In keeping with good ethical standards, parents should be informed of the purpose and scope of the research, and permission to use their feedback should be obtained from them.

As you sift through your various pieces of data, you may find instances that demonstrate evidence of where you are now living more closely to your values. These pieces of data can then be presented as evidence of improvement, resulting from changes you have implemented in your practice. You could convene a validation group, perhaps from among your colleagues or from teachers in neighbouring schools, to whom you would present your evidence. The validation group could assess the validity of your claim to have achieved improvement through implementing change, by engaging in a process of critically examining your data for evidence of the realisation of your values in your practice. The group would then be in a position to say whether you had fulfilled the criteria, drawn from your values, for assessing your research. Having a validation group, as well as a critical friend, and including evidence from students, colleagues and parents, will contribute to, and strengthen, the triangulation of your data, which we discussed in Chapter 5.

Each time you unearth evidence of positive change in your practice or in your thinking, you are demonstrating your agency and autonomy as a professional committed to a process of educational improvement.

Pause and reflect

How can you track your learning to show changes as they occur in your research process?

Expand on your thoughts about how students might provide evidence of change.

Describe how colleagues and parents might contribute to establishing whether change has occurred in your practice.

New learning resulting from the changes that you have initiated in your practice

In previous chapters you have been guided through the process of collecting and examining data. We have shown you how you can analyse your data in terms of what it is you are trying to achieve. For example, if your aim was to ensure that your students took a more active part in their own education, you might examine your store of information to see where you could point to instances that showed students actively engaged in their own learning. You can also analyse your information with reference to your values by looking for evidence to show situations where you are, or are not, living to your values. If, for example, inclusion is one of your educational values, you may be able to show that you have found ways to integrate all children, including those with learning difficulties and those from different ethnic backgrounds, in your teaching practice. In the vignette below, McDonagh (2007) explains how, through her valuing of, and respect for, the voices of research participants, her students with specific learning difficulties were empowered to create personal knowledge around their individual learning styles.

> **Vignette**
>
> As a researcher and teacher I have come to believe that I cannot give participants a voice but rather my work provides participants with opportunities for voice. Through my search for an appropriate form of voice I have come to accept that there are multiple ways of learning and knowing. As the Platonic view proposes, there is no one 'right' way of knowing and I have found that the acceptance of multiple ways of knowing can lead to dialogue. Such an acceptance also creates a freedom, which grows from informed choice because it involves exploring many ways and excluding none. In investigating the learning experiences of children with specific learning disability, I have provided a practice-based emancipatory methodology of research in which opportunities were made for children's voices to be heard.
>
> I gained significant insights into the nature of teaching children with specific learning difficulties by listening and allowing them to formulate ideas together. The children voiced a theory of learning spellings and created personal knowledge dialogically. They also demonstrated the value of metacognition in learning. As a result of permitting my children to represent their personal learning orally, I as a teacher ceased to perceive myself as the professional 'knower' in the classroom and realised that I too was a learner. This follows the thinking of Zeichner (1999), who places the teacher as a learner in his USA studies of the power of self-study in educational research.

From her initial position of wishing to provide students with opportunities for their voices to be heard, McDonagh (2007) has recounted a number of other instances of new personal and professional knowledge from her research, including a recognition of multiple ways of knowing, the importance of dialogue and the concept of the teacher as learner.

You could also discover, as you analyse the information you have collected, that there are other positive outcomes besides those you had set out to achieve. These unplanned or unintended findings can be very valuable in terms of contributing to your own learning and can add to the personal and professional enhancement of your practice, as can be seen in the vignette above. Kemmis *et al.* (2014) suggest that we should be alert to the possibility of anticipated and unanticipated outcomes, intended and unintended findings and any side effects. In a similar vein, Pine (2009) reminds us to keep notes on any new ideas that are unanticipated, and to be aware of any findings that were not planned. Reflecting on the causes of any intended or unintended effects will help you to determine if the outcomes are the result of actions undertaken by you, and if you have had an educational influence on the outcomes. Furthermore, the acknowledgement and scrutiny of any unintended outcomes can contribute to the rigour and robustness of the research process.

> **Pause and reflect**
>
> How might you now perceive yourself as an agent of change?
>
> Why is it important to be aware of any unintended effects of your action research?
>
> Do you agree with McDonagh (2007) on the importance of children's voices being heard?

Significance of your new learning for yourself

The information that you have gathered methodically and systematically can provide robust evidence that you have had agency in bringing about improvement in your practice or in your understanding of your practice. It can show what changes have taken place in your practice, and these changes are usually an indication of improvement. Improvement can occur at various levels. Different versions of these levels can be found in many action research literatures (Bradbury 2015; McDonagh *et al*. 2012; McNiff and Whitehead 2010; Noffke 1997).

We have summarised the different levels of improvement as follows:

- Improvement at a practical level, where you can show that you have improved some aspect of your teaching practice
- Improvement at a personal level, where you may have changed or clarified your views or your understanding of your practice
- Improvement at a theoretical level, where your new thinking can provide you with new knowledge and enable you to develop a new theory of your practice.

An example of improvement at a *practical* level might occur in a situation where, initially, you had been using a didactic approach in your teaching, presenting knowledge to your students as a ready-made package, which they were expected to assimilate in a passive and uncritical manner. Through your engagement in critical self-reflection, you may have come to realise that a better option might be to adopt a pedagogic approach that would allow the students the opportunity to discover the information for themselves, and so become more active and independent learners. In the process, they could demonstrate their potential to become knowledge creators (Dewey 1966; Freire 1972; Sullivan 2004). The change that has occurred in your practice represents a significant improvement on the original situation.

At a *personal* level, you may have been of the opinion that the teacher, as the person possessing the knowledge, should do most of the talking in the classroom. Through your critical self-reflection and self-evaluation, you may now have reached the conclusion that your students could learn more, and also have a greater opportunity of consolidating their learning, if they were to do more of the talking and questioning in the classroom. Your new approach indicates an increase in your understanding of the importance of a dialogical relationship between teaching and learning in your classroom (Glenn 2006, 2011; McDonagh 2007; Roche 2007, 2015). It can also contribute to an enhancement in your personal thinking processes.

When you have articulated the improvements that have taken place at a practical or personal level, you can formulate your findings as a new theory of your practice, drawing on the new knowledge developed during your research. A number of authors, including ourselves (McDonagh *et al*. 2012), attest to the potential of an action research approach to result in the development of new knowledge. For example, Greenwood and Levin (2014: 7) write 'We believe that AR [action research] is one of the most powerful ways to generate new research knowledge.' Coghlan and Brannick (2014: xiii) express a similar view, stating that 'Action research is an approach to research which aims at both taking action and creating knowledge or theory about that action as the action unfolds.' Writing about teacher researchers engaging in enquiry, Alexakos (2015: 3) believes 'they must be concerned that their knowledge is real and meaningful – that, as teachers, their knowledge as it emerges out of their everyday experience does matter'.

Using the above example of improvement at a practical level, you could develop a theory that a self-discovery or experiential approach to learning can result in your students becoming more independent learners and thinkers, in control of their own learning. You will, of course, have provided sound explanations and critical analysis for the research findings that underpin your emergent theory. The example of improvement at a personal level could help you to generate a theory of the importance of creating a dialogical environment in your classroom, with students and teacher having equal opportunity to voice their opinions in classroom discourses. Through such thorough and perceptive analysis of your research, and through the development of new knowledge about your educational practice, you will be able to articulate the significance of your findings at a *theoretical* level.

Significance of your research for others

In traditional forms of research, the researchers presented their findings to others at the end of the research project. In contrast, in a self-study action research approach the practitioner researcher begins to share the emerging ideas with others from the outset. This is achieved through sharing ideas and reflections, which you may have noted in your reflective journal, with other participants, and through engaging in dialogue with critical friends and colleagues. In an action research approach, therefore, new learning, leading to new knowledge, becomes apparent throughout, rather than at the end of the process. Bradbury (2015) articulates the relationship between action research and knowledge creation succinctly in the following statement: 'Action research is a democratic and participatory orientation to knowledge creation. It brings together action and reflection, theory and practice, in the pursuit of practical solutions to issues of pressing concern' (p. 1).

Learning is most beneficial when it is shared with others. If learning remains in the sole possession of a single learner, its effect can be somewhat limited. However, if the social dimension of learning is actively and assiduously promoted, the new learning can have widespread educational influence. The ripple effect from the dissemination of new knowledge can be of benefit to other teachers and may inspire them to begin the process of taking action to improve their practice also. This could form the basis for a more collaborative and cooperative approach among staff and may result in the transformation of your school environment. The TALIS (2013) report (OECD 2014) suggests that, where there is cooperation, collaboration and openness to sharing ideas among teachers, the learning outcomes for students are increased.

Opportunities for educational discussions with colleagues do not readily present themselves in the busy lives of teachers, so we need to find the space for such professional conversations (Clark 2001; Glenn *et al.* 2012; Glenn *et al.* forthcoming). Staff meetings could be the first port of call. You could ask for time to outline your learning from critically reflecting on your practice at a staff meeting. Your colleagues may be looking for ways to improve some aspect of their classroom practice and so could be interested in hearing of your research experiences. School planning days could also provide an opportunity for you to share the narrative of your learning with colleagues, particularly if the agenda includes the topic of self-evaluation, as this is now a required component in many educational systems worldwide. You could demonstrate how this concept is linked to reflection on one's practice, and how self-evaluation can be achieved in an effective and beneficial way through engaging in critical self-reflection.

You may wish to extend the benefits of your learning beyond the boundaries of your particular educational establishment, thereby having an influence on social formations, as described by Whitehead (2004). There are a number of ways in which you could achieve this. You could write an article based on your experiences for publication in an educational journal, or produce a chapter for inclusion in an edited book. You could also present the narrative of your learning at an educational conference or seminar. As you can see, the potential for your personal and professional learning to have a far-reaching influence on other educators is considerable. The insights gained through undertaking your research can have substantial significance, which Bradbury (2015: 8) describes as 'having meaning and relevance beyond their immediate context in support of the flourishing of persons, communities and the wider ecology'.

Knowledge creation and theory emanating from your improvement in your practice

Knowledge comes in many forms and from various sources, but none is as enriching or as deep as the knowledge you create for yourself through critical reflection on your thinking and on your actions. The field of epistemology is a complex one, and engaging with ideas about forms of knowledge, who is considered to be a knower, knowledge acquisition, knowledge generation and knowledge creation are all important epistemological concepts (for good explorations of these ideas read Dewey 1933; Foucault 1980; Polanyi 1958; Schön 1983; Whitehead and McNiff 2006. We also have practical examples of some of these seminal ideas in our theses – see www.eari.ie).

Until we get on the inside of these ideas, we may mistakenly think of knowledge as something 'out there', separate from ourselves – in a book, on the internet, in the minds of experts – something ready-made and reified as a product to be transmitted, as opposed to something dynamic, internal and personal that we generate for ourselves. These assumptions may stem from a tendency to overlook some important facts about knowledge, such as that it is a process; that it is constantly evolving and developing; that it can be created through engaging in critical self-reflection; that it can result from participating in critical discourse with others.

One of the outcomes of critically reflecting on your practice is the development of new knowledge or new learning, and this can evolve from the process of analysing the information or data gathered during the course of your research, as described in the previous section. The new learning can manifest itself in a number of ways. It can be:

- Something new that you have discovered about your teaching practice
- Increased knowledge in relation to your students' learning styles
- Personal knowledge around your educational values
- A change of direction in a pedagogical area.

Each of these ideas is explained in the paragraphs below.

Your teaching practice may have been representative of a situation where you, as the teacher, did most of the talking, and the students' roles were mainly as listeners. The realisation that this is not an equitable situation, and that it does not value students' voices, may have resulted in a change of approach, whereby you now try to ensure that students are given ample opportunity, and actively encouraged, to voice their opinions. Your new approach around empowering students and recognising their right to have their voices heard, as a feature of classroom discourse, represents new knowledge concerning your teaching practice.

Let's assume that you have claimed that you value inclusion. Throughout your teaching career, you may have employed teaching skills that were suited to particular learners. You may now be aware that some of your students learn best when other approaches are used, and this may have resulted in a change in your teaching strategies. The adaptation of your teaching style, in order to accommodate various learners, can be regarded as new knowledge acquired through taking into consideration your students' differing learning needs. Documenting this process is important, as it provides evidence of how you have realised your value of inclusion through implementing a change in your practice, as a result of your critical reflection on the issue.

Another of your educational values may be around valuing the individuality of each student in your class. However, due to the 'busyness' of daily life in the classroom and the pressures of a demanding curriculum, the easiest option can often be to consider the class as a homogeneous unit for much of your teaching time. The realisation that you need to focus on each student as an individual, and to take account of each individual's learning needs, may lead you towards further new knowledge around your educational values and around the importance of living to those values. Kristeva (Kristeva and Lechte 2002: 162) recognises the importance of attending to individuality when she says, 'Each person has the right to become as singular as possible and to develop the maximum creativity for him or herself.'

A further example of how new knowledge may be developed could be that, in your approach to the teaching of reading skills, you may have a tendency to rely on a singular method – for example, one based on phonics. Through your critical reflection on your practice, it may have come to your attention that some students are not making much progress through the use of phonics. You may, therefore, come to the realisation that other methods could be equally valid – for example, using a whole-word strategy. Your willingness to try out a new approach, that could benefit some of your students, can be considered as new knowledge for you in a pedagogical area.

Drawing on any of the four examples above, it could now be said that you have discovered new knowledge about your teaching practice. If you make this new claim to knowledge, you can say that you have generated a theory from your practice. This can be achieved by reflecting critically on your claim, subjecting it to the scrutiny and challenge of others, whereby it is validated when you provide robust and rigorous evidence for your claim. You can then present it in a public forum as your valid theory of your practice. This could have relevance, not only in your particular institutional context, but also for the wider educational community. You also have the option of submitting your research for academic accreditation, such as for a Masters degree or for a PhD.

Pause and reflect

What new personal knowledge have you generated from your reflections on your educational practice?

What new pedagogical and/or practical knowledge have you created?

What new professional knowledge have you gained?

Describe how the new knowledge that you have created can develop into a theory of practice.

Conclusion

In this chapter, you have been introduced to the idea that it is important to be open to the possibility of change, and to embrace any opportunities for achieving change in your practice. You have learned how to gather information so that you have evidence of when and where change has occurred, and to view any positive change, no matter how insignificant it might appear to you, as improvement. You are now aware of how improvement in your practice can influence both your teaching and your students' learning. The wider implications of your educational influence, both on colleagues and on educators in general, have been discussed. You have been introduced to methods of disseminating your research findings and, in the process, having an influence on social formations (Whitehead 2004). Epistemological issues have been discussed, in relation to how new knowledge can be created through critical reflection on your practice, and how you can develop a new theory of your educational practice. We agree with Somekh and Zeichner (2009) in relation to the various benefits from engaging in action research, when they state: 'All educators who conduct action research are interested in improving their own practice. In addition, some of them are also interested in sharing their learning with others and/or in contribution to social reconstruction' (p. 10).

In this chapter:

- You have examined the concept of change as a signifier of improvement.
- You have come to view yourself as an agent of change.
- You have learned how to track your learning through the research process.
- You have become aware of how new knowledge can evolve from your reflection and action on your practice.
- You have discovered the significance of your research in terms of influencing yourself, your students, your colleagues and other educators.
- You have realised the potential of your research to lead to the development of a theory of your practice.

Recommended reading and resources

Kemmis, S., McTaggart, R. and Nixon, R. (2014) *The Action Research Planner: Doing Critical Participatory Action Research*, Singapore: Springer-Verlag.

Noffke, S. and Somekh, B. (2009) *The Sage Handbook of Educational Action Research*, London: Sage.

Pine, G. J. (2009) *Teacher Action Research: Building Knowledge Democracies*, Thousand Oaks, CA: Sage.

Sachs, J. (2003) *The Activist Teaching Profession*, Buckingham: Open University Press.

Whitehead, J. and McNiff, J. (2006) *Action Research: Living Theory*, London: Sage.

www.eari.ie

www.arnaconnect.org/

8 Sharing and sustaining your action research

Introduction

When you have carried out an action research project, you may be inclined to think that you are now finished with the process. You have completed all the necessary elements, such as identifying a research question, engaging with the literature, gathering and analysing data, providing evidence of your claim to knowledge and validating your claim through feedback from critical friends or research participants. You may also have reflected on the process, uncovered some new questions that you would like to research further and so you may have begun another cycle of action and reflection. There is, however, one other step that you can take, and that is to put your research into the public domain, where it will be available to a wider listenership and readership than it would have reached if confined to your immediate location. This extra process will bestow on your work additional validation through the critical evaluation of the other voices to which it will now have been exposed. The communication of your research through a public forum can secure the endorsement of your ideas by others and thus has the potential to add considerably to the significance of the research.

Assuming that you were passionate about your research as you engaged in the process, it would be invaluable if your passion, integrity and commitment could shine through in your written document. This may not be easy to achieve because we often know something at an intuitive level but may have difficulty in verbalising our knowledge or in writing about it. Polanyi (2009: 4) says, 'We can know more than we can tell': it is equally true that we can know more than we can write. Notwithstanding the difficulties involved, we contend that you, as a teacher researcher, are better placed to give a true and accurate account of your research, from an insider perspective, than is an external researcher interpreting your research solely from a non-participant vantage point. In this chapter, then, we will provide guidelines for you on the writing up of a self-study action research project from the point of view of a practitioner researcher.

Another issue that we discuss in this chapter is the possibility of continuing to engage in self-study action research in order to ensure the sustainability of the improvement already achieved. One approach that we feel could be useful in this regard would involve the setting up of learning communities, such as those proposed by Wenger (1998). Such communities of practice would contribute to the expansion of your educational influence, as we explained in Chapter 7, as well as to the continuation of achieving improvement in your practice.

The purpose of this chapter is to:

- Guide you in beginning the task of writing an account of your research.
- Demonstrate how you might match the story of your learning with the headings normally provided by academic institutions.
- Provide you with tips to help you with the writing process.
- Encourage you to work towards the sustainability of your research.
- Suggest how you might establish learning communities in your workplace.
- Outline the benefits of continuing the process of achieving improvement in your practice.

Beginning the task of writing an account of your research

If you wish to extend the influence of your research through publishing it in an educational journal, in an online format, or as a chapter in a book, or if you plan to present an account of your research at a conference, you will need to engage in a formal writing process. Likewise, if you are undertaking research for academic purposes, such as a Masters or PhD qualification, you will be required to write a dissertation or thesis. This can be a daunting task, especially if you have not produced any academic writing in recent years. You may feel quite competent in talking about your research and you may feel comfortable in presenting your work orally. However, when it comes to producing a written document, a different set of skills is required in order to communicate your ideas clearly and with conviction. Greenwood and Levin (2014: xi) allude to the difficulty faced by researchers as they attempt to engage with the process of writing about their research when they state, 'We were stunned to learn how difficult it was for practitioners of AR [action research] both to communicate research findings in writing and to get a firm handle on epistemological issues.'

Where to begin the writing task and how to structure the report can be major stumbling blocks initially, as can a lack of knowledge of the precise requirements for writing up a research project. We would advise you, therefore, to begin writing at the earliest opportunity, before you have come to the end of your research project. If you are writing for academic qualifications, you may have some prior experience of formal writing. For example, you may have been required to submit a research proposal, outlining your research in terms of aims, purposes, contexts, research design and ethical issues. Producing a proposal will have prepared you somewhat for the task of writing your dissertation or thesis, though these will need to be much more detailed, more structured and of a higher academic standard. Reading academic papers, journals and books will provide you with examples of the standards and the language required in academic writing. At a more basic level, you may have begun the practice of keeping a journal of your reflective writing, as we recommended in earlier chapters. This practice represents writing that is of a personal nature, whereas the formal academic writing, with which you are now about to engage, will require a much more stringent style of language and will need to be a coherent and comprehensive document.

You can begin drafting your report at an early stage in the research process. You will then have time to redraft this original writing in light of your learning as you carry out your research, and you will be able to take account of the insights you gain as you progress through your research. We suggest that it is in your interest to study the requirements for writing up the research that are specific to your situation before you begin, and we refer to these in more detail below. Our guidelines are concerned with producing a written text, which was the traditional, and often the only, format acceptable for academic accreditation until recent times.

Pause and reflect

Can you think of creative ways of presenting your action research project?

Would the following ways of presenting your research sit well with the values that you hold around education: a formal paper report, portfolios, artefacts, performances and multimedia presentations?

As many academic institutions continue to require some written text from the researcher, we will now focus on the specific requirements for this particular task.

Matching the story of your learning with the headings from academic institutions

Having a definite structural framework can help you to feel more confident as you undertake the writing process. The structure depends, to a large extent, on the purpose of the writing. For example, if, on the one hand, you are writing a paper for a journal or a chapter for a book, the publishers will have their own guidelines for structuring your writing. If, on the other hand, you are producing an account of your research for accreditation purposes, your college or university will probably have specific requirements that you need to fulfil. Each source of publication will have its own suggestions in regard to the word count, the format for presentation and the style and font to be used, and these guidelines should be adhered to meticulously. It is in your interest to scrutinise the relevant requirements before you embark on your writing.

The structure we describe here is more in line with that used for academic writing for accreditation purposes, but this format may also be acceptable to the majority of publishers. We propose, therefore, to guide you in organising your research under the following headings that are frequently used in academic research writing. We include 'Literature review' as a heading, even though this is not normally a requirement for an action research report. The rationale for not having a literature review is that, in an action research approach, the literature is interwoven throughout the text, and is specifically utilised for the purpose of discussing the conceptual frameworks within which the research is located. Our reason for the inclusion of a literature review here is that we wish to emphasise the importance of critically engaging with the literature, and to stress the necessity of ensuring that the relevant literature permeates the whole document and frames your emergent ideas.

1   Abstract
2   Introduction

You can, of course, use alternative and more creative headings, if your institution allows it, but you need to ensure that the above sections are adequately attended to within your structure. Before we proceed with our elaboration of the above headings, you might like to take time to reflect on the issues below.

Pause and reflect

What is to be gained from writing up your action research project?

Can you see the difference between writing in your reflective journal and academic writing?

What are the main stumbling blocks to the writing process?

Outline the advantages of beginning the writing early in the research process.

Why is a literature review not a necessary component of an action research document?

---

1. Abstract

Even though the abstract appears at the beginning of your action research document, it is usually the last piece to be written. It contains a brief description of the action research project and a succinct account of your claim to knowledge. From our experience as practitioner researchers, we have found that this is easier to do when you have completed your research, as it may be only then that you have a complete picture of the theory you have generated and of its significance. At that stage of your action research also, you are well-positioned to be able to take a step back and give an overview of the whole process. As the abstract is the first section to be read, it needs to capture the immediate interest of the reader. There are often specific requirements around the word count and formatting of the abstract, so you may need to check with your supervisor or publisher.

2. Introduction

The introduction to your research indicates for the reader the rationale behind your research project and explains why you wished to investigate the particular topic you have chosen. As you outline the reasons for your choice of research topic, you can link them specifically to your espoused values. The introduction provides details of the background to your research, as well as the contextual, conceptual or theoretical frameworks that may be applicable to your particular circumstances. The frameworks may be summarised as follows:

- Contextual frameworks – these include personal details that could have an impact on your research, or that could have inspired you to undertake your research. You could refer to your location, or that of your educational institution, and how this might influence your research. There may also be policy contexts that could frame your research.
- Conceptual frameworks – these involve the concepts or themes that are relevant to your research, such as democracy, freedom, love, equality and social justice. Conceptual frameworks are usually grounded in your educational values in an action research approach.
- Theoretical frameworks – these are often drawn from the literature that you have engaged with and will inform all aspects of your research. They too can be inspired by your ontological and epistemological values.

Your research question is included in the introduction, and it is important that you state it clearly and unambiguously in terms of 'How do I…?' or 'How can I…?' (McNiff and Whitehead 2006). This ensures that the focus of your research is self-improvement in relation to your teaching practice, and that you are working more in the direction of your values, rather than attempting to bring about improvement in your students: the latter might well be an outcome of your research, but the initial motivating factor in a self-study action research project is improvement of the self. The introduction, then, could be said to set the scene for your research project as it addresses the issues of what you wanted to do and why you wanted to do it. These issues can be addressed by posing the questions, 'What is my concern?' and 'Why am I concerned?' (McDonagh *et al.* 2012; Whitehead and McNiff 2006). You need also to outline for the reader what they may expect to find in the rest of the document. In contrast to traditional research writing, the introduction to your action research report is one of the most complex pieces in your account, and great care needs to be taken with it. The final draft of your introduction might not be completed until the end of the entire writing process, so that your learning from undertaking your research may be reflected in it.

3. Literature review

In a literature review, you have an opportunity to discuss in detail concepts and themes that are relevant to your research. You will have read a wide range of literature on your chosen topic, and also on your research approach, and this is your chance to display your knowledge of the literature. Sources of literature could include books and peer-reviewed journals available from college or university libraries: these may be available online if accessing a library physically is not possible. You may be able to source relevant government publications, educational policies and dissertations and theses on your particular topic. The authors you quote might support your particular viewpoint; some authors may hold opinions that are in conflict with your views. In either case, it is important to engage critically with the literature, explaining why you agree or disagree with the opinions expressed, rather than simply quoting the views of others and allowing those views to go unchallenged. The demonstration of critical engagement with the literature is one of the most important aspects of your work and is also one of the criteria used by academic institutions to assess the quality of research theses and dissertations. Academic institutions generally offer higher grades for higher levels of critical engagement with the literature. Many institutions also require that sources cited are up to date, unless they are seminal texts. There may also be a preference for citing from refereed journals, rather than from textbooks.

Referencing is essential to ensure integrity around the acknowledgement of intellectual property. A version of the Harvard referencing system is used in many educational institutions. It generally requires the year of publication each time you quote an author, whose surname only is used in the reference, and whenever you use a direct quote, the relevant page number should also be given. If a book or journal article was co-authored by more than two authors, it is referenced by using the name of the first author, followed by *et al*. It is important to remember that you should not confine your engagement with the literature to the literature review section: the literature should be incorporated throughout your document, informing your insights and framing your emergent theories. Pine (2009) outlines the various benefits to be accrued from undertaking a review of the relevant research literature as follows:

> A good literature review can help in focusing your research question, developing your research methodology and data collection procedures, identifying a conceptual framework for your research, making you more critical about your assumptions, situating your inquiry within context, identifying gaps in previous studies, identifying flawed methodologies or theoretical approaches, and identifying controversies in the research literature. (p. 250)

As we mentioned earlier in this chapter, in some situations of writing up a self-study action research account, a stand-alone literature section is not considered adequate or appropriate. It is expected that the researcher demonstrates critical engagement with the relevant literatures in the discussion of the conceptual and theoretical frameworks, as well as weaving the literatures throughout the whole document. The following vignette from my research (Sullivan 2006) shows how I proposed, in my introduction, to engage with the literature through a discussion of the conceptual issues that were central to my research.

Vignette

In the area of equality and social justice I refer to the ideas of, among others, Rawls (1971), Young (1990), Connell (1993), Drudy and Lynch (1993) and Griffiths (1998). I discuss the democratic, life-enhancing and positive views of Dewey (1966), McLaren (1999) and Zappone (2002), as containing the potential for a greater measure of equality and social justice. My analysis of issues of power and control takes account of the theories of Foucault (1980), Rabinow (1991) and Moss (1998). In proposing an intercultural approach to education, as opposed to a monocultural, oppressive perspective that often predominates in the educational system, I engage with the ideas of Kenny (1997), Berlin (2000) and Said (2002).

When I got to the stage of writing about my conceptual frameworks, I discussed my main themes in detail, drawing on the relevant theories in the literature as outlined above.

4. Methodology

The methodology section of your research document includes a description of your self-study action research approach and your justification for choosing that approach, in terms of your ontological and epistemological commitments. Ethical considerations need to be stated and explained, including permissions that you sought and consent forms that you have received. You need to spell out how you have taken anonymity and confidentiality into account. As we explained in Chapter 6; all of these issues have an added significance when minors are involved in the research. Mockler (2014) suggests that participants should be fully apprised of the purpose and processes of the research, and that they should be informed as to how they were chosen to be invited to participate in the project. Your account needs to show that, as an action researcher, your approach allows for research participants to be treated with respect and dignity, and to be regarded as co-researchers, on an equal footing with you, the researcher, rather than as disempowered and voiceless research subjects (Cox and Robinson-Pant 2008; Garvis *et al.* 2015; Kellett 2005; Ruddock and McIntyre 2007; Sullivan 2000).

An outline of your research design forms part of the methodology section, and this includes a description of the research tools you used and the purpose for which they were used. Remember that, in self-study action research, a discussion of values will form a key part of your written account; this distinguishes it from traditional research accounts. You may have used questionnaires or interviews as sources of data and these, and the reasons for using them, need to be foregrounded in your methodology. Qualitative and quantitative methods of data collection need to be mentioned, and also triangulation opportunities that you intend to use. You may, for example, have a critical friend or teaching colleague who may be able to provide critical feedback on your research and corroborative evidence of your findings. It would be useful to include the timeframe you outlined for your research, giving details of the actions that you proposed taking and when you intended to undertake them. It is important to remember that an action research project does not follow a linear trajectory from beginning to end: there are many twists and turns as you reflect on the process, change direction in light of your reflections and engage with the messiness (Cook 2009; Mellor 2001) of real-life research. A timeframe may be required when submitting a research proposal. The following is an example of a possible timeframe to help you plan your research project, but bear in mind that timeframes are provisional and always subject to change.

Table 8.1 Sample timeframe

January 2015	Identify research topic. Engage critically with literature. Keep reflective journal. Invite participants to take part. Begin writing.
February 2015	Formulate research question. Draw up action plan. Decide on methodology. Ethical issues. Research design. Gather initial data.
March 2015	Identify critical friend. Implement plan. Continue data-gathering. Reflect on process. Set up validation group. Continue writing.
April 2015	Continue data-gathering. Data analysis. Get feedback from critical friend and other participants. Critical reflection.
May 2015	Establish findings. State claim to knowledge. Provide evidence. Continue writing. Check references.
June 2015	First complete draft of project. Get feedback on it.
July 2015	Final document ready for submission.

You may have engaged in more than one cycle of reflecting, planning, acting and reviewing in your action research. If, for example, you had reached the stage of reviewing your plan of action and discovered that your plan was not having the desired effect, you could develop another plan, thus beginning another cycle of action research. You would need to describe both cycles in your methodology, explaining the necessity for the change in direction.

We have emphasised the importance of keeping a reflective journal and have recommended that you use it to track the narrative of your research and your learning from it. You need to mention that you are keeping a reflective journal in the methodology, as it may form a key part of your data collection. It would also be appropriate to mention in this section the criteria by which your research project will be assessed. The criteria can evolve from two sources: you can develop your own criteria based on your educational, ontological and epistemological values, as described in earlier chapters, or, if you are writing up your research for academic accreditation, your college or university will have specific criteria that you need to meet as well. Whichever criteria are applicable to your situation, and in action research it is quite in order to use both, it would be advisable to outline them clearly in your methodology section. Examples of research accounts that do this can be found on www.eari.ie, www.actionresearch.net and www.jeanmcniff.com. In my PhD thesis (Sullivan 2006), besides fulfilling the University of Limerick main criterion of making an original contribution to the field of study by generating new knowledge, I formulated my own criteria and standards of judgement, which evolved from my embodied values in a process that I describe in the vignette below.

Vignette

Ideas of generalisability and replicability are the conventional criteria for judging traditional social science research. However, I am arguing for a new living form of theory that engages with new forms of criteria and standards of judgement. I am locating my work within the new scholarship which, as Schön (1995) says, requires new kinds of epistemologies and new standards of judgement. Whitehead (2000) has responded to the call for innovative epistemologies by suggesting that the standards of judgement could be grounded in an individual's embodied values that underpin the research process. I engage with these new epistemologies in formulating my living theories from the lived reality of my educational practice, and ground my living standards of judgement in my ontological values of social justice and equality that are reflected in my practice.

Subsequently, in my thesis, I demonstrated how I met both the criteria of the university and my own criteria, drawn from my ontological values.

Pause and reflect

Explain why the introduction is such an important section of your written document.

What ethical considerations need to be discussed in your methodology section?

What extra precautions are needed when children are participants in the research process?

Describe how criteria can be established for the assessment of action research projects.

---

5. Findings

It is in this section that you articulate your learning from undertaking your research and demonstrate how your new knowledge can be expressed in terms of a theory of practice. In action research it is difficult to write a section on findings in one chapter and have the discussion of findings in another. It may be worth negotiating with your supervisor to establish whether it is possible to combine these two chapters. However, we accept that this may not be possible for everyone. If not, then your findings can be outlined in detail in the findings section of your written document. Articulating your findings will enable you to make a claim to knowledge. You can make this claim through identifying the learning that is evident from your engagement in your research. Examples of how to make a claim to knowledge can be found in the action research theses on our website, www.eari.ie

The findings in terms of your new learning begin to emerge as you analyse the data that you have gathered throughout the research process, and as you engage in meaning-making in relation to your research question. Asking questions such as, 'What have I learned from my research?' or 'What insights have I gained from undertaking my research?' can help you to articulate your new learning with clarity and precision. You then need to describe the pieces of data from your data archive that can be used to provide evidence for the learning that you have identified. Do not feel that you have to use every piece of data – only use data that supports explicitly and unequivocally the particular claim to knowledge that you are outlining. If you have tables, charts or graphs to illustrate your findings, it would be appropriate to include them here. You also have the evidence from your critical friend and from your validation group, a process that we explained in Chapter 7, and these two sources of critical feedback can help to triangulate your findings.

You should be able to provide instances of where you have succeeded in living to your values and this will then count as evidence of having fulfilled your criteria. It would be good practice to list your findings here and name each claim to knowledge. For example, you could outline the changes that have taken place in your own learning and in the learning of your students. In the discussion section, you would then develop each of these findings in detail. It is important to remember that your findings are always tentative, rather than conclusive, and that you need to be open to the possibility that others may interpret your data differently. Kincheloe (2003: 150) alerts us to this situation when he suggests, 'As teacher researchers, we can display our findings and argue for their value, but always with one hesitation, a stutter, a tentativeness – never as the truth.'

To preserve the integrity of the research, it is important that you write about negative as well as positive findings: you might, for example, give an account of occasions where you failed to live to your espoused values, or of where your expected outcomes did not materialise. This approach will ensure that you are not writing what MacLure (1996) calls a victory narrative, in which you only write about your successful outcomes, and which results in your research report lacking authenticity and trustworthiness. Instead, you should aim to include the messiness of your action research project, with all its problems, pitfalls and setbacks, as described by Cook (2009) and Mellor (2001). In acknowledging the negative aspects of your research, you are highlighting your own perceptiveness and integrity by demonstrating your openness to critical self-reflection and self-evaluation, and signifying the unadulterated development of new learning about your practice or your understanding of your practice.

6. Discussion

Having outlined your findings in the previous section, you are eminently positioned to be able to analyse them and draw conclusions from them in the discussion section. You can discuss each of your findings, as listed in the previous section, in turn and try to link each of them to your espoused educational values. You can add to the scholarly status of your written document by linking your discussion to relevant literature and by demonstrating your critical engagement with the literature. The implications of your new learning for you, for your students and for the wider educational community will form part of your discussion. As you elucidate these implications, you will be able to articulate the significance of your research at various levels – personal, professional and theoretical – as we have explained in Chapter 7. The new learning that you identify, through communicating the significance of your research, represents new knowledge about your practice that can be developed into a new theory of your practice. This process requires a robust and rigorous approach in providing strong and incontrovertible evidence to support your practice-based theory, and your written account must clearly show this evidence. The vignette below shows the rigorous approach adopted by Glenn (2006) as she developed her living theory of practice in her PhD thesis.

Vignette

At a theoretical level, I believe that the ideas developed by Bohm about a stream of understanding (2004) began to flow between my class and myself as we engaged in dialogical approaches to learning. I began to see learning as a dynamic, organic and fluid process (Bentley 1998) and continue to do still. The classroom became an 'integral, interactive part of reality, not a place apart' (Palmer 1993: 35). I have learned from my engagement with my practice and with living educational theory that my emergent ontological values provide me with underpinning explanations and purposes, for education and for how I live my life. I express these living ontological values in my work and in the educational relationships I establish with and for people, as they become enacted in living practice (McNiff 2005). I have not taken this learning lightly because

I am aware of the serious implications of the communicative actions I have undertaken; I assume in acting communicatively that I must speak in ways that are comprehensible, truthful, sincere and appropriate for the context (Habermas 1987). I believe that I have spoken in this manner as I share my theory of practice with others and as I demonstrate academic rigour as outlined by Winter's (1989) criteria of reflexive critique, dialectical critique, risk, plural structure, multiple resources and theory practice transformation.

7. Conclusion

In this final section of your action research report, you have an opportunity to display the knowledge and expertise you have garnered through your engagement in the research process.

Pause and reflect

Imagine you are a supervisor about to read the conclusion of a research account.

What will you expect to find in the conclusion?

What aspects or characteristics of the report will you be looking for?

What will grab your attention and leave you informed and uplifted?

At this point of the writing process, researchers are often exhausted and have little energy for writing a robust conclusion. Take time, then, to ensure that you give some thought to this important section and that you produce a strong finish. This will be the last piece of writing that your reader or examiner will experience, so you should aim to leave a lasting impression of a scholarly and worthwhile account of your research project in the mind of your reader or examiner.

In your conclusion, you draw together the various threads woven throughout the research process. It would not be appropriate to introduce any new concepts or theories at this stage, as the purpose of this section is to provide a coherent summary of your project. As you summarise your research, you will be able to engage in meaning-making in relation to your teaching practice, your own learning and your students' learning. These themes are instrumental in providing a catalyst for assessing the educational influence of your research, for identifying issues that, with hindsight, you might have handled differently and for making recommendations as to how you might engage in further research on your practice in the future. For example, your research may have raised questions that you now wish to investigate further, so you may begin another cycle of action research. Your commitment and dedication to the process may influence readers of your research report to undertake similar research on their individual educational practices. You would then be justified in claiming to have had an educational influence on social formations (Whitehead 2000).

8. References

It is usual practice to provide a list of references at the end of a research document. The list includes all the authors whose work you have quoted throughout the writing process. The authors should be listed in alphabetical order and the following details should be supplied: author's surname, initial of first name, year of publication, title of book or journal article, place of publication and publishing company. We mentioned earlier in this chapter that, when citing more than two authors, you would give the first surname, followed by *et al*. However, in the references section, you need to write the name of each author. Again, if you are writing for accreditation, we urge you to scrutinise the particular requirements of your institution. In the case of a journal article, you need to include the title of the journal, the number of the particular issue and the relevant page numbers for the article you have quoted. It would be advisable to refer to the guidelines of your institution or publisher to ensure conformity on these issues.

Sometimes, appendices can be placed after the references. This is not an obligatory part of the written document but it can be a useful strategy in some instances. For example, if you are likely to exceed the recommended word count, you could place some items such as questionnaires and interview questions in the appendices. You could also use an appendix for the purpose of showing samples of permission letters and consent forms. A further use of appendices could be to provide transcripts of tape-recordings or video-recordings.

Tips to help you with the writing process

It is very tempting to defer taking action, or to use delaying tactics, especially when faced with a new challenge. We can all choose to be procrastinators when we want to avoid engaging in a difficult task, and we will use all kinds of excuses to postpone beginning the task, even to the extent of preferring to do jobs that we normally try to shirk. We would advise you, then, not to fall into this trap when confronted with the task of writing about your research project. There is no point in trying to delay the inevitable: you will have to begin sooner or later. The following tips might help you to get started:

- Negotiate with your supervisor or tutor how often they will expect to receive written work from you, and whether these submissions are acceptable as rough drafts or need to be edited prior to submission.
- Set aside a specific writing time – begin with a short period of time and you can extend it as your confidence grows and the writing begins to flow.
- Ensure that you will not be disturbed during your writing time – you do not want to be tempted to down tools and abandon your task.
- Start by writing a small piece of text on a topic that you are familiar with, such as what you like about your teaching practice.
- Progress to a short piece of more academic writing, such as a review of one of the books that you have read on your research topic.
- Begin writing your first draft by writing down all the ideas that you have around your research topic.
- Structure your ideas into a logical and coherent sequence.
- Give this initial attempt at writing to a critical friend or colleague who will give you constructive feedback.

At this stage, you should be well on your way to completing a first draft of your text. It is important to emphasise that it is only a first draft, and that you will redraft it a number of times before you reach the final product. Try to avoid viewing the drafting process as a tiresome chore: instead, view it as an opportunity for continuous improvement of your research report through incorporating your learning throughout your research, your critical reading of the literature and the feedback from other participants in the research. You might take some consolation from what Polanyi (1958) says about the struggle to articulate and communicate our thoughts and ideas in a way that is intelligible to our readers:

> Speaking and writing is an ever renewed struggle to be both apposite and intelligible, and every word that is finally uttered is a confession of our incapacity to do better; but each time we have finished saying something and let it stand, we tacitly imply also that this says what we mean, and should mean it therefore also to the listener or reader. Though these ubiquitous tacit endorsements of our words may always turn out to be mistaken, we must accept this risk if we are ever to say anything. (p. 207)

Working towards the sustainability of your research

We have already discussed the various benefits from undertaking action research in your educational practice, and have indicated the main beneficiaries from the process: yourself as teacher researcher, your students as co-researcher participants and the wider educational community whom you have influenced through the dissemination of your research findings. There is a possibility that these benefits could end up being short-lived. For example, if your research project was a one-off and your critical enquiry stance ceased on completion of your project, then there could be a discontinuity in relation to achieving ongoing improvements. However, McNiff and Whitehead (2009) suggest that, when an action research project is completed, it raises issues that lead to the beginning of another research project, in accordance with the cyclical nature of action research. It is important, therefore, to continue the process of critical reflection and action in order to keep the momentum going and to extend the culture of improvement that existed during the course of your action research. Stringer (2014) indicates the benefits of sustaining improvement, resulting from engagement in action research, as follows:

> action research provides a flexible and practical set of procedures that are systematic, cyclical, solutions orientated, and participatory, providing the means to devise sustainable improvements in practice that enhance the lives and well-being of all participants. (p. 5)

How, then, can you sustain an orientation towards improvement that could result in a culture of enquiry leading to enhancement in your practice on a continuous basis for the foreseeable future? That is the question that we propose to address now.

Pause and reflect

What can you, as an individual, do to sustain the climate of improvement in your practice?

What can you, as a participant in a learning community, do to contribute to the sustainability of your enhanced practice?

We will now address these two significant questions.

Individual contribution to sustaining the culture of improvement in your practice

Our individual experiences of engaging in action research over a number of years have brought us to a situation where we authors now regard action research as a life-enhancing way of being for us that is commensurate with our ontological stance in life. When we undertook our initial research projects – and, in the process, experienced the benefits for ourselves and for our students – we each felt compelled to continue our journey of action research leading to improvement. This stance is understandable, in light of the fact that teachers generally want to make a difference in the lives of their students – a difference that will lead to greater educational opportunities for all students, irrespective of social class, ethnic status or geographical location. Teachers may also have a desire for the empowerment of their students so that the students can become independent learners and critical thinkers. We authors have a passionate commitment towards achieving this aim for our students, and this is what has sustained and motivated us to carry on with our enquiry projects.

A passion for the work that you do and a commitment to doing it better are two of the qualities that will help you to continue with your action research undertakings. Perseverance is another quality that would stand you in good stead, as it can be tempting to give up if the research is not progressing as you had expected. As we have emphasised throughout, another strategy that could motivate you towards continuation would be to live your educational values in your everyday practice. For example, if you hold ontological values, such as inclusion, social justice and equality, you may experience a strong desire or compulsion to have those values realised in your practice, and this could provide the impetus that you need to continue with your research. In this vignette from her PhD thesis, Roche (2007) explains how her quality of perseverance, coupled with an increase in her self-confidence, inspired her to continue with her research enquiry.

Vignette

I encountered several difficulties, not least my own lack of confidence around my practice. I was conscious that, in my new institutional context, my three colleagues had high standards of professionalism. At times I lost confidence and became fearful that I had been mistaken in considering my discrete classroom discussion circles an innovative practice and that facilitating them was, in fact, causing disruption. However, I did persevere with Thinking Time, and gradually my confidence in the programme as a means of establishing a culture of dialogue in my classroom was restored.

You may feel isolated and unsupported if you are engaging in an individual research project, and there may be times when you feel that you are ploughing a lonely furrow. However, the fact that you are working on your own does not preclude you from becoming part of a supportive environment. As we have mentioned in previous chapters, one of the features of an action research approach is that it is a collaborative undertaking, so it would be to your advantage to seek out like-minded and supportive colleagues who would be willing to collaborate with you. We authors provided support and encouragement for one another as we pursued our individual research studies. Our face-to-face meetings were infrequent, but the sense of social cohesion and emotional well-being engendered through shared concerns and constructive advice sustained us until the next meeting. In between meetings, we maintained contact by email and telephone conversations, through which we provided critical feedback on one another's work, seeking explanations and clarifications, and challenging new ideas as they emerged from our practice. In the process, we developed what was, in effect, a learning community, a phenomenon which we now discuss.

Learning communities contributing to the sustainability of your enhanced practice

At its most fundamental level, a learning community is a space where people come together to share their learning experiences with one another. The participants are usually colleagues with a common interest, who wish to explore areas of practical significance in a dialogical space. In this shared space, both fledgling and established ideas can be put out into a public domain, where they can be discussed and critiqued in a supportive environment. As learning communities are based on the idea of sharing knowledge with others, they tend to be characterised by qualities such as cooperation and collaboration. These qualities are also constituents of an action research approach, so it would seem that action research could be effectively and efficiently undertaken under the mantle of a learning community (see Glenn *et al.* forthcoming).

Learning is a social activity. We learn with and from one another, through our interactions and communications with other learners. Vygotsky (1978) views learning as a social constructivist activity in which one learner provides the necessary scaffolding to support the learning of another. Freire (2013: 101–2) also acknowledges the value of social communication when he says, 'Dialogue is the loving encounter of people, who, mediated by the world, "proclaim" that world.' Through your involvement in a learning community, you can create a space where you can exchange your ideas with others and communicate your meanings to them. There are various methods of achieving this, such as face-to-face meetings, teach meets, research meets, blogs, discussion groups, emails, online shared documents, networks and Skype conversations, among others. The dialogue that ensues, as ideas are teased out, deconstructed and modified, can add significantly to your learning experience. You will also benefit through obtaining a different perspective on your views, as others give their critical opinions on them.

It is important that a learning community is underpinned by a number of guiding principles, to ensure that it benefits all participants. An understanding of group dynamics is essential to the smooth running of a learning community. Relationships are at the heart of learning communities, and these need to be conducted in a spirit of mutual respect, trust and honesty. Members of a learning community need to feel safe and secure when they put forward their ideas for scrutiny in a public forum. They also need to feel that their individual contributions are welcomed, appreciated and treated in a respectful manner. Values of equality and fairness should be evident in the conduct of activities in a learning community, so that all participants can share a sense of belonging and of ownership of the process. Participants also need to feel empowered by their experience of belonging to the learning community, and to feel that their voices are being listened to. The values that underpin your action research would also be appropriate as the guiding principles for framing learning communities.

Wenger (1998) has written widely about learning communities, or communities of practice, which, he says, are groups of people who share a concern or a passion for something they do, and who learn how to do it better as they interact regularly. According to Wenger, communities of practice require a shared domain of interest, to which members are committed, and in which they value each other's contributions and learn from each other. Members of communities of practice engage in joint activities and discussions, help each other, share information, interact with each other and learn together. Members can be described as practitioners who share resources: tools, experiences, stories and ways of addressing problems.

Establishing learning communities in your workplace

If there is not in existence a learning community in your area of interest, you could begin the process of establishing one. If you have enlisted the services of a critical friend or colleagues for the purpose of providing critical feedback on your research, they may be willing to participate in a learning community. Forming a learning community is not a difficult task, but it needs to be structured carefully to ensure its continuity and sustainability. Bear in mind that communication can be face-to-face or online. The following guidelines could help you in this endeavour:

- Make contact with colleagues who share your interest in improving practice through action research
- Agree a date, time and place for an initial meeting of all interested parties
- Have an agenda in place for the first meeting, if possible drawn up with the cooperation of others who have expressed an interest in the group
- At the first meeting, decide on the principles according to which the learning community will be organised
- Agree on the educational values that should underpin the thoughts and actions of the group.

The benefits of continuing to try to achieve improvement in your practice

Having set up a learning community, you will have in place a group of colleagues who, besides engaging in research to improve their own classroom practice, could have the potential to support you in your continuing research endeavours. The small-scale projects undertaken in the learning community can have a substantial influence on your learning and on the learning of your colleagues. Through sharing the narratives of your individual action research experiences, you and your fellow researchers are eminently positioned to contribute to the enhancement of classroom practice. The learning community, once it has been set up, should be relatively easy to maintain in existence, provided members can continue to remain focused on, and committed to, their objective of achieving improvement in their practice.

Some members of the learning community may wish to become part of a validation group, which, as we explained in Chapters 5 and 7, can be useful when you get to the stage of seeking evidence for your findings. It would be important, therefore, to keep the group informed of all aspects of your research and to invite their critical feedback on it at regular intervals. You could, for example, make a presentation of your research to the learning community, who could provide critical feedback, perhaps even conducting a mock viva, which would be of immense benefit if you were undertaking your research for academic accreditation.

Your participation in a learning community, and contributions to it, would benefit you in your efforts to fulfil your action research commitments. You would have a sounding board for your emergent ideas and would be able to get critical and honest feedback on these ideas. In this scenario, you would be able to continue with your action research projects on a long-term basis, with the support and cooperation of the learning community. You could then be said to have achieved sustainability of improvement in your educational practice. You would also have ample opportunity for influencing the thinking and learning of the other members of the community. This would enable you to provide evidence of your influence on the education of social formations (Whitehead 2000), which can add substance to the significance of your research.

Conclusion

In this chapter, we have given detailed guidelines for writing an account of your self-study action research project, both for publication purposes and for academic accreditation. We have outlined the specific requirements of academic institutions, and we have indicated the headings under which you could organise your research writing. You have been made aware of the importance of beginning the writing process at the earliest opportunity, so that you would be able to include your learning from undertaking the research in your written account, and to allow for redrafting of the report. Convinced of the importance of continuing the ethos of improvement in practice, we have discussed how you might engage in the sustainability of your action research. One approach to achieving continuity is the setting up of a learning community, and we have outlined the reciprocal benefits, to you and to the learning community, from participating in it.

In this chapter:

- You have become acquainted with the basic elements for writing up your action research document.
- You have acquired a structure for framing your research project.
- You have been made aware of the necessity for a drafting process.
- You have learned how to ensure the sustainability of research on your practice.
- You have been introduced to the idea of participation in a learning community.
- You have become aware of the significance of continuity of improvement.

Recommended reading and resources

Glenn, M., Roche, M., McDonagh, C. and Sullivan, B. (forthcoming) *Learning Communities in Educational Partnerships*, London: Bloomsbury.

McNiff, J. (2014) *Writing and Doing Action Research*, London: Sage.

McNiff, J. and Whitehead, J. (2009) *Doing and Writing Action Research*, London: Sage.

Polanyi, M. (1958) *Personal Knowledge: Towards a Post Critical Philosophy*, London: Routledge and Kegan Paul.

Wenger, E. (1998) *Communities of Practice: Learning, Meaning and Identity*, Cambridge: Cambridge University Press.

Whitehead, J. (2000) 'How Do I Improve My Practice? Creating and Legitimating an Epistemology of Practice', *Reflective Practice*, 1(1), 91-104.

www.alarassociation.org/pages/education

Conclusion

Now that we have finished writing our book, we take time once more to pause and reflect on the process. Our purpose in writing it was to enhance the learning experience for you, our reader, as you undertook critical reflection and action on your educational practice. It has also been a learning experience for us, as authors. Teasing out our ideas, as we articulated them through our writing, has clarified our thinking around the potential of action research to promote critical self-reflection for teacher researchers. As you will have gathered from reading our book, self-study action research has the potential to be a rigorous and robust methodology and, when undertaken with sincerity and integrity, it can be a life-changing and life-enhancing experience for the committed researcher.

We hope that the structure of this book supported you, as a teacher researching your practice, with the aim of improving it. The format we used was designed to track the path you might follow if you wished to undertake an action research project. We explained that your research may not necessarily follow a smooth path from beginning to end, but that you would probably encounter many twists and turns along the way. These divergent paths contribute to the idea of action research as a cyclical, rather than a linear, process and have the potential to add to your learning experience from engaging in your research.

We reminded you that teacher researchers are in a unique position to conduct insider action research. We looked at how critical reflection could be embedded in your everyday practice. We explored the notion of reflective practice and its implications for us as teacher researchers. We believe that engaging in action research on your practice has the potential to rekindle and sustain the enthusiasm you felt when you began your professional journey as a teacher.

As we took you through the practicalities of critically reflecting on your practice from different perspectives, we engaged in the process of exploring your values and forming a focus for your research. We helped you to establish the groundwork for your project. The preparatory stages included examining concepts such as meta-reflection, experiencing oneself as a living contradiction or identifying areas of practice that are not commensurate with your values. We subscribe to the view that every project has to be based on firm foundations of critical analysis and the articulation of values as overarching principles of practice.

We made suggestions as to how you might develop an action plan. This involved showing how to gather data in a consistent and thorough way, and in a manner that would reflect a critical approach to the process. We discussed how you could use data to generate evidence of your new learning. We believe that the approaches we have suggested will ensure rigour and validity in your classroom-based research. The new learning that emerges from your research has the potential to empower teacher researchers to become creators of theory and to contribute to the knowledge base of the teaching profession.

The teacher researcher as an agent of change is an important aspect of the action research process. We outlined how the teacher researcher can enact change leading to improvement in their own practice or in their understanding of it. This process is significant in that it has the potential for you to have an influence not only on your own learning, but also on that of your students, your colleagues and the wider educational community. You were given practical advice on how to present a written report of your action research project. We indicated how you could share your new learning with others through participating in a learning community. We are convinced of the significance of engaging in dialogue as a means of continuing professional conversations and extending your learning.

In this book we have taken care not to be prescriptive, but, in order to provide a structure for your research project, we have introduced you to our personal model for framing your research. We have taken care in explaining the various stages of our model, such as how to identify your educational values, how to formulate a research question, what critical engagement with the literature involves, the importance of critical self-reflection right from the outset, the necessity of keeping a reflective journal from the start of the process, how to collect and analyse various forms of data, how to articulate your findings and the process of developing new theory from your learning through carrying out your research.

Our approach to action research is one based on the concept of developing theory from your practice, rather than applying existing theory to your practice, which is often a characteristic of traditional forms of research. Academic researchers operating out of a traditional paradigm believe that it is their remit to develop or create new theory, and that the role of practitioners is to implement that theory in their practice. We would be strong advocates of the view that practitioner researchers are eminently capable of, and qualified to, create their own theories from their practice. This view has been one of the core tenets of this book, and we hope that we have inspired you, the reader, to see yourself as a knowledge creator and theory developer. This stance can be expanded to the extent that you might regard your research participants as co-researchers and, therefore, co-creators of knowledge in partnership with you.

We place great emphasis on the significance of action research as a sustainable form of continuing professional development (CPD) for the teacher researcher. We have indicated the potential influence of an individual teacher's action research project on wider social and educational practices. We firmly believe that it is important for teacher researchers to have a space wherein they can participate in professional conversations around their educational practice. It is widely acknowledged that teachers can enhance their learning through discussions with colleagues (Clark 2001; Glenn *et al.* 2012), but finding opportunities to do so can often be a problem. With this in mind, we have suggested that forming learning communities could fill the lacuna that currently exists for many teachers in this area.

Teachers who participate in learning communities are open to experiencing a sense of cooperation and collaboration in a supportive and inclusive environment where all opinions and contributions are valued. Some of the benefits engendered through a collaborative approach by participants in learning communities are articulated by Zuber-Skerritt *et al.* (2015: 36): 'As we engage collaboratively with communities, we co-create knowledge; we research new contextually and culturally relevant ways to improve social circumstances.' This idea of creating spaces to become communities of learning and enquiry will be the focus of our next book (Glenn *et al.* forthcoming). Because we perceive action research as an ongoing process and as a dialogue between everyone who is interested in action research and who participates in it, we invite you to continue the conversations that have begun in this book – on our blog at http://www.eariblog.edublogs.com and our website at http://www.eari.ie

Throughout this book we have encouraged you to reflect critically on your own day-to-day practice as well as on wider contexts of education. We have encouraged you to engage in theorising your own practice. In so doing, we hope that the knowledge you have generated for yourself will have implications for you personally and professionally, as well as for the 'macro' of education – beginning, perhaps, with your own school context, and maybe even broadening out to include the wider educational context and the profession as a whole. We have encouraged you to become the kind of professional who is a generator of educational theory, and an agent of change and transformation.

If we take our professional development seriously and we critically reflect on our practice in order to continuously seek to become better at what we do, while all the while trying to deepen our understanding of what we do and why, then we are well on the way to becoming the kind of a professional who is an effective, reflective, enquiring and transformative teacher. We may find too, what Arendt (1958: 30) calls a 'sphere of freedom' and become what Greene (1988: 3) calls more than our 'minimal selves'. We each want to make student learning our central focus, to help each individual become their best selves, so we research our practice and critically reflect so as to strengthen our scholarship and creative work all the time with a bigger picture in view.

And we ask you, finally, now to pause and reflect, and decide for yourself: what is education all about? Why should I try to become a better educator? And that brings us right back to where we began – to our educational values.

Bibliography

Alderson, P. and Morrow, V. (2011) *The Ethics of Research with Children and Young People: A Practical Handbook*, London: Sage.

Alexakos, K. (2015) *Being a Teacher/Researcher: A Primer in Doing Authentic Inquiry Research on Teaching and Learning*, Rotterdam: Sense.

Alhadeff, M. (2003) 'Rethinking Transformative Learning and the concept of "Critical Reflection" through the Paradigm of Complexity'. Paper presented at the 5th International Transformative Learning Conference 'Transformative Learning in action: Building Bridges Across Contexts and Disciplines', Teachers College, Columbia University, New York.

Altrichter, H., Posch, P. and Somekh, B. (2005) *Teachers Investigate Their Work: An Introduction to the Methods of Action Research*, London: Routledge.

Altrichter, H., Feldman, A., Posch, P. and Somekh, B. (2008) *Teachers Investigate Their Work: An Introduction to Action Research Across the Professions*, 2nd edn, Abingdon: Routledge.

Arendt, H. (1958) *The Human Condition*, Chicago: University of Chicago Press.

Argyris, C. and Schön, D. (1978) *Organizational Learning: A Theory of Action Perspective*, Reading, MA: Addison Wesley.

Association of American Educators (1994-2014) *Code of Ethics for Educators*, Association of American Educators Advisory Board, California. Available at http://www.aaeteachers.org/

Australian Government (2007, updated May 2015) *National Statement on Ethical Conduct in Human Research*, Canberra: NHMRC and Australian Research Council.

Ballantine, J. H. and Spade, J. Z. (2015) *Schools and Society: A Sociological Approach to Education*, Thousand Oaks, CA: Sage.

Bassey, M. (1990) *On the Nature of Research in Education*, Nottingham: Nottingham Polytechnic.

Bassey, M. (1999) *Case Study Research in Educational Settings*, Birmingham: Open University Press.

Bentley, T. (1998) *Learning Beyond the Classroom*, London: Routledge.

Berlin, I. (2000) *The Power of Ideas*, ed. H. Hardy, London: Chatto and Windus.

Biesta, G. (2014) 'Who Knows? The Ongoing Need to ask Critical Questions About the Turn Towards', in K. B. Petersen, D. Reimer and A. Qvortrup (eds) *Evidence-based Education in Denmark: The Current Debate*, CURSIV, Aarhus University: Department of Education (DPV).

Bloom, B. S. (ed.) (1956) *Taxonomy of Educational Objectives, Handbook I: The Cognitive Domain*, New York: David McKay Co. Inc.

Bohm, D. (2004) *On Dialogue*, London: Routledge.

Bolton, G. (2014) *Reflective Practice: Writing and Professional Development*, 4th edn, Los Angeles and London: Sage.

Boud, D. (2010) 'Relocating Reflection in the Context of Practice', in H. Bradbury, N. Frost, S. Kilminster and M. Zukas (eds) (2010), *Beyond Reflective Practice: New Approaches to Professional Lifelong Learning*, Abingdon: Routledge.

Boud, D. and Walker, D. (1998) 'Promoting Reflection in Professionals Courses: The Challenge of Context', *Studies in Higher Education*, 23(2), 191-206.

Bourke, R. and Loveridge, J. (2014) 'Exploring Informed Consent and Dissent Through Children's Participation in Educational Research', *International Journal of Research & Method in Education*, April, 37(2), 151-65.

Bradbury, H. (ed.) (2015) *The Sage Handbook of Action Research*, 3rd edn, London: Sage.

Briggs, A. R. J. and Coleman, M. (2007) *Research Methods in Educational Leadership*, London: Sage.

British Education Research Association (BERA) (2014) *Research and the Teaching Profession: Building the Capacity for a Self-improving Education System - Final Report of the BERA-RSA Inquiry into the Role of Research in Teacher Education*, London: BERA.

Britzman, D. P. (2003) *Practice makes Practice: A Critical Study of Learning to Teach*, Albany: State University of New York.

Broch, H. B. (2014) 'Anthropological Field Experiences from Work with Children in Natural Settings on Three Continents', in H. Fossheim (ed.), *Cross-Cultural Child Research Ethical Issues*, Norway: Norwegian National Research Ethics Committees, pp. 45-71.

Brookfield, S. (1995) *Becoming a Critically Reflective Teacher*, San Francisco: Jossey-Bass.

Brookfield, S. (2000) 'The Concept of Critically Reflective Practice', in A. L. Wilson and E. R. Hayes (eds), *Handbook of Adult and Continuing Education*, San Francisco: Jossey-Bass.

Brookfield, S. (2009) 'The Concept of Critical Reflection: Promises and Contradictions', *European Journal of Social Work*, 12(3), 293-304.

Brookfield, S. (2012) *Teaching for Critical Thinking: Tools and Techniques to Help Students Question their Assumptions*, San Francisco: Jossey-Bass.

Brookfield, S. (2014), in G. Bolton, *Reflective Practice: Writing and Professional Development*, 4th edn, Los Angeles and London: Sage, pp. xiii-xiv.

Bruce Ferguson, P. (2015) 'Who am I Who Teaches?' *Educational Journal of Living Theories*, 8(1), 49-66.

Brydon-Miller, M., Greenwood, D. and Maguire, P. (2003) 'Why Action Research?', *Action Research*, 1(1), 9-28.

Buber, M. (1958) *I and Thou*, 2nd edn, Edinburgh: T. and T. Clark.

Bullough, R. V. and Pinnegar, S. (2004) 'Thinking about the Thinking about Self-study: An Analysis of Eight Chapters', in J. J. Loughran, M. L. Hamilton, V. K. LaBoskey and T. Russell (eds), *International Handbook of Self-study of Teaching and Teacher Education Practices*, 1, 313-42.

Burbules, N. C. and Berk, R. (1999) 'Critical Thinking and Critical Pedagogy: Relations, Differences, and Limits', in T. S. Popkewitz and L. Fendler (eds), *Critical Theories in Education, Changing Terrains of Knowledge and Politics*, London: Routledge.

Carr, W. and Kemmis, S. (1986) *Becoming Critical: Education, Knowledge and Action Research*, London: RoutledgeFalmer.

Carroll, T. W. and Gutmann, M. P. (2011) 'The Limits of Autonomy: The Belmont Report and the History of Childhood', *Journal of the History of Medicine and Allied Sciences*, 66(1), 82-115.

Centre for Children and Young People, Southern Cross University, Childwatch International Research Network, Unicef Office of Research, University of Ontago New Zealand (2013) *Ethical Research Involving Children: Research Support*. Available at childethics.com/wp-content/uploads/2013/10/ERIC-compendium-Researcher-support-section-only.pdf

Chomsky, N. (2000) *Chomsky on Miseduation*, Oxford: Rowman and Littlefield.

Chomsky, N. (2013) *The Purpose of Education* [online]. Available at http://www.thedailyriff.com/articles/noam-chomsky-the-purpose-of-education-869.php. Accessed 18 July 2015.

Clark, C. (ed.) (2001) *Talking Shop: Authentic Conversation and Teacher Learning*, New York: Teachers College Press.

Cloninger, K. (2006) 'Making Institution Practical', *Curriculum & Teaching Dialogue*, 81(2), 15-28.

Cochran-Smith, M. and Lytle, S. L. (2009a) *Inquiry as Stance: Practitioner Research for the Next Generation*, New York: Teachers College Press.

Cochran-Smith, M., and Lytle, S. L. (2009b) 'Teacher Research as Stance', in S. Noffke and B. Somekh, *The Sage Handbook of Educational Action Research*, London: Sage.

Coghlan, D. and Brannick, T. (2014) *Doing Action Research in your own Organization*, 4th edn, London: Sage.

Cohen, L., Manion, L. and Morrison, K. (2007) *Research Methods in Education*, 6th edn, Abingdon and New York: Routledge.

Cohen, L., Manion, L. and Morrison, K. (2011) *Research Methods in Education*, 7th edn, Abingdon: Routledge.

Connell, R. W. (1993) *Schools and Social Justice*, Philadelphia: Temple University Press.

Cook, T. (2009) 'The Purpose of Mess in Action Research: Building Rigour through a Messy Turn', *Educational Action Research*, 17(2), 277-91.

Cox, S. and Robinson-Pant, A. (2008) 'Power, Participation and Decision Making in the Primary Classroom: Children as Action Researchers', *Educational Action Research*, 16(4), 457-68.

Cremin, T. (2011) 'Reading Teachers/Teaching Readers: Why Teachers Who Read Make Good Teachers of Reading', *English Drama Media*, 19, 11-18.

Dadds, M. (1993) 'The Feeling of Thinking in Professional Self-study', *Educational Action Research*, 1(2), 287-303.

Dadds, M. (2001) 'The Politics of Pedagogy', *Teachers and Teaching: Theory and Practice*, 7(1), 43-58.

Dadds, M. and Hart, S. (2001) *Doing Practitioner-based Research Differently*, London: RoutledgeFalmer.

Dalli, C. and Te One, S. (2012) 'Involving Children in Educational Research: Researcher Reflections on Challenges', *International Journal of Early Years Education*, 20(3), 224-33.

Darder, A., Baltodano, M. and Torres, R. D. (eds) (2003) *The Critical Pedagogy Reader*, New York and London: Routledge.

David, M., Edwards, R. and Alldred, P. (2001) 'Children and School-based Research: "Informed Consent" or "Educated Consent"?', *British Educational Research Journal*, 27(3), 347-65.

Day, C. (2004) *A Passion for Teaching*, London: RoutledgeFalmer.

Day, C. (2012) 'New Lives of Teachers', *Teacher Education Quarterly*, Winter, 6-26.

Dewey, J. (1933) *How We Think: A Restatement of the Relation of Reflective Thinking to the Educative Process*, Chicago: Henry Regnery.

Dewey, J. (1966) *Democracy and Education*, New York: Free Press.

Drudy, S. and Lynch, K. (1993) *Schools and Society in Ireland*, Dublin: Gill and Macmillan.

Di Stefano, G., Gino, F., Pisano, G. and Staats, B. (2015) *Learning by Thinking: Overcoming The Bias For Action Through Reflection*, Harvard Business School NOM Unit Working Paper No. 14-093, Harvard Business School Technology and Operations. Available at http://papers.ssrn.com/sol3/papers.cfm?abstract_id=2414478. Accessed October 2015.

Dick, B. (2002) *Action Research* [online]. Available at http://www.alarassociation.org/pages/al-and-ar/action-research. Accessed 18 July 2015.

Duncan, R., Drew, S., Hodgson, J. and Sawyer, S. (2009) 'Is My Mum Going to Hear This? Methodological and Ethical Challenges in Qualitative Health Research with Young People', *Social Science and Medicine*, 69, 1691-9.

Dyment, J. and O'Connell, T. (2011) 'Assessing the Quality of Reflection in Student Journals: A Review of the Research', *Teaching In Higher Education*, 16(1), 81-97.

Economic and Social Research Council (ESRC) (2010, updated 2015) ESRC Framework for Research Ethics. Available at http://www.esrc.ac.uk/

Education Act 1998 (1998) No. 51/1998, Dublin: Stationery Office.

Elliott, J. (1978) 'What is Action Research in Schools?', *Journal of Curriculum Studies*, 10(4), 355-7.

Elliott, J. (1990) 'Teachers as Researchers: Implications for Supervision and for Teacher Education', *Teaching and Teacher Education*, 6, 1-26.

Elliott, J. (1991) *Action Research for Educational Change*, Milton Keynes: Open University Press.

Elliott, J. (2007) 'Assessing the Quality of Action Research', *Research Papers in Education*, 22(2), 229-46.

Foucault, M. (1980) *Power/Knowledge: Selected Interviews and Other Writings 1971-1977*, trans. C. Gordon, Brighton: Harvester.

Freire, P. (1972) *Pedagogy of the Oppressed*, London: Sheed and Ward.

Freire, P. (1973) *Cultural Action for Freedom*, Harmondsworth: Penguin.

Freire, P. (2003) 'From Pedagogy of the Oppressed', in A. Darder, M. Baltodano and R. D. Torres (eds), *The Critical Pedagogy Reader*, London: Routledge, pp. 57-68.

Freire, P. (2013) *Education for Critical Consciousness*, London: Bloomsbury.

Garrison, D. R. (1991). 'Critical Thinking and Adult Education: A Conceptual Model for Developing Critical Thinking in Adult Learners', *International Journal of Lifelong Education*, 10(4), 287-303.

Garvis, S., Ødegaard, E. E. and Lemon, N. (2015) *Beyond Observations: Narratives and Young Children*, Rotterdam: Sense.

Gibbs, G. (1988) *Learning by Doing: A Guide to Teaching and Learning Methods*, Oxford: Further Education Unit.

Glenn, M. (2006) 'Working with Collaborative Projects: My Living Theory of a Holistic Educational Practice', unpublished PhD thesis, University of Limerick. Available at http://www.eari.ie

Glenn, M. (2011) 'Developing Holistic Practice Through Reflection, Action and Theorising', *Educational Action Research*, 19(4), 489-502.

Glenn, M. (2015) 'Session 3: Practitioner Research', MTeach, Module 2, Professional Practitioner Research Methods I, 23 October, St Patrick's College, Drumcondra, unpublished.

Glenn, M., McDonagh, C., Roche, M. and Sullivan, B. (2008) 'Exploring Practitioner-based Action Research for the Ongoing Professional Development of Teachers as we Create a New Knowledge Base for the Teaching Profession', paper presented at Education Studies Ireland Conference, Galway, March.

Glenn, M., McDonagh, C., Sullivan, B. and Roche, M., with Morgan, M. (2012) *Practice-based Research Encompassing Professional Development Project: Action Research Supported by the Teaching Council of Ireland* [online]. Available on www.eari.ie and http://www.teachingcouncil.ie/en/Publications/Research/Documents/Practice-based-Research-Encompassing-Professional-Development-Project.pdf

Glenn, M., Roche, M., McDonagh, C. and Sullivan, B. (forthcoming) *Learning Communities in Educational Partnerships*, London: Bloomsbury.

Gore, J. M. (1993) *The Struggle for Pedagogies, Critical and Feminist Discourses as Regimes of Truth*, New York: Routledge.

Government of Ireland, Data Protection Act (1988 and 2003, updated 2014) *Number 25 of 1988 Data Protection Act 1988 Revised Updated to 14 October 2014*, Dublin: Government Publication.

Government of Scotland (2010) *Literature Review on Teacher Education in the 21st Century* [online]. Available at http://www.gov.scot/Publications/2010/09/24144019/0. Accessed 2 November 2015.

Gramsci, A. (1971) *Selections from the Prison Notebooks*, London: Lawrence and Wishart.

Greene, M. (1978) *Landscapes of Learning*, New York: Teachers College Press.

Greene, M. (1984) 'How Do We Think About Our Craft?', *Teachers College Record*, 86(1), 55–67.

Greene, M. (1988) *The Dialectic of Freedom*, John Dewey Lecture Series, New York: Teachers College Press.

Greene, M. (1995) *Releasing the Imagination: Essays on Education, The Arts and Social Change*, San Francisco: Jossey-Bass.

Greene, M. (2001) *Variations on a Blue Guitar*, The Lincoln Center Institute Lectures on Aesthetic Education, New York: Teachers College Press.

Greenwood, D. J. and Levin, M. (2014) *Introduction to Action Research: Social Research for Social Change*, 2nd edn, Thousand Oaks, CA: Sage.

Griffiths, M. (1998) *Educational Research for Social Justice: Getting Off the Fence*, Buckingham: Open University Press.

Guba, E. G. and Lincoln, Y. S. (1989) *Fourth Generation Evaluation*, Beverly Hills, CA: Sage.

Habermas, J. (1976) *Communication and the Evolution of Society*, trans. McCarthy (1979), London: Beacon Press.

Habermas, J. (1987) *The Theory of Communicative Action, Volume Two: The Critique of Functionalist Reason*, Oxford: Polity Press.

Hadfield, M. (2014) 'Becoming Critical Again: Reconnecting Critical Social Theory with the Practice of Action Research', *Educational Action Research*, 20(4), 471–585.

Hammersley, M. (1993) 'On the Teacher as Researcher', *Educational Action Research*, 1(3), 425–45.

Harford, J., Hudson, B. and Niemi, H. (eds) (2012) *Quality Assurance and Teacher Education: International Challenges and Expectations*, Bern: Peter Lang.

Hatton, N. and Smith, D. (1995) 'Reflection in Teacher Education: Definition and Implementation', *Teaching and Teacher Education*, 11(1), 33–49.

Hayes, K. Steinberg, S. and Tobin, K. (eds) (2011) *Key Works in Critical Pedagogy: Joe L. Kincheloe*, Rotterdam: Sense.

Hayes, C., Daly, J., Duncan, M., Gill, R. and Whitehouse, A. (2014) *Developing as a Reflective Early Years Professional*, Northwich: Critical.

Hocking, B., Haskell, J. and Linds, W. (2001) *Unfolding Bodymind*, Vermont: Foundation for Educational Renewal.

hooks, b. (2003) *Teaching Community: A Pedagogy of Hope*, New York: Routledge.

Hopkins, D. (2014) *A Teacher's Guide to Classroom Research*, 5th edn, Maidenhead: Open University Press.

Hoyle, E. (1975) 'Professionality, Professionalism and Control in Teaching', in V. Houghton, R. McHugh and C. Morgan (eds), *Management in Education: The Management of Organisations and Individuals*, London: Ward Lock Educational in association with Open University Press.

Humphreys, J. (2015) *Unthinkable: Great Ideas for Now*, Dublin: Irish Times Books.

Ireland, Department of Children and Youth Affairs (DCYA) (2011) *Children First: National Guidance for the Protection and Welfare of Children*, Dublin: Government Publications.

Ireland, Department of Education and Science (1999) *Primary School Curriculum*, Dublin: Government Publications.

Ireland, Department of Education and Skills (2014) *Further Education and Training Strategy 2014-2019*. Available at https://www.education.ie/en/Publications/Policy-Reports/Further-Education-and-Training-Strategy-2014-2019

Kasl, E. and Yorks, L. (2002) 'An Extended Epistemology for Transformative Learning Theory and Its Application through Collaborative Inquiry', *TC Record Online*. Available at http://www.tcrecord.org/Content.asp?ContentID=10878. Accessed October 2015.

Kellett, M. (2005) *Children as Action Researchers: A New Paradigm for the 21st Century?*, ESRC. Available at http://www.ncb.org.uk/media/895543/children_as_active_researchers_m_kellett_2005.pdf

Kemmis, S. (2009) 'Action Research as a Practice based Practice', *Educational Action Research*, 17(3), 463-74.

Kemmis, S. and McTaggart, R. (eds) (1988) *The Action Research Planner*, 3rd edn, Victoria: Deakin University Press.

Kemmis, S., McTaggart, R. and Nixon, R. (2014) *The Action Research Planner: Doing Critical Participatory Action Research*, Singapore: Springer-Verlag.

Kenny, M. (1997) *The Routes of Resistance: Travellers and Second-Level Schooling*, Aldershot: Ashgate.

Kincheloe, J. L. (1991) *Teachers as Researchers: Qualitative Paths to Empowerment*, New York: Falmer.

Kincheloe, J. L. (2003) *Teachers as Researchers: Qualitative Inquiry as a Path to Empowerment*, 2nd edn, London: Routledge.

Kincheloe, J. (2004) *Critical Pedagogy*, New York: Peter Lang.

Kincheloe, J. and Berry, K (2004) *Rigour and Complexity in Educational Research: Conceptualizing the Bricolage*, Columbus, OH: McGraw Hill.

Kolb, D. A. (1984) *Experiential Learning*, Englewood Cliffs, NJ: Prentice Hall.

Koshy, V. (2010) *Action Research for Improving Educational Practice: A Step-by-Step Guide*, London: Sage.

Kristeva, J. and Lechte, J. (2002) 'Interview: Sharing Singularity', in J. Lechte and M. Margaroni (eds) (2004), *Julie Kristeva: Live Theory*, London: Continuum, pp. 143-63.

Labov, W. (1973) 'The Logic of Nonstandard English', in N. Keddie (ed.), *Tinker, Tailor: The Myth of Cultural Deprivation*, London: Penguin.

Larrivee, B. (2000) 'Transforming Teaching Practice: Becoming the Critically Reflective Teacher', *Reflective Practice*, 1(3), 293-307.

Lassonde, C. A., Galman, S. and Kosnik, C. (2009) *Self-Study Research Methodologies for Teacher Educators*, Rotterdam: Sense.

Lindsey, D., Lindsey, B., Hord, S. and von Frank, V. (2015) *Reach the Highest Standard in Professional Learning: Outcomes*, Thousand Oaks, CA: Corwin Press.

Lingard, B. and Renshaw, P. (2009) 'Teaching as a Research-informed and Research- informing Profession', in A. Campbell and S. Groundwater-Smith (eds), *Connecting Inquiry and Professional Learning*, London: Routledge, pp. 26-39.

Lomax, P. (1994) 'Standards, Criteria and the Problematic of Action Research within an Award Bearing Course', *Educational Action Research*, 2(1), 113-26.

Lortie, D. (1975) *Schoolteacher: A Sociological Study*, London: University of Chicago Press.

Loughran, J. (2002) 'Effective Reflective Practice: In Search of Meaning in Learning about Technology', *Journal of Teacher Education*, 53(1), 33-43.

Loughran, J. (2006) *Developing a Pedagogy of Teacher Education: Understanding Teaching and Learning about Teaching*, Abingdon: Routledge.

MacDonald, K. and Greggans, A. (2008) 'Dealing with Chaos and Complexity: The Reality of Interviewing Children and Families in Their Own Homes', *Journal of Clinical Nursing*, 17, 3123-30.

MacLure, M. (1996) 'Telling Transitions: Boundary Work in Narratives of Becoming an Action Researcher', *British Educational Research Journal*, 22(3), 273-83.

Marshall, J., Coleman, G. and Reason, P. (2011) *Leadership for Sustainability*, Sheffield: Greenleaf.

McDonagh, C. (2003) 'Presenting Voice in Action Research', paper presented at the Invitational Seminar 'Critical Debates in Action Research', 8-10 May, University of Limerick. Available at www.jeanmcniff.com

McDonagh, C. (2004) 'Learning With and From Pupils', paper presented at the American Educational Research Association Annual Meeting as part of the interactive symposium, 'Self-Study of Teacher Education Practices: The Transformative Potentials of Individuals', Collaborative Self-Studies for Sustainable Global Networks of Communication, San Diego 16 April.

McDonagh, C. (2007) 'My Living Theory of Learning to Teach for Social Justice: How do I Enable Primary School Children with Specific Learning Disability (Dyslexia) and Myself as their Teacher to Realise our Learning Potentials?', unpublished PhD thesis, University of Limerick. Available at http://www.eari.ie

McDonagh, C. and Sullivan, B. (2003) 'Making the Invisible Visible: Giving a Voice to the Marginalised', paper presented at the Collaborative Action Research Network Conference, Manchester, September.

McDonagh, C., Roche, M., Sullivan, B. and Glenn, M. (2012) *Enhancing Practice through Classroom Research: A Teacher's Guide to Professional Development*, Abingdon: Routledge.

McDonagh, C., Sullivan, B. and Roche, M. (2015) 'Self-Study Action Research Project Workshop', Module MB5033: Pedagogy, National Centre for Excellence for Maths and Science Teaching and Learning, University of Limerick, unpublished.

McIntosh, P. (2010) *Action Research and Reflective Practice: Creative and Visual Methods to Facilitate Reflection and Learning*, London: Routledge.

McLaren, P. (1999) 'A Pedagogy of Possibility: Reflecting Upon Paulo Freire's Politics of Education', *Educational Researcher*, March, 49–54.

McLaughlin, C. (2004) 'Partners in Research: What's in it for You?', *Teacher Development*, 8(2 and 3), 127–36.

McMahon, T. and Jefford, E. (2009) 'Assessing Action-research Projects within Formal Academic Programmes: Using Elliott's Context-related Criteria to Resolve the Rigour Versus Flexibility Dilemma', *Educational Action Research*, 17(3), 359–71.

McNiff, J. (2002a) 'What Peace Means for Us, What Conflict Means for Us: Understanding Education for Mutual Understanding in the Northern Ireland Curriculum', paper presented to the Special Interest Group Peace Education at the American Educational Research Association Annual Meeting, New Orleans, 1–5 April. Available at http://www.jeanmcniff.com/items.asp?id=37

McNiff, J. (2002b) *Action Research for Professional Development*. Available at http://jeanmcniff.com/ar-booklet.asp. Accessed 31 July 2015.

McNiff, J. (2005) 'Pedagogy, Theory of Mind, and Educative Influence: How do I Contribute to the Education of Sustainable Social Formations?', paper presented at the EARLI Conference SIG Invited Symposium, Teaching and Teacher Education, Demonstrating Accountability Through our Self-study Practices as Teacher Educators? Nicosia. Available at http://www.jeanmcniff.com/items.asp?id=59. Accessed 14 September 2005.

McNiff, J. (2013) *Action Research: Principles and Practice*, 3rd edn, Abingdon: Routledge.

McNiff, J. (2014) *Writing and Doing Action Research*, London: Sage.

McNiff, J. and Whitehead, J. (2002) *Action Research: Principles and Practice*, London: RoutledgeFalmer.

McNiff, J. and Whitehead, J. (2006) *All You Need To Know About Action Research*, London: Sage.

McNiff, J. and Whitehead, J. (2009) *Doing and Writing Action Research*, London: Sage.

McNiff, J. and Whitehead, J. (2010) *You and Your Action Research Project*, 3rd edn, London: RoutledgeFalmer.

McNiff, J. and Whitehead, J. (2011) *All You Need to Know About Action Research*, 2nd edn, London and Thousand Oaks, CA: Sage.

McNiff, J., Lomax, P. and Whitehead, J. (1996) *You and Your Action Research Project*, London: Routledge and Hyde.

McTaggart, R. (1997) *Participatory Action Research: International Contexts and Consequences*, New York: State University of New York.

Meaux, J. B. and Bell, P. L. (2001) 'Balancing Recruitment and Protection: Children as Research Subjects', *Issues in Comprehensive Pediatric Nursing*, 14, 241–51.

Mellor, N. (1998) 'Notes from a Method', *Educational Action Research*, 6(3), 453–70.

Mellor, N. (2001) 'Messy Method: The Unfolding Story', *Educational Action Research*, 9(3), 465–84.

Mellor, N. (2015) *The Untidy Realities of Research*, PowerPoint: Slide 76. Available at https://sites.google.com/site/nigelsbitsandbobs/Home/messy-method--the-secrets-of-the-doctorate. Accessed 1 November 2015.

Mezirow, J. (1990) *Fostering Critical Reflection in Adulthood: A Guide to Transformative and Participatory Learning*, San Francisco: Jossey-Bass.

Mezirow, J. (1991) *Transformative Dimensions of Adult Learning*, San Francisco: Jossey-Bass.

Mezirow, J. (1998) 'On Critical Reflection', *Adult Education Quarterly*, 48(3), 185–98.

Mezirow J. (2000) 'Learning to Think Like an Adult', in J. Mezirow and Associates, *Learning as Transformation: Critical Perspectives on a Theory in Process*, San Francisco: Jossey-Bass, pp. 3–33.

Mills, G. E. (2011). *Action Research: A Guide for the Teacher Researcher*, 3rd edn, Upper Saddle River, NJ: Merrill/Prentice Hall.

Mockler, N. (2014) 'When "Research Ethics" become "Everyday Ethics": The Intersection of Inquiry and Practice in Practitioner Research', *Educational Action Research*, 22(2), 146–58.

Moon, J. (1999) *Reflection in Learning and Professional Development: Theory and Practice*, London: Kogan Page.

Moon, J. A. (2001a) *Learning Journals: A Handbook for Reflective Practice and Professional Development*, London: Routledge.

Moon, J. A. (2001b) *Reflection in Higher Education Learning*, PDP Working Paper 4, Exeter: Learning and Teaching Support Network, University of Exeter. Available at http://www.sussex.ac.uk/education/ctlr/documents/jenny-moon-workshop---reflection-in-higher-education-learning.docx

Moon, J. A. (2004) *A Handbook of Reflective and Experiential Learning: Theory and Practice*, Oxford: RoutledgeFalmer.

Morrison, M. (2007) 'What Do We Mean by Educational Research?', in A. Briggs and M. Coleman, *Research Methods in Educational Leadership and Management*, London and Thousand Oaks, CA: Sage, pp. 13–35.

Morrow, V. and Richards, M. (1996) 'The Ethics of Social Research with Children: An Overview', *Children and Society*, 10, 90–105.

Moss, J. (ed.) (1998) *The Later Foucault*, London: Sage.

Nagel, T. (1986) *The View From Nowhere*, New York and Oxford: Oxford University Press.

National Commission for the Protection of Human Subjects (1977) *Research Involving Children: Report and Recommendations*, Washington: Dhew.

National Council for Curriculum and Assessment (2007) *Assessment in the Primary School* Available at http://www.ncca.ie/en/Curriculum_and_Assessment/Early_Childhood_and_Primary_Education/Primary-Education/Assessment/

Nias, J. (1996) 'Thinking about Feeling: The Emotions in Teaching', *Cambridge Journal of Education*, 26(3), 293–306.

Niemi, H. and Kemmis, S. (2012) 'Communicative Evaluation for Improvement in Education', in J. Harford, B. Hudson and H. Niemi (eds), *Quality Assurance and Teacher Education: International Challenges and Expectations*, Bern: Peter Lang, pp. 53–82.

Niemi, H., Harford, J. and Hudson, B. (2012) 'Introduction: From Quality Assurance to Quality Culture', in J. Harford, B. Hudson and H. Niemi (eds), *Quality Assurance and Teacher Education: International Challenges and Expectations*, Bern: Peter Lang, pp. 1–11.

Noddings, N. (1984) *Caring: A Feminine Approach to Ethics and Moral Education*, Berkeley: University of California Press.

Noddings, N. (1997) 'Accident, Awareness and Actualization', in A. Newmann and P. L. Peters (eds), *Learning From Our Lives: Women, Research and Autobiography in Education*, New York: Teachers College Press.

Noffke, S. E. (1997) 'Professional, Personal, and Political Dimensions of Action Research', in M. W. Apple (ed.), *Review of Research in Education*, Washington: American Educational Research Association.

Noffke, S. and Somekh, B. (2009) *The Sage Handbook of Educational Action Research*, London: Sage.

O'Donohue, J. (1999) *Anam Ćara: Spiritual Wisdom from the Celtic World*, London: Bantam Books.

OECD (2014) *TALIS 2013 Results: An International Perspective on Teaching and Learning*, Paris: OECD. Available at http://dx.doi.org/10.1787/9789264196261-en. Accessed 2 November 2015.

Office of Research Integrity and the Office for Human Research Protection (2014) *The Research Clinic* 9video). Available at https://www.youtube.com/watch?v=iUiosu0YlcQ

Ó Ruairc, T. (2014) 'The Preparation of Teachers for STEM Education in Ireland', proceedings in Teaching Council Public Consultation Forum on Review of STEM, Dublin, 17 April. Available at http://www.teachingcouncil.ie/en/Publications/Promoting-Teaching/education-papers

Oxford Dictionary of English (2010) 3rd edn, Stevenson, Oxford University Press Online, published 2010. Available at http://www.oxfordreference.com/view/10.1093/acref/9780199571123.001.0001/acref-9780199571123

Palmer, P. J. (1993) *To Know as We are Known: Education as a Spiritual Journey*, New York: HarperCollins.

Pine, G. J. (2009) *Teacher Action Research: Building Knowledge Democracies*, Thousand Oaks, CA: Sage.

Pinnegar, S. (1998) Introduction, in M. L. Hamilton (ed.), *Reconceptualizing Teaching Practice: Selfstudy in Teacher Education*, London: Falmer Press.

Polanyi, M. (1958) *Personal Knowledge*, London: Routledge and Kegan Paul.

Polanyi, M. (2009) *The Tacit Dimension*, Chicago: University of Chicago Press.

Pollard, A. (ed.) (2002) *Readings for the Reflective Practitioner*, London: Continuum.

Pollard, A., Anderson, J., Maddock, M., Swaffield, S., Warin, J. and Warwick, P. (2008) *Reflective Teaching*, 3rd edn, London: Continuum International.

Powell, M. A., Fitzgerald, R., Taylor, N. J. and Graham, A. (2012) *International Literature Review: Ethical Issues in Undertaking Research with Children and Young People* (Literature review for the Childwatch International Research Network). Lismore: Southern Cross University, Centre for Children and Young People/Dunedin: University of Otago, Centre for Research on Children and Families.

Progoff, I. (1992) *At a Journal Workshop: Writing to Access the Power of the Unconscious and Evoke Creative Ability*, Los Angeles: J. P. Tarcher.

Quinlan, O. (2014) *The Thinking Teacher*, Carmarthen: Independent Thinking Press.

Rabinow, P. (ed.) (1991) *The Foucault Reader: An Introduction to Foucault's Thought*, London: Penguin.

Rawls, J. (1971) *A Theory of Justice*, London: Oxford University Press.

Raz, J. (2001) *Value, Respect and Attachment*, Cambridge: Cambridge University Press.

Reason, P. and Bradbury, H. (eds) (2001) *Handbook of Action Research: Participative Inquiry and Practice*, London: Sage.

Reason, P. and Bradbury, H. (eds) (2008) *Handbook of Action Research: Participative Inquiry and Practice*, 2nd edn, London: Sage.

Reason, P. and Bradbury, H. (eds) (2013) *The Sage Handbook of Action Research: Participative Inquiry and Practice*, 3rd edn, London: Sage.

Reid Banks, L. (1982) *The Indian in the Cupboard*, New York: HarperCollins.

Riel, M. (2010) Understanding Action Research, Center for Collaborative Action Research, Pepperdine University (last revision September 2013) [online]. Available at http://cadres.pepperdine.edu/ccar/define.html. Accessed 30 October 2015.

Roche, M. (2000) 'How can I Improve My Practice so as to Help My Pupils to Philosophise?', Master of Arts dissertation, University of the West of England, Bristol. Available at http://www.eari.ie

Roche, M. (2007) 'Towards a Living Theory of Caring Pedagogy: Interrogating My Practice to Nurture a Critical, Emancipatory and Just Community of Enquiry', unpublished PhD thesis, University of Limerick. Available at http://www.eari.ie

Roche, M. (2011) 'Creating a Dialogical and critical classroom: reflection and action to improve practice', *Educational Action Research*, 19(3).

Roche, M. (2014) 'Developing Researcherly Dispositions in an Initial Teacher Education Context: Successes and Dilemmas', *International Journal for Transformative Research*, 1(1).

Roche, M. (2015) *Developing Children's Critical Thinking through Picturebooks: A Guide for Primary and Early Years Students and Teachers*, Abingdon: Routledge.

Rudduck, J. (1991) 'The Language of Consciousness and the Landscape of Action: Tensions in Teacher Education', *British Educational Research Journal*, 17(4).

Rudduck, J. and McIntyre, D. (2007) *Improving Learning Through Consulting Pupils*, London: Routledge.

Russell, B. (1971) *Education and the Social Order*, London: Unwin Books.

Sachs, J. (2003) *The Activist Teaching Profession*, Buckingham: Open University Press.

Said, E. (2002) *The End of the Peace Process*, 2nd edn, London: Granta Books.

Sartre, J. P. (1966) *Being and Nothingness*, London: Routledge.

Schön, D. A. (1983) *The Reflective Practitioner: How Professionals Think in Action*, New York: Basic Books.

Schön, D. A. (1995) 'Knowing-in-Action: The New Scholarship Requires a New Epistemology', *Change*, November/December, 27-34.

Schulte, A. K. (2002) 'Do As I Say!', *Making a Difference in Teacher Education through Self-Study*, proceedings from Herstmonceux IV: The 4th International Conference on Self-Study of Teacher Education Practices, Vol. 2, August, Herstmonceux Castle, East Sussex, 101-6.

Shamoo, A. E. and Resnik, B. (2009) *Responsible Conduct of Research*, New York: Oxford University Press.

Shipman, M. D. (1997) *The Limitations of Social Research*, London: Longman Social Research Series.

Shipman, M. D. (2014) *The Limitations of Social Research*, 4th edn, London: Routledge.

Shor, I. and Freire, P. (1987) *A Pedagogy for Liberation: Dialogues On Transforming Education*, New York: Bergin and Garvey.

Skilbeck, M. (1983) 'Lawrence Stenhouse: Research Methodology "Research is Systematic Inquiry Made Public"', *British Educational Research Journal*, 9(1), 11-20.

Smith, M. K. (2001, 2011) 'Donald Schön: Learning, Reflection and Change', *The Encyclopedia of Informal Education*. Available at www.infed.org/thinkers/et-schon.htm. Accessed 31 July 2015.

Somekh, B. and Zeichner, K. (2009) 'Action Research for Educational Reform: Remodelling Action Research Theories and Practices in Local Contexts', *Educational Action Researcher*, 17(1), 5-21.

Spriggs, M. (2010) 'Understanding Consent in Research involving Children: The Ethical Issues', in *A Handbook for Human Research Ethics Committees and Researchers*, Melbourne: Children's Bioethics Centre, The Royal Children's Hospital, Melbourne.

Stenhouse, L. (1975) *An Introduction to Curriculum Research and Development*, London: Heinemann.

Stenhouse, L. (1980) *The Teacher as Focus of Research and Development*, notes for a paper, Vancouver. Available at https://www.uea.ac.uk/documents/4059364/4994243/Stenhouse-1980-Site+Lecture.pdf/89c0c1ac-e685-4ad4-ae3a-cd13a806ef58. Accessed October 2015.

Stenhouse, L. (1981) 'What Counts as Research?', *British Journal of Educational Studies*, 29(2), 103–14.

Stevens, D. and Cooper, J. (2009) *Journal Keeping: How to Use Reflective Writing for Learning, Teaching, Professional Insight and Positive Change*. Sterling, Virginia: Stylus.

Stringer, E. (2014) *Action Research*, 4th edn, Thousand Oaks, CA: Sage.

Sullivan, B. (2000) 'How can I Help My Pupils to Make More Effective Use of their Time in School?', unpublished MA dissertation, University of the West of England, Bristol.

Sullivan, B. (2004) 'The Transformative Potential of an Educational Practitioner's Engagement in Emancipatory Practices', paper presented at the British Educational Research Association symposium, Have We Created a New Epistemology for the New Scholarship of Educational Enquiry Through Practitioner Research? Developing Sustainable Global Networks of Communication, Manchester, September.

Sullivan, B. (2006) 'A Living Theory of a Practice of Social Justice: Realising the Right of Traveller Children to Educational Equality', unpublished PhD thesis, University of Limerick. Available at http://www.eari.ie. Accessed 2 August 2015.

Taylor C. and White, S. (2000) *Practising Reflectively in Health and Welfare*, Milton Keynes: Open University Press.

Teaching Council Ireland (2012) *Code of Professional Conduct* [online]. Available at www.teachingcouncil.ie. Accessed 2 July 2015.

Torrey, J. (1973) 'Illiteracy in the Ghetto', in N. Keddie (ed.), *Tinker, Tailor: The Myth of Cultural Deprivation*, London: Penguin.

UK Department of Education (2005) *Children's Workforce Strategy: A Strategy to Build a World-class Workforce for Children and Young People*, Nottingham: DfES Publication. Available at https://www.education.gov.uk/consultations/downloadableDocs/5958-DfES-ECM.pdf

UK, Department of Education (2011, updated 2013) *Teachers' Standards: Guidance for School Leaders, School Staff and Governing Bodies*. Available at https://www.gov.uk/government/publications/teachers-standards

University of Limerick (2010) *Child Protection Guidelines Policy: Protocols and Procedures* [online]. Available at http://www.ul.ie/ehs/node/80

US Department of Education (n/d) *Policy Planning and Innovation*, Office of Postsecondary Education. Available at www2.ed.gov/about/offices/list/om/fs_po/ope/policy.html#skipnav2

USA Commission for the Protection of Human Subjects (1979) *The Belmont Report: Ethical Principles and Guidelines for the Protection of Human Subjects of Research*, Washington, DC: National Commission for the Protection of Human Subjects of Biomedical and Behavioral Research.

Usher, R., Bryant, I. and Johnston, R. (1997) *Adult Education and the Postmodern Challenge: Learning beyond the Limits*, London: Routledge.

Vanassche, E. and Kelchtermans, G. (2015) 'The State of the Art in Self-Study of Teacher Education Practices: A Systematic Literature Review', *Journal of Curriculum Studies*, 47(4), 508–28.

Vygotsky, L. (1978) *Mind in Society: The Development of Higher Psychological Processes*, Cambridge: Harvard University Press.

Waters-Adams, S. (2006) *Action Research in Education* [online]. Available at http://www.docfoc.com/action-researchdocx. Accessed 21 February 2016.

Webb, G. (1996) 'Becoming Critical of Action Research for Development', in O. Zuber-Skerritt (ed.), *New Directions in Action Research*, London: Falmer Press.

Welikala, T. and Atkin, C. (2014) 'Student Co-inquirers: The Challenges and Benefits of Inclusive Research', *International Journal of Research & Method in Education*, 37(4), 390–406.

Wenger, E. (1998) *Communities of Practice: Learning, Meaning and Identity*, Cambridge: Cambridge University Press.

Whitehead, J. (1985) *An Analysis of an Individual's Educational Development: The Basis for Personally Orientated Action Research* [online]. Available at http://www.actionresearch.net/writings/jack/jw1985analindiv.pdf. Accessed 1 August 2015.

Whitehead, J. (1989) 'Creating a Living Educational Theory from Questions of the Kind, "How Do I Improve My Practice?"', *Cambridge Journal of Education*, 19(1), 137–53.

Whitehead, J. (1993) *The Growth of Educational Knowledge: Creating Your Own Living Educational Theories* [online]. Available at http://www.actionresearch.net/writings/jwgek93.htm. Accessed 1 October 2015.

Whitehead, J. (2000) 'How Do I Improve My Practice? Creating and Legitimating an Epistemology of Practice', *Reflective Practice*, 1(1), 91–104.

Whitehead, J. (2004) 'What Counts as Evidence in Self-studies of Teacher Education Practices?', in J. J. Loughran, M. L. Hamilton, V. K. LaBoskey and T. Russell (eds), *International Handbook of Self-Study of Teaching and Teacher Education Practices*, Dordrecht: Kluwer Academic, pp. 871–903.

Whitehead, J. (2005a) 'Creating Educational Theories from Educational Enquiries of the Kind, "How do I improve my educational influence?"', response to Gorard and Nash's paper for submission to *The Journal of Educational Enquiry*, 14 March.

Whitehead, J. (2005b) 'Living Critical Standards of Judgment in Educational Theorising', paper presented to a Symposium on Creating and Testing Inclusional and Postcolonial Living Educational Theories at the 2005 Conference of the British Educational Research Association, University of Glamorgan, 29 July [online]. Available at http://actionresearch.net/writings/bera05all/jwbera05pap.htm. Accessed 25 June 2015.

Whitehead, J. (2007) *Communicating Meanings of the Expression of Life-affirming Energy with Values in Educational Relationships and in Explanations of Educational Influences in Learning*. Available at http://actionresearch.net/writings/jack/jwenergywithvalues.htm. Accessed October 2015.

Whitehead, J. (2008) 'Using a Living Theory Methodology in Improving Practice and Generating Educational Knowledge in Living Theories', *Educational Journal of Living Theories*, 1(1), 103–26.

Whitehead, J. (2009) 'Generating Living Theory and Understanding in Action Research Studies', *Action Research*, 7(1), 85–99.

Whitehead, J. (2010a) 'Creating an Educational Epistemology in the Multi-Media Narratives of Living Educational Theories and Living Theory Methodologies', *Action Researcher in Education*, 1(1), 89–109.

Whitehead, J. (2010b) *How did you Develop your Living Theory Approach? Jack Whitehead Interviewed.* Available at https://www.youtube.com/watch?v=DzXHp9M39BM. Accessed 1 June 2015.

Whitehead J. (2015a) 'The Practice of Helping Students Find Their First Person Voice in Creating Living Theories for Education', in H. Bradbury (ed.), *The Sage Handbook of Action Research*, 3rd edn, London and Thousand Oaks, CA: Sage, pp. 246–54.

Whitehead J. (2015b) 'Educational Researchers and their Living-educational-theories', *The BERA Blog: Research Matters* [online]. Available at https://www.bera.ac.uk/blog/educational-researchers-and-their-living-educational-theories. Accessed 12 September 2015.

Whitehead, J. and McNiff, J. (2006) *Action Research: Living Theory*, London: Sage.

Wilcox, S., Watson, J. and Peterson, M. (2004) 'Self-study in Professional Practice', in J. J. Loughran, M. L. Hamilton, V. K. LaBoskey and T. Russell (eds), *International Handbook of Self-Study of Teaching and Teacher Education Practices*, Vol. 1, Dordrecht; Kluwer Academic, pp. 273–312.

Winkler, G. (2001) 'Reflection and Theory: Conceptualising the Gap Between Teaching Experience and Teaching Expertise', *Action Research*, 9(3), 437–51.

Winter, R. (1989) *Learning from Experience: Principles and Practice in Action-Research*, Lewes: Falmer Press.

Winter, R. (1996) 'Some Principles and Procedures for the Conduct of Action Research', in O. Zuber-Skerritt (ed.), *New Directions in Action Research*, London: Falmer Press, 13–27.

Winter, R. (2002) 'Truth or Fiction: Problems of Validity and Authenticity in Action Research', *Educational Action Research*, 10(1), 143–55.

World Map Action Learning and Action Research Around the World, ALARA (2015) http://www.alarassociation.org/pages/networks/around-the-world

Young, I. M. (1990) *Justice and the Politics of Difference*, Princeton, NJ: Princeton University Press.

Yoshida, A. (2002) 'Martin Buber, Education as Holistic Encounter and Dialogue', in J. Miller and Y. Nakagawa (eds), *Nurturing our Wholeness: Perspectives on Spirituality in Education*, Brandon, Vermont: Foundation for Educational Renewal.

Zappone, K. (2002) 'Achieving Equality in Children's Education', *National Forum Primary Education: Ending Disadvantage*, Dublin: St Patrick's College.

Zeichner, K. (1999) 'The New Scholarship in Teacher Education', *Educational Researcher*, 28(9), 4–15.

Zeichner, K. M. and Liston, D. P. (1996) *Reflective Teaching: An Introduction*, Mahwah, NJ: Lawrence Erlbaum.

Zuber-Skerritt, O., Wood, L. and Louw, I. (eds) (2015) *A Participatory Paradigm for an Engaged Scholarship in Higher Education: Action Leadership from a South African Perspective*, Rotterdam: Sense.

Zwozdiak-Myers, P. (2012) *The Teacher's Reflective Practice Handbook: Becoming an Extended Professional through Capturing Evidence-informed Practice*, Abingdon: Routledge.

Index